Aeschylus's *Suppliant Women*

Publication of this volume has been made possible, in part, through the generous support and enduring vision of WARREN G. MOON.

Aeschylus's *Suppliant Women*

The Tragedy of Immigration

Geoffrey W. Bakewell

The University of Wisconsin Press

The University of Wisconsin Press
1930 Monroe Street, 3rd Floor
Madison, Wisconsin 53711-2059
uwpress.wisc.edu

3 Henrietta Street
London WC2E 8LU, England
eurospanbookstore.com

Printed in the United States of America

Library of Congress Cataloging-in-Publication Data

Bakewell, Geoffrey W.
Aeschylus's Suppliant women : the tragedy of immigration / Geoffrey W. Bakewell.
p. cm. — (Wisconsin studies in classics)
Includes bibliographical references and index.
ISBN 978-0-299-29174-7 (pbk. : alk. paper) — ISBN 978-0-299-29173-0 (e-book)
1. Aeschylus. Suppliants—Criticism and interpretation. 2. Metics. 3. Athens (Greece)—Emigration and immigration. I. Title. II. Series: Wisconsin studies in classics.
PA3829.B35 2013
882'.01—dc23

2012032674

For Rosie

Contents

	Preface	ix
	Introduction	3
1	Charter Myth for Metoikia	17
2	Spoken Like a Metic	34
3	The Cypriote Stamp	59
4	Sons of Earth	87
	Conclusion	122
	Notes	127
	References	179
	Index	193

Preface

Questions of where, to what, and to whom we belong are central to our lives. Yet they are not new. The inhabitants of classical Athens found them equally compelling, and explored them in numerous ways. Two of their most important vehicles for such reflection were the tragic stage and the democratic assembly. This book works the seam between these complementary means of collective self-definition. Its main contention is that Aeschylus's *Suppliant Women* offers an invaluable perspective on Athenian attempts at establishing their own identity in the late 460s BCE. Because it is often harder to say what one is than what one is not, Aeschylus operated at a number of removes. He set his suppliant drama in the fictionalized city of Argos and had its inhabitants offer an ambivalent welcome to exotic immigrants. The displaced self-portrait of Athens that results is not entirely flattering. The citizens' wariness toward outsiders and their fears about the newcomers' political, sexual, and economic leanings have clear, if complex, echoes in our contemporary debates about immigration. I leave it to ears better trained and attuned than mine to trace such reverberations. But I confess to having considerable sympathy for the Athenians and their tragic democracy: they had to think through pressing and perilous questions without the benefit of their own example. Should we now make different choices than they did, we do so in large part via the political and intellectual instruments they invented.

Though I sympathize with the Athenians, I empathize still more with the metics who lived among them. Like many academics today, I was led far from home by the exigencies of the job market. And I've seen first-hand how conscience and creed, class and color, can affect one's membership in various tight-knit communities. Along the way I've been blessed with abundant guest-friendship: Michael Brown, Bill Carroll, Julia Hejduk, and Niall Slater have been steadfast *xenoi*. At times, friendship and intellectual obligation overlap. And so I thank Greg Anderson and Jennifer Wise not only for their *philia*, but also for the expert advice they gave me on various portions of the manuscript. Ted Lendon and Elizabeth Meyer cheerfully read the whole thing with their characteristic generosity and aplomb: their profound learning saved me from many errors, and their intellectual rigor sets an example to which I aspire. I likewise thank the anonymous referees, the staff at the University of Wisconsin Press, and Jane Barry: this book is the better for their careful attentions. I am solely responsible for any remaining errors.

Portions of chapter 1 and chapter 4 are indebted to my article "Μετοικία in the *Supplices* of Aeschylus," which appeared in *Classical Antiquity* 16.2 (1997): 209–28, © 1997 by the Department of Classics, UC Berkeley. Likewise, part of the argument in chapter 2 was previously published as "Aeschylus' *Supplices* 11–12: Danaus as Πεσσονομῶν" in *Classical Quarterly* 58.1 (2008): 303–7, © 2008 by The Classical Association. I am grateful to the University of California Press and to Cambridge University Press, respectively, for their permission to reprint.

I close by acknowledging the support of my family over the years. My parents have been a constant source of affection, and my children, of joy. But my greatest thanks go to Rosie, who has once again joined me in making a new life in a new land. This book is dedicated to her with much love.

Aeschylus's *Suppliant Women*

Introduction

Aeschylus's tragedy *Suppliant Women* is above all a drama about the limits to and perils of civic incorporation. It must be understood in light of an important phenomenon in the years surrounding its production: large-scale immigration to Athens in the fifth century BCE. Under the Peisistratids in the sixth century, the city experienced an increased flow of foreigners from the Mediterranean and beyond. Following liberation from the tyrants, the reforms of Cleisthenes, and the victories of the Persian Wars, the flow of immigrants became a flood. As fifth-century Athenians became increasingly conscious of their collective identity, their ongoing attempts at self-definition involved the exclusion of others.[1] Among their most important actions in this regard was the creation of a formal legal status to designate the free non-citizens living among them. These people were termed *metics* ("livers with," μέτοικοι), and their status *metoikia* (μετοικία). When Aeschylus staged the flight of Danaus and his daughters from Egypt, he did so in light of his own time and place. Time and again, directly and indirectly, the poet casts the newcomers as metics, and their stay in Greece as metoikia.

Suppliant Women takes as its subject matter a venerable Bronze Age myth. The fifty daughters of Danaus want to avoid marrying their fifty cousins, the sons of Danaus's brother Aegyptus, and together with their father arrive in the territory of Argos seeking refuge. The basis of their claim is descent from Io, an Argive priestess once courted by Zeus. Transformed into a cow and driven to Egypt, she was there touched by the god and restored to human form, subsequently giving birth to a son, Epaphus. Now returned to their ancestral homeland, the Danaids seat themselves at a local altar and are advised by their father on how to behave. They are soon confronted by a body of local warriors led by the Argive king, Pelasgus. After mutual introductions and a discussion of the situation, the king refuses to grant them asylum on his own authority, although he is sympathetic to their claim. When the women threaten to kill themselves, however, he relents and refers the matter to the citizen assembly. He and his men then depart to escort Danaus to the meeting. Shortly thereafter their father returns alone, bearing the good news that the Argives have approved the request. But the Danaids' jubilation is interrupted by the arrival of their pursuers from Egypt. With their foes approaching, Danaus goes to summon help. As the Egyptian herald and his men prepare to drag the women off to their ships, Pelasgus and the Argives return to save the day. A confrontation ensues, and the Egyptians angrily depart, threatening to return in force. The play ends as newcomers and natives depart together for the city center of Argos, considering what the future may hold.

Scholars have traditionally been hard-pressed to establish a single dominant theme for the play. As R. D. Murray notes, various interpreters have emphasized one or more of the following motifs: "(1) the struggle of the Danaids against marriage; (2) the formal establishment of the institution of matrimony and the concomitant change in the status of women; (3) the emancipation of women; (4) the question of the right of women to refuse forced marriage, and the establishment of the Thesmophoria; (5) the sanctity of marriage; (6) the question of exogamy versus endogamy; (7) the rights of the suppliant; (8) the conflict between divine custom and state law; (9) the conflict between human rights and the divine ordinance . . . ; (10) the will of Zeus, which brings harmony out of chaos."[2] Since this summary in 1958, the list of possible themes has only grown longer. Noteworthy recent additions include: Athens's treatment of Themistocles and its relationship with Argos;[3] the impossibility of escaping fate;[4] the "'refracted' nature" of citizenship;[5] and the acculturation and incorporation of foreigners.[6] Despite the advances brought by these newer readings, no one interpretation has driven the others from the field.[7] Even in comparison with other Greek tragedies, the meaning of *Suppliant Women* remains unusually open to dispute.

My own approach is closest to that of Froma Zeitlin, who emphasizes the play's treatment of its newcomers.[8] But she thinks it an example of successful integration and reconstructs the trilogy to which it belongs as an aetiological celebration of marriage and the Thesmophoria. For her the drama depicts "the beginning of [the Danaids'] education into the rules of this 'civilized' society into which they will be incorporated."[9]

I place the emphasis quite differently. If the play is about anything, it is about the limits to civic incorporation and the anxieties and dangers that attend the process.

The starting point for my interpretation is *Suppliant Women*'s use of terminology related to metics and metoikia. Although Aeschylus explicitly refers to the Danaids' stay in Argos with the verb μετοικεῖν (609),[10] most scholars have either skipped over the term[11] or not read it literally.[12] According to Holger Friis Johansen and Edward Whittle, for instance, "the terms μετοικεῖν, μέτοικος are not insisted upon by any character in the play and no interest is shown in their precise definition."[13] Even David Whitehead, who agrees that "all three major tragedians were drawing upon the characteristics and implications of a contemporary institution"[14] when it came to metoikia, nevertheless reads such references metaphorically.[15] For him metic terminology is above all a means of accentuating pathos.[16] By contrast, I urge that the metic references in *Suppliant Women* be given their full technical weight. Aeschylus's Danaids are foreigners who arrive from Egypt and take up residence in Greece *without* becoming citizens. And the spectators doubtless understood them in light of the metics inhabiting classical Athens.[17]

Athenian Self-Definition

This book draws on a number of scholarly advances regarding Athenian literature and history over the last half-century. On the literary side, the progress made in the study of tragedy is remarkable. As late as the mid-1980s, the idea that the genre could be "political" still seemed radical to many. Even those who conceded the possibility often restricted themselves to the search for topical allusions. For a sense of the distance traveled, consider just four of the important works published in the period from 1985 to 1989. In the grand scheme of things, Christian Meier argued that through its appropriation of myth, tragedy allowed the Athenians to think through what it meant to run a democracy and control an empire, and to do so at a safer remove. For him, the genre was essential "for the mental venture of politics . . . refresh[ing], regenerat[ing], and further develop[ing] [its] ethical basis,"[18] above all in the period between the Persian and Peloponnesian Wars. Meanwhile, Simon Goldhill was making an equally compelling case for tragedy's ideological nature. He claimed that "the four moments of ceremonial preceding the dramatic festival [at the City Dionysia] are all deeply involved with the city's sense of itself. The libations of the ten generals, the display of tribute, the announcement of the city's benefactors, and the parade of state-educated boys, now men, in full military uniform, all stress the power of the *polis*, the duties of an individual to the *polis*."[19] Yet Goldhill also stressed that tragedy was not straightforwardly patriotic. On the contrary, its content routinely subverted "key words in the discourse of social order,"[20] with deeply problematic results. At roughly the same time, Zeitlin showed that displacement was one of tragedy's key strategies. By making the disruptions its plays depicted products of geography and of gender, the genre reinforced a strong sense of male citizen identity.[21] And in 1989 Edith Hall showed that tragedy employed this approach not just via Theban settings and female characters, but with its use of foreigners more generally. According to her, the tragic theater's "barbarian" from the East was above all a stereotyped agent of male Athenian self-definition.[22] Since then, political readings of tragedy have proliferated; this book is indebted to these pioneers and their successors.

In the meantime, equally fundamental reshapings were underway in the study of Athenian history. The publication of P. J. Rhodes's monumental commentary on the Aristotelian *Athenaion Politeia* placed the analysis of Athenian constitutional developments on a new footing,[23] while the ongoing work of Mogens Hansen and the Copenhagen Polis Centre located Athens' particulars in a descriptive, pan-Hellenic framework. Within this context, scholars devoted increased (and increasingly sympathetic) attention to the classical democracy.[24] Whitehead marshaled literary and epigraphical evidence to treat its fundamental building block, the *deme* ("local village"), in exhaustive detail.[25] Other scholars undertook a searching reexamination of Pericles's famous law of 451/50 restricting citizenship to those having two Athenian parents. While their analyses differed in important ways, all of them concluded that the law was closely bound up with increased efforts at Athenian self-definition.[26] At the same time, there was a growing recognition that these emerging Athenian self-portraits were to a considerable extent arbitrary. Literary genres such as the *epitaphios* ("funeral oration"), for instance, were an important means of "inventing" and solidifying a community's identity.[27] The city's efforts on the ground were equally revisionist: its building (and rebuilding) programs simultaneously adapted history and remade topography.[28]

The Athenian process of self-definition was accompanied by the delineation of the *polis*'s perimeter[29] and the consolidation of power in its center.[30] By demarcating its geographical and human boundaries, the city created both "insiders" and "outsiders."[31] Athenians had originally differentiated themselves from slaves and transients with relative ease:[32] among long-standing residents of Attica, the primary distinctions were economic.[33] But in the course of the sixth and especially the fifth centuries, the number of foreigners residing in Athens increased exponentially.[34] At first the Athenians accommodated the influx with recourse to traditional concepts: their city had been a place of refuge from the earliest days,[35] and ties of guest-friendship (*xenia*) already linked its leading families to those of other *poleis*. But as the democratic character of the city deepened, its ideology shifted: aristocratic practices became increasingly suspect and were supplanted. Soon the idea of autochthony emerged as a kind of civic glue.[36] Citizens were urged to differentiate themselves from the "Others" living among them,[37] and to do so primarily along "national" rather than economic lines.[38]

Metics and Metoikia

The scholarly study of Athens's resident foreigners entered the modern era with Ulrich von Wilamowitz's twin articles of 1887.[39] In them he demonstrated that the epigraphical formula οἰκῶν ἐν ("living in") plus the name of a deme did more than mark a metic's place of residence; it also identified him as a legal member of that community. On his understanding, the development of metoikia as a legal institution was linked to the greatness of the host polis: "the state wanted to gain for itself fresh blood by making entrance easier, and by offering immigrants an *incomparably favorable* legal situation. We are dealing with one of the measures that led to *the overwhelming greatness* of Athens."[40] Michel Clerc's book *The Athenian Metics*, published six years later,[41] further explored the juridical and moral status of metics at Athens. It also mapped out the substantial role they played in the life of the city. As Clerc put it, "the history of Athens in the fifth and fourth centuries can only be completely explained if one pays the greatest attention to the foreign population that was incorporated into the city."[42]

Whitehead undertook a searching reexamination of the entire subject in his 1977 monograph *The Ideology of the Athenian Metic*. His careful collection and analysis of the surviving contemporary sources forms the basis of the current *communis opinio* about metics. In general, he accepts the basic definition proffered by Aristophanes of Byzantium (fr. 38): "a metic is whoever comes from a foreign land and dwells in the city, paying a fee toward some established needs of the city. For a stay of up to so many days he is termed a visitor and owes no fee, but when he stays past the stated time, he becomes a metic and owes it." To paraphrase, metics were those who stayed in Athens beyond a fixed limit (perhaps thirty days)[43] and thereby owed an annual payment called the *metoikion* (fixed at twelve drachmas for men and six for women).[44] Among other requirements, they had to acquire a citizen sponsor (*prostates*)[45] and register with the *polemarch*; they were subject to various liturgies,[46] liable for military service under some circumstances,[47] and barred from owning houses and land.[48] In exchange, they received limited legal protection for themselves and their movable possessions.[49]

Whitehead's work on the specifics of metoikia remains invaluable. But more important still is his understanding of the broader shape of the evidence. For one thing, he recognized better than others the extent to which "metic" was a catch-all term obscuring a complex reality. Real-life immigrants came to Attica from many places for many reasons, and stayed for varying lengths of time; nevertheless, the same legal classification applied to them all. "The ordinary observer saw what the *polis* ignored: the utter heterogeneity of these *metoikoi* in every possible respect other than juristic status."[50] For another, Whitehead challenged the prevailing piety that metoikia was a quasi-citizenship, a generous concession extended by the city to the less fortunate.[51] On his view, the legal status was not an expression of *noblesse oblige* rooted in Athenians' sense of political, aesthetic, and moral superiority. It was rather a matter of enlightened self-interest. Metics made crucial contributions to Athens in multiple ways, and so had to be tolerated and even encouraged at times. Yet these same people were outsiders and had to remain so; by their very nature they constituted an existential threat to the democratic city and its self-understanding. Metoikia was therefore an ambiguous blend of concession and obligation, a deal struck by a city eager to maximize gain and minimize risk.

In the generation since its appearance, Whitehead's work has prompted one major challenge. In *The Athenian Nation*, Edward Cohen argued that Athens should be understood as a "nation" (*ethnos*) as well as a polis.[52] He further claimed that scholars have exaggerated the distinctions Athenians drew between themselves and non-citizens, and have thereby created "the shibboleth that Athenian *politai* constituted an impenetrable group of scions of *politai*, an autochthonous club sealed forever by doubly endogamous barriers."[53] On Cohen's view, the separation between citizens and metics mattered less than that between locals and strangers regardless of juridical status. His argument relies on a sweeping redefinition of the word ἀστός (traditionally considered a synonym for πολίτης, "citizen")[54] to mean "free local person."[55] According to him, "a great variety of persons permanently domiciled in Attika would be recognizable as *astoi*: most, if not all, of the *politai*; some of those registered as metics; the offspring of *politai* who had not been born 'in accordance with the laws' . . . the scions of *astoi* who had been rejected when evaluated by their demes . . . the *apepsephismenoi* . . . and potentially many others."[56]

Cohen correctly emphasizes the many types of inhabitants residing in Attica, the practical difficulty in determining their various civic statuses, and the invisibility of many legal distinctions amid the bustle of daily life. In all these regards, he has performed an important service. Yet in attempting to separate *astos* from *polites*, he has gone too far. For J. H. Blok has shown that "the meaning of *politai* . . . can hardly be distinguished from that of *astoi*. In the archaic and early classical records, the *astoi* are involved in exactly the same activities as the *politai*. The main difference appears to be that *astoi* is used more frequently than *politai* as a contrast-term."[57] Cohen rightly notes that the popular saying "today a slave, tomorrow a demesman of Sounion" implies a degree of "mobility and anonymity" in Athenian life.[58] Yet the phrase does not mean that the legal line separating citizen from metic was unimportant.[59] On the contrary, the Athenians must have regarded the distinction as significant; otherwise the saying would lose its bite. Elizabeth Meyer's recent study of the corpus of vases known as *phialai exeleutherikai* drives home the point. Her demonstration that these numerous "freedom" vases were dedicated by metics acquitted of *graphai aprostasiou* (charges that they failed to have a citizen sponsor) implies that there was no shortage of citizen volunteers ready to prosecute.[60] Both individually and collectively, Athenians were acutely attuned to the differences separating them from metics, and keen to maintain them.[61] Whitehead's treatment of metoikia remains definitive.[62]

Suppliant Women: Date, Text, Commentary

The last fifty or so years have put the study of *Suppliant Women* on a much more secure footing. The play was once thought to be the earliest surviving work of Aeschylus, and hence the oldest extant tragedy; it was accordingly scrutinized with an eye to reconstructing the earlier days of the genre.[63] But then the mid-century discovery of the didascalic information contained in Oxyrhynchus Papyrus 2256 led to a significant downdating of the play.[64] One fragment states that in a year paraphrased as ἐπὶ ἀρ[. . .] (fr. 3.1.1), Aeschylus was victorious with his Danaid trilogy, while Sophocles placed second and Mesatus third. Scott Scullion rightly notes that the dating formula is more plausibly restored as ἐπὶ ἄρ[χοντος . . .] ("in the archonship of . . .") than ἐπὶ Ἀρ[χεδημίδου] ("in the [archonship of] Ar[chedemides],"[65] i.e. 464/63).[66] If Plutarch is correct in his assertion (*Cimon* 8.8) that Sophocles defeated Aeschylus with his first production in 468,[67] we have a *terminus post quem* for the play.[68] Other didascalic information claims that Aeschylus's *Seven against Thebes* was produced in the following year. A. F. Garvie notes that if C. W. Müller is correct that tragedians could not offer plays at the City Dionysia in two successive years, then 466 is thereby also excluded.[69] And the fact that the play makes no use of any scene building (*skene*) argues for a date prior to 459.[70] In assigning the play to the latter half of the 460s, we are on solid ground.

Shortly after the publication of the Oxyrhynchus fragment, Garvie put forth his careful study of the trilogy as a whole.[71] In 1977 Alan Sommerstein published an important set of textual notes. And in 1980 Friis Johansen and Whittle came out with a massive three-volume edition and commentary that Mark Griffith rightly described as "the most comprehensive ever attempted (longer even than Fraenkel's *Agamemnon*) . . . a remarkable monument of learning and industry, . . . its coverage of matters lexical, morphological, grammatical, syntactical, orthographical, and palaeographical is marvellous, as is the careful use of scholia and ancient lexica."[72] Learned and important as this edition (hereafter referred to as *FJW*) is, it has nevertheless been seen to fall short in critical areas, particularly with regard to interpretative questions.[73] Martin Sicherl, Froma Zeitlin, Wolfgang Rösler, Alan Sommerstein, and Mary Bachvarova have all helped narrow this gap.[74] And Pär Sandin has recently published the first volume of the next generation of full-length commentary on the play.[75] These are propitious times for the study of *Suppliant Women*.

Summary of the Argument

Chapter 1, "Charter Myth for Metoikia," offers a detailed argument for treating Aeschylus's Danaids as metics. It begins with a brief historical overview of immigration to Athens, focusing on the period between Cleisthenes and the latter half of the 460s. The performance of *Suppliant Women* is seen to provide a firm *terminus ante quem* for the existence of metoikia as a formal legal status at Athens. The play's stagecraft, including costuming, blocking, and props, emphasizes its themes of immigration and incorporation. The Danaids' departure from Egypt, their crossing of the boundary into Argos, the terms of their acceptance by the Argive assembly, and the final *exeunt* to the walled city center all reflect the play's debt to Athenian metoikia. *Suppliant Women* thus provides an *aition* for a crucial historical development in classical Athens. In short, the play gives the metic a distinguished pedigree, making him in some senses the political successor of the ritual suppliant. At the same time he is also the beneficiary of the *demos*, which has appropriated and adapted for its own use the aristocratic custom of guest-friendship (*xenia*).

Despite its aetiological dimension, *Suppliant Women* is nevertheless not a civic celebration. The play explicitly reminds its audience of the challenges that newcomers pose to the identity and well-being of the city that takes them in. Chapter 2, "Spoken Like a Metic," focuses on the political difficulties involved in accommodating newcomers. It considers in particular the speech norms posited by the play: according to *Suppliant Women*, citizens should talk one way and metics another.[76] The Danaids prove prone to violent speech, and their father deceptive; together they represent the antithesis of persuasion (*peitho*). Pelasgus is by contrast forthright and free-spoken, embodying both the principle of *isegoria* and the democratic rhetorical ethos more generally. While the newcomers use bold speech to pursue their self-interest, Pelasgus puts his city's well-being first. Although much about the subsequent trilogy remains unclear, the dramatic action certainly featured war, multiple changes of regime, and a significant alteration in the Argive body politic. Read in this light, *Suppliant Women* is suggestive about the context surrounding the enactment of Pericles's citizenship law a decade or so later in 451/50. The play's newcomers provide an example of the political dangers a city ran by accepting metics: one implication is that their speech should be controlled and their political participation curtailed. Significantly, Pericles's measure denied metics the ability to serve on the *ekklesia*, *boule*, and *dikasteria*.

Many previous interpreters of *Suppliant Women* have examined the Danaids' reluctance to wed. Chapter 3, "The Cypriote Stamp," frames the marriage issue somewhat differently, focusing on the erotic complications the women create for Argos.[77] In their relative independence from their father and their insistence on their own agency, the Danaids undermine the *kyrios*-centered values of the polis. Moreover, their exotic appearance lends them a potentially promiscuous allure. Their threat to disrobe and hang themselves in front of the Argives reveals just how outlandish their behavior is. In the remainder of the trilogy, they first marry and then murder their cousins. In addition, hints in *Suppliant Women* and the surviving fragments of *Danaids* suggest that the Danaids are purified and eventually remarried, this time to Argive men. There is, however, little evidence to support Zeitlin's claim that the trilogy ends with the women's transformation into citizen wives and the foundation of the Thesmophoria.[78] Such a conclusion might perhaps be conceivable in Athens, the traditional locale for the genre's "happy" endings. But the Danaid trilogy transpires in Argos and features a radical remaking of the civic order attended by defeat, death, and destruction. *Suppliant Women* thus highlights the negative consequences of marriage to exotic, troublesome, foreign women like the Danaids.

The difficulties the newcomers raise extend to the economic realm as well. Chapter 4, "Sons of Earth," considers the relations between natives, newcomers, and the earth in *Suppliant Women*. Pelasgus's definition of his ancestry and of his land are intertwined. In depicting the Argives as eponymous "land-sharers" (γαμόρων, 613), *Suppliant Women* borrows liberally from a fifth-century ideological staple at Athens, the notion of citizen autochthony.[79] Solon's census created a legal link between citizen and soil; this in turn provided a conceptual justification for the ban on *enktesis* (ownership of real property) by metics. Noncitizens consequently tended to live in different places and manners than citizens, earn their livelihood in different ways, and store their assets in alternative forms. All these differences between natives and newcomers inform the play's focus on where the Danaids are to live. As metics they are denied the right to houses of their own and are lodged in a new sort of accommodation being pioneered in the metic-heavy demes of Athens at the time of the play's production.

The Tenor and Tenure of Metoikia

The numerous challenges posed by metics help to explain why classical Athenians all too often proved reluctant hosts.[80] Generally speaking, they took little official notice of the numerous non-citizens among them, and when they did so, were often slow to acknowledge the benefits they derived from them. In [Xenophon's] *Constitution of the Athenians* (1.10), for example, the Athenian narrator comments that "slaves and metics at Athens are brazen in the extreme. It is not permitted to strike them there; a slave will not even step to the side for you. The reason for the custom is this: if there were a law allowing a free man to strike a slave or metic or freedman, he would often have struck an Athenian, thinking him a slave." According to him, metics are ubiquitous at Athens and arrogantly usurp the place of their superiors. Though Pseudo-Xenophon grudgingly admits (1.12) the city's reliance on their technical skills and naval contributions, he wishes it were otherwise and yearns (1.11) for the freedom to manhandle non-citizens the way they do at Sparta.

On those rare occasions when Athenians lauded metics, they tended to do so faintly. In his own *Suppliant Women*, Euripides offers a portrait of the metic Parthenopaeus that at first glance appears sympathetic (890–900):

He was an Arcadian, but having come to the streams of Inachus
was raised in Argos. Brought up there,
he was, first of all (in keeping with how metics should act),
not obnoxious or ostentatious, nor quarrelsome,
which makes citizen and stranger alike burdensome.
He stood in the ranks and protected the land
as if he had been born an Argive, rejoicing
when the city fared well, and grieving when it suffered.
Having many male and female lovers,
he was careful to do no harm.

As Whitehead notes, this is "explicitly a blueprint for the ideal [Athenian] metic (892), permanently installed and permanently on his best behavior."[81] Yet note how much of this praise is stated negatively: the focus is arguably less on good done than harm averted. The play's Argives had such low expectations for metics that Parthenopaeus was able to surpass them. Whitehead concludes that this was likely the best a metic could aspire to: the chance to keep his head down, "to[e] all possible lines,"[82] and receive in return a grudging toleration.[83]

Although classical Athenians benefited from the immigrants among them, they still feared their effects in *inter alia* the political, sexual, and economic realms.[84] It is worth remembering that in Aeschylus's *Suppliant Women*, Pelasgus's convocation of the Argive assembly and its grant of metoikia are not an entirely free choice, but the *ad hoc* response to a crisis. As Pelasgus puts it (407–11):[85]

There is need of deep, saving thought
to go down into the depths like a diver,
casting a sober gaze,
how all these matters may bring no harm to the city
and may turn out well for us . . .

δεῖ τοι βαθείας φροντίδος σωτηρίου,
δίκην κολυμβητῆρος εἰς βυθὸν μολεῖν
δεδορκὸς ὄμμα μηδ' ἄγαν ᾠνωμένον,
ὅπως ἄνατα ταῦτα πρῶτα μὲν πόληι,
αὐτοῖσί θ' ἡμῖν[86] ἐκτελευτήσει καλῶς . . .

Metoikia ultimately proved an imperfect solution to the problem of large-scale immigration. Historically speaking, the Athenians stuck with it as long as they did because of the lack of better alternatives.[87]

Methods

I conclude this section with a brief apologia. Three aspects of my approach to *Suppliant Women* may cause some concern. The first involves the play's dramatic setting. The Danaids state in their entering song (*parodos*) that they have come to the land of Argos (Ἄργους γαῖαν, 15), and further remarks scattered throughout the play refer to some of its recognizable topographical features (e.g. the streams of Inachus). Nevertheless, I analyze the drama in light of metoikia at Athens. How is this justifiable, given that there were almost certainly real-life foreigners resident in classical Argos as well?[88]

Whitehead has shown that metics and metoikia were not unique to Athens, but a fact of life in many if not most cities.[89] He adds that while "the classical Athenian metoikia was unique . . . [it] can (and should) serve as our model of the immigrant communities not that other cities *did* have but that, given Athens' circumstances and history, they *could* have had; a model, that is, of how metic-like groups came into existence in the poleis, and of the series of practical questions posed to the poleis thereby."[90] In other words, Athenian metoikia can safely serve as a guide to the theoretical and practical issues posed by metics throughout the Greek world. And the surviving evidence for Athenian metoikia, though scanty enough, is nevertheless orders of magnitude fuller than that from any other polis.

Equally important in this vein is the Athenocentric nature of tragedy. According to Zeitlin, the genre consistently presented Thebes as a foil, an "anti-Athens" constructed in response to the latter city's preoccupations.[91] Suzanne Saïd has produced a variation on the same theme regarding Argos as *topos*. On her view the city lacks a firm identity in tragedy and its depiction is often "contaminated by typically Athenian elements."[92] Upon reflection, the fact that life on-stage in Athens resembled life off-stage should come as no surprise. Despite tragedy's aversion to "metatheater,"[93] its poets had few resources as they went about their business of recreating the vanished Heroic Age. Lacking eyewitnesses, archives, and libraries, and only dimly aware of most of the material remains surrounding them, Aeschylus and his peers relied on analogy with the present to resurrect the past.[94] In many instances their recourse to the here and now was admittedly intuitive rather than conscious. In the case of the Danaids, Aeschylus had no way of knowing whether and how specific Bronze Age Greek communities had incorporated immigrants from elsewhere. What he did know, and could not but use as a point of reference, was how his own city did so. In creating plays steeped in Athenian points-of-view and particulars, the tragic poets not only represented their community on stage but helped it think through its most pressing issues.[95] Aeschylus's fictive metics at Argos thus performed important conceptual work for his audience. Victoria Wohl has argued that tragic women are a primary means "through which the male subject thinks about himself and his place in the world."[96] *Nominibus mutatis*, the same holds true for tragic metics, who helped the spectators figure out how to be citizens.

A second methodological point involves the relationship of *Suppliant Women* to Aeschylus's other Danaid plays. The paucity of fragments from *Sons of Aegyptus* (Αἰγύπτιοι),[97] together with the fact that the two substantial fragments from *Danaids* (Δαναίδες)[98] are shorn of context, makes any detailed reconstruction of the trilogy extremely hazardous.[99] Nevertheless, working primarily from a number of later sources, including *Prometheus Bound* and Pausanias, and from analogy with the *Oresteia*,[100] scholars have arrived at a broad outline agreeable to many if not all.[101] The departure of the Egyptian herald was likely followed by a war encompassing the death of Pelasgus[102] and the siege or defeat of Argos.[103] Danaus then became ruler of Argos and ended hostilities by agreeing that his daughters would marry the sons of Aegyptus after all. At the same time he secretly urged the women to kill their grooms on the wedding night. Forty-nine of them did so. But Hypermestra spared her husband, Lynceus, and together with their offspring founded a new dynasty at Argos. Meanwhile her sisters were cleansed of their blood-guilt and remarried, this time to Argive men.[104] This skeletal reconstruction of the trilogy undergirds portions of the analysis in chapters 2 and 3 especially. To venture further seems neither warranted nor wise.

A final methodological issue involves my use of external evidence. Anyone foolhardy enough to undertake a book on this play faces a severe challenge. As Griffith notes, "no work of Greek literature is more daunting to editor and commentator than Aeschylus' *Suppliants*, a drama rich and fascinating, but so poorly preserved that text and interpretation (to say nothing of the rest of the trilogy) are often beyond hope of recovery."[105] And anyone seeking to study the play in light of metoikia has in effect doubled down on his bet. For as Whitehead remarks, "a 'history' of the Athenian metic can never be written: the *data* are so sparse that vast expanses of metic history are totally undocumented, even in the classical period."[106] I have therefore, upon occasion and of necessity, resorted to other types of evidence drawn from earlier or later periods. I am more hesitant than the Danaids to cross boundaries, and try to be more observant of the appropriate formalities when I do. For instance, the distinctions between literary and material evidence, between various epochs, and among different literary genres are all important and worth noting. But it is the crossing of just such boundaries that may help to fill the lacunae of trilogy and history alike. The reader will decide whether the effort was well-omened.

1

Charter Myth for Metoikia

Suppliant Women depicts the arrival of barbarian newcomers in Greece. Although the play is set in Argos, critics have long noted that its themes, characters, and language point toward democratic Athens.[1] In the aftermath of the Persian Wars, this city struggled to cope with an influx of thousands of new residents hailing from elsewhere in Greece and the Mediterranean world. It did so in substantial part by creating the formal juridical status known as metoikia. Shortly thereafter, in the second half of the 460s,[2] Aeschylus staged this drama focused on a Bronze Age migration myth. He did so with clear recourse to his own time and place: a citizen assembly grants the Danaids the privilege μετοικεῖν τῆσδε γῆς ("to live as metics in this land"). In addition to using legal terminology relating to metoikia, the playwright deployed all the tricks of his trade—movement, theatrical space, blocking, costumes, props, gestures—to demonstrate the liminal nature of the newcomers' status at Argos. They have been accepted as metics, true; but they have also been rejected as citizens. At play's end, their incorporation into the polis remains partial, not full. *Suppliant Women* is *inter alia* an aetiological drama investing a contemporary political and social phenomenon with a Bronze Age pedigree.

Historical Context

Suppliant Women dates from an eventful stretch of Athenian history, after the costly triumph in the Persian Wars and prior to the reforms of Ephialtes and Pericles. The tribal reorganization of Cleisthenes and the navy championed by Themistocles had acquitted themselves superbly at Salamis and formed the basis for the city's subsequent rise to empire. At home Athenians were busy rebuilding their city walls, expanding and fortifying the Piraeus, and clearing and restoring the Acropolis.[3] To these economic labors Athenian military and democratic activity added others. Sailors and soldiers were needed to lead the Delian League's fight against the Great King and to discipline recalcitrant allies; meetings of the council and assembly may have increased in importance and frequency;[4] the law courts took on greater precedence and prominence.[5] There was much work to do, more than citizens could accomplish even with the help of slaves. The introduction of payments to citizens for various military and civic duties during the mid-fifth century reflects in part the increased burdens posed by these numerous civic obligations.[6]

The rise of the *metoikion* (the annual fee owed by metics) counterbalanced the emergence of the *misthos* (state payments to citizens).[7] Although Athens had had a long history of immigration,[8] the end of the sixth century marked a new era in this regard. In *Politics* 1275b36–37, Aristotle says that following the expulsion of Hippias, Cleisthenes πολλοὺς . . . ἐφυλέτευσε ξένους καὶ δούλους μετοίκους. The grammar and meaning of this phrase are much disputed. At the philological level, the most difficult questions surround the use of the word μετοίκους. Is it being used as a direct object with asyndeton ("he distributed among the tribes[9] many foreigners and slaves [and] metics")? Is it being used to supplement the meaning of both ξένους and δούλους ("he distributed among the tribes many metics who were once foreigners and slaves")?[10] Or is it being used in apposition to ξένους καὶ δούλους ("he distributed among the tribes many foreigners and slaves [as] metics")? The second and third are the more likely of the three alternatives.[11] Further complicating matters is the fact that Aristotle's use of the term *metic* here is almost certainly anachronistic.[12] Above all, we need to remember that the phrase occurs in the context of the creation of citizens, not metics.[13] What the *Politics* passage thus seems to say is that in 508/7, Cleisthenes incorporated many foreigners and slaves into the city during the creation of his new tribal system.[14] J. K. Davies has gone further and suggested that all those resident in Attica at the time may have been enrolled in demes.[15] Although Aristotle does use the word *metic* in connection with this process, he is probably retrojecting details of the status as he knew it in the fourth century back into a period prior to its official creation.

The silver strikes at Laureion and elsewhere early in the fifth century, the minting of archaic Athenian tetradrachms, the development of a two-hundred-ship navy, and the burgeoning market for Attic ceramics all brought additional immigrants to Athens. Moreover, the Persian War showed that some of the newcomers meant to stay. In 480, as Xerxes's host marched toward Athens, many non-citizens doubtless sought safety elsewhere.[16] But others remained and fought bravely, evincing considerable devotion to their new home. In the aftermath of victory, the expansion of the Piraeus and consequent economic boom produced unprecedented immigration to Attica.[17]

At the time *Suppliant Women* was produced, Athens was thus working through at a communal level many of the issues surrounding newcomers. For all the good immigrants did the city, they were a potentially disruptive presence as well. This was partly due to their considerable numbers. Working from limited data, Hansen has calculated that in 450 the population of Athens may have included something like 60,000 adult male citizens.[18] While reliable evidence about metic numbers is even scarcer, responsible estimates suggest that metics made up 20–50 percent of the total free population during roughly the same time period.[19] By any reckoning, between 480 and 450 the metic population at Athens swelled into the tens of thousands, with metics outnumbering citizens in some demes.[20]

It was not just metic numbers that were threatening. Many of the earliest immigrants had been fellow Hellenes sharing the same basic language, cults, and customs.[21] Yet sixth- and fifth-century colonization in the Black Sea region, the Persian Wars and subsequent Delian League campaigns, and attempts to expand into Thrace around Ennea Hodoi all brought Athens into protracted contact with numerous non-Greeks. As a result increased numbers of Phrygians, Lydians, Lycians, Carians, Egyptians, Thracians, and Scythians made their way to the Piraeus and elsewhere. Some came to trade and leave; others to stay. This generation of newcomers brought with them different mother tongues, appearances, accents, and cultural practices.[22] And their visibility helped accelerate Athenian attempts to fashion and sharpen a sense of civic identity.[23]

The Invention of Metoikia

Without careful supervision, all these newcomers might threaten Athens's identity and well-being.[24] The citizens therefore sought to secure for themselves the benefits of immigrants and immigration while limiting their potential harm. At one level, their concern was ideological: they needed to distinguish themselves from "Others" in ways consonant with their history and traditions. But practical considerations were also involved. The solution the Athenians arrived at was the invention of metoikia. The available evidence suggests that the institution emerged as a formal practice sometime between the mid-470s and approximately 460. Despite Cleisthenes' apparent enfranchisement of all free residents of Attica in 508/7, subsequent immigrants were not made citizens but instead referred to as ξένοι (xenoi). For instance, the Themistocles decree uses this term to describe non-citizens during the preparations for the battle of Salamis in 480.[25] By contrast, the first technical use of the word μέτοικος at Athens occurs in the 460s.[26] *IG* i^3 244 is dated by David Lewis to approximately 460[27] and records a set of laws from the deme of Scambonidae. It contains a provision for the demarch and *hieropoioi* (sacrificial officials) to sacrifice to the eponymous tribal hero as part of a celebration involving both demesmen and metics (lines 5–10):

Let there be an allotment of . . .
obols to each
of the Scambonids; let
the metics obtain
a share in the marketplace
of the Scambonids.

λεχ[σιν . . .]
[ὀ]βολον· hε[κάστοι]
Σκαμονι[δον καὶ]
τὸς μετοίκ[ος λαχ]—εν· ἐν ἀγορα[ι τει Σ]—[κ]αμβονιδο[ν].

The opposition in lines 7 and 8 between Σκαμβονι[δον] and μετοίκ[ος] suggests a technical distinction between the two groups. In Aeschylus's *Eumenides*, performed just a few years later, newcomers explicitly described as μέτοικοι also take a prominent part in the religious life of the city.[28] The play's production in 458 thus provides an apparent *terminus ante quem* for the existence of formal metoikia at Athens.

Dramaturgy and Immigration

The first and last movements of *Suppliant Women* dramatize its themes of immigration and incorporation.[29] At the start, Danaus and his daughters[30] enter alone via one *eisodos*, coming from the harbor to the territory of the Greek polis where they hope to dwell.[31] The absence of prologue and the anapestic meter enhance the sense of movement. Significantly, the newcomers enter in single file, with the women preceding their father.[32] And at the end of the play (1018–1073), the Danaids depart via the opposite *eisodos* for the fortified city center of Argos, accompanied by their new citizen sponsors. What happens in the orchestra between these framing movements constitutes the central action of the drama.

Caught between the harbor and the *asty*, the Danaids possess a geographically liminal status.[33] The importance of where they will end up is emphasized by the fact that they are the only figures visible throughout the whole performance. Danaus and Pelasgus, Egyptians and Argives all come and go; yet the women spend the bulk of the play poised around an altar centrally located in the orchestra.[34] At line 21 they claim to be suppliants (ἱκέται), people whose immediate need for assistance prompts them to engage in a religiously sanctioned social ritual. In exchange for recognizing the authority of a powerful superior, they may lay a claim to his protection.[35] The rite was a familiar one in ancient Greece, enacted both on- and off-stage. Thus when the audience heard the women call upon the local gods to "welcome [as a] suppliant / this female / expedition" (δέξασθ' ἱκέτην / τὸν θηλυγενῆ / στόλον, 27–29), they had no doubt about the type of play they were attending.[36] Given the conventions of Greek tragedy, they could shortly expect the women's pursuers to issue from one *eisodos* and their protectors from the other.[37] The poet literally heightens the suspense surrounding these imminent arrivals by having Danaus twice mount a platform (perhaps the altar itself) and look about.[38] His gaze, punctuated with bold gestures, was directed first toward the city and later in the opposite direction toward the sea. The Danaids are thereby marked as neither fully Egyptian nor fully Argive: they are trapped between the two worlds.

Aeschylus uses outland-ish costuming to make a similar point. As Henri and Micheline van Effenterre note, in ancient Greece "the mark of the stranger is above all his physical aspect: his size, his features, the color of his skin, eyes, or hair. . . . It is also his accessories."[39] When Pelasgus encounters the Danaids, his first reaction is amazement (234–37):

What sort of un-Greek crowd
do I address, that delights
in barbarian mantles and headbands?

For your clothing is not that
of Argive women, nor from
Greek climes.

ποδαπὸν ὅμιλον τόνδ' ἀνελληνόστολον
πέπλοισι βαρβάροισι κἀμπυκώμασιν
χλίοντα προσφωνοῦμεν; οὐ γὰρ Ἀργολὶς
ἐσθὴς γυναικῶν οὐδ' ἀφ' Ἑλλάδος τόπων.

The women's mantles (πέπλοισι) and headbands (ἀμπυκώμασιν) are foreign in appearance (βαρβάροισι).[40] Their overall attire (ἐσθής) is not native to the area around Argos (οὐ . . . Ἀργολίς), nor even remotely Greek (ἀνελληνόστολον, οὐδ' ἀφ' Ἑλλάδος τόπων). Their dark complexions, likely created by masks and skin blackened with paint,[41] are visible to all; Pelasgus later likens the women to those from sultrier climes (279–90). Yet amid all this foreignness, the Danaids nevertheless carry in their left hands a sure sign of Greek custom and thus identity: the wool-tipped olive boughs routinely employed by suppliants (21–22). Like their position in the orchestra, the Danaids' physical appearance poses the question of which world they belong to: barbarian or Greek?

According to Aristotle, tragic figures are largely products of the choices they make and the actions they perform.[42] In Aeschylus, prominent props and gestures often serve as a kind of shorthand linked to these essential characterizations.[43] Throughout *Suppliant Women*, Aeschylus makes particular use of his actors' hands.[44] The Danaids entreat Pelasgus by laying their branches at altars (241–42) and threaten him by fingering their girdles (457–65). The Argives define themselves by raising their right hands in assembly and voting to accept the Danaids (604, 607–8). The Egyptian herald and his companions[45] reach out to drag the women away from the altar (909). And some sort of prominent gesture, such as an extended arm and pointing finger or outstretched palm, must have accompanied Pelasgus's interception of the Egyptian herald at line 911.[46] Aeschylus's emphasis on hands and handiwork likely increased in the remainder of the trilogy.[47] A cursory outline of *Suppliant Women* might even be sketched by what passes through the Danaids' hands.[48]

Careful consideration of the interaction between Pelasgus and the Egyptian herald reveals an important detail. Oliver Taplin has noted that after the latter arrives, the play's text contains only "threat and intended action. . . . [The herald's] last words before Pelasgus' intervention imply that he is still only on the point of using force."[49] While much of the play's energy derives from confrontations between its *dramatis personae*, the actors in any one scene never seem to touch.[50] There is no textual evidence that the Danaids ever supplicate Pelasgus by grasping his knees or chin;[51] that the king raises them from the central altar himself; that the herald touches the women; that the king and the herald ever come to blows. Put differently, in *Suppliant Women* it is proximity rather than physical contact that generates dramatic tension. An electrical analogy is apt: the poet creates a voltaic tension, and the audience waits to see if a spark will arc across the gap. In sum, Aeschylus employs movement, theatrical space, blocking, costumes, props, and gestures to identify the Danaids as newcomers and emphasize their isolation. The times when they approach or are approached by others are marked moments important for the meaning of the play.[52] Will they be dragged back to their homeland, or welcomed into a new land?

Out of Egypt

When the Danaids enter the theater, they claim that their departure from Egypt proceeds from their unwillingness to marry their cousins (9–11). But they leave the reason for their refusal unstated.[53] Some scholars trace the women's aversion to a prior power struggle between their father and their uncle. Others associate it with the violence displayed by their cousins as suitors. Still others see deeper gender issues at work and endow the women with a broader antipathy to marriage. And a fourth group argue that their primary motivation is filial piety, as their father attempts to forestall an oracle linking their marriage to his death. These explanations will be taken up again in a subsequent chapter; for now it is enough to note that all are consistent with the Danaids' description of their "flight" (φεύγομεν, 5; φεύγειν, 13) and their claim that they (unlike many exiles) are ritually clean (οὔτιν' ἐφ' αἵματι δημηλασίαν / . . . γνωσθεῖσαι, 6–7).

At first glance, the possible explanations for their flight distinguish the Danaids from historical metics at Athens, many of whom were prompted by economic motives.[54] The women's silence about financial matters certainly conforms to the conventions of tragedy. Adopting the bygone Heroic Age as its usual backdrop, the genre took a dim view of commerce. Its choruses routinely celebrated agriculture and the joys of one's homeland while cautioning against the search for excessive wealth.[55] To be tied too closely to money and the pursuit of personal gain was ignoble and might invite scorn or worse.[56] In addition, tragedians were tightly constrained by the basic outlines of myth handed down and hallowed by tradition. While a poet might tinker with individual elements of a particular story, he was bound to follow its central features. In the case of the Danaids, this meant that Aeschylus had to situate their flight to Argos within the context of their relationships with their father and cousins.

Yet Richard Seaford has shown that tragedy is not indifferent to the financial concerns of the fifth century. According to him, "the world represented by Homeric epic contains neither coinage nor even (except for a few indications) money, nor is its representation of events influenced by money, whereas the world represented by tragedy does, anachronistically, contain (precious metal) money . . . and is . . . in various non-obvious ways shaped by money."[57] When we look closely at *Suppliant Women*, we find Aeschylus has here and there introduced elements that might tie Danaus and his family to more lucrative (and historically attested) promptings toward metoikia. According to some ancient traditions it was Danaus who invented the ship, that wretched instrument that first breached divinely sanctioned natural boundaries in search of gain.[58] In *Suppliant Women* Aeschylus makes Danaus the sailor par excellence: at lines 714–18 and 764–72, for instance, he describes ships and seafaring at a level of detail baffling to landlubbers like Pelasgus. In confronting these sea-borne arrivals, the Argives are out of their element.[59] As Pelasgus laments, "I have waded into this bottomless, uncrossable sea / of folly, and nowhere is there a harbor from evils" (ἄτης δ' ἄβυσσον πέλαγος οὐ μάλ' εὔπορον / τόδ' εἰσ⟨β⟩έβηκα, κοὐδαμοῦ λιμὴν κακῶν, 470–71).

Also relevant is the Danaids' homeland. From the last quarter of the seventh century, Greeks maintained an emporium at Naucratis in the Nile delta. The traders hailed from a wide range of communities, including various Ionian, Dorian, and Aeolian poleis.[60] While some settled there more or less permanently, others visited for shorter periods of time.[61] In the sixth century the Egyptian king Amasis granted the emporium exclusive rights to maritime trade with his country.[62] These Greeks and their Egyptian neighbors had much in common, including their women.[63] Thus when Aeschylus's Danaids refer to their flight as "a naval expedition raised up from the fine-sanded mouthings of the Nile" (στόλον ἡμέτερον νάϊον ἀρθέντ' / ἀπὸ προστομίων λεπτο⟨ψα⟩μάθων / Νείλου, 2–4), the spectators perhaps likened them to people coming from Naucratis.[64] The women's dark complexions and claims of mixed ancestry would only have strengthened the Egyptian associations.

One of the most important products exported through Naucratis was papyrus (βύβλος).[65] Plato explicitly associates the trading emporium with Theuth and the invention of writing.[66] And another ancient tradition tied Danaus himself to the origins of script.[67] Throughout *Suppliant Women*, Aeschylus frequently associates people from Egypt with writing and writing materials. For instance, Danaus twice encourages his daughters to write down his words on tablets.[68] They in turn threaten to "decorate" the statues of the Argive gods by making themselves into πίνακες, tablets inscribed with prayers and hung on divine effigies.[69] And at lines 944–49 Pelasgus prefaces his dismissal of the Egyptian herald with a programmatic statement:

The nail of [the decree] has been
driven in forcefully, to remain fast.
These things are not written on *pinakes*
nor sealed up in folds of papyrus,[70]
but you hear them clearly
from a free-speaking tongue. Get out of my sight immediately.

. . . τῶνδ' ἐφήλωται τορῶ⟨ς⟩
γόμφος διαμπάξ, ὡς μένειν ἀραρότως.
ταῦτ' οὐ πίναξίν ἐστιν ἐγγεγραμμένα,
οὐδ' ἐν πτυχαῖς βύβλων κατεσφραγισμένα,
σαφῆ δ' ἀκούεις ἐξ ἐλευθεροστόμου
γλώσσης. κομίζου δ' ὡς τάχιστ' ἐξ ὀμμάτων.

Phiroze Vasunia interprets Pelasgus's first two lines in light of "the notices 'nailed up' in the Athenian agora for all residents to see."[71] On his understanding, Argive writing is thereby limited to public inscriptions on durable media recording, for example, decrees of the assembly, which are orally disseminated, independently verifiable, and openly discussed.[72] Egyptian writing, by contrast, is a matter of wax tablets and sealed letters, private and secretive by nature.[73] While Pelasgus's democratic Argos is a place dependent on oral transactions (ἐλευθεροστόμου / γλώσσης),[74] despotic Egypt is "the graphic space par excellence."[75]

One of the most important uses of writing was to direct and document commercial transactions. Given this fact, Pelasgus's disparagement of the Egyptian herald and his attendants as ξυνέμποροι (939) is significant. While the word literally means "fellow travelers" or "companions,"[76] the context and tone here suggest something pejorative. The herald has been insisting that he is simply reclaiming his runaway property (τἄμ' ὀλωλόθ' εὑρίσκων ἄγω, 918).[77] When forced to depart empty-handed, he wants to know whom to blame. He demands Pelasgus's name, swearing that the war god Ares will settle things, and not with testimony from witnesses or the payment of a fine (935–36). This focus on property and money prompts Pelasgus to respond that the herald and his ilk (⟨σύ⟩ τ' αὐτὸς χοἰ ξυνέμποροι σέθεν, 939) will learn his identity in time. One implication is that the king and his fellow Argives have little in common with traders (ἔμποροι) and their commerce (ἐμπορία).[78]

While mythic tradition and the conventions of tragedy required Aeschylus to set the Danaids' flight to Argos in the long-distant Heroic Age, and to couch it in non-economic terms, his *Suppliant Women* contains discordant notes, perhaps reminding the Athenian audience of other, more contemporary immigrants from Egypt. Indeed, a substantial presence of Egyptian metics seeking both freedom from tyranny and economic opportunity in the years following 480 might help explain Athens's intervention in support of the rebel Inarus shortly after the play's production.[79] The ultimate failure of his revolt would only have increased emigration. The gravestone of one Dionysius, a metic from Naucratis, was apparently found in the Piraeus and is generally dated to the end of the fifth century on the basis of its letter forms.[80] At some point prior to 333, Egyptians residing in the Piraeus became so numerous that the city granted them permission to establish a temple to Isis.[81] By the middle of the fourth century, no fewer than four Egyptian deities were being worshiped in the port deme.[82] And while these developments admittedly occurred later than the production of *Suppliant Women* (some significantly so), Robert Parker has argued that they capped a process of immigration spanning several generations.[83]

Border Crossing

When the Danaids enter from Egypt via the *eisodos*, they encroach upon Argive territory.[84] Boundary crossings were fraught acts for the Greeks, and so their father makes an initial scouting foray. He shortly spots the dust raised by the approaching Argives and counsels his daughters to occupy the nearby hill (πάγον προσίζειν τόνδ'[85] ἀγωνίων θεῶν, 189) and take up positions as suppliants.[86] The ability of a stranger unfamiliar with Argos to recognize a local shrine dedicated to the gods suggests that it was demarcated in one way or another.[87] Its description as belonging to the ἀγώνιοι θεοί implies that the place is not just a sacred space, but has a communal dimension as well.[88] When the chorus's members occupy its altar and effigies, they thus enter a public sanctuary without observing any of the customary ritual preparations.[89]

The play's theme of boundary-crossing is emphasized again when the Argives arrive. Pelasgus marvels that the Danaids have dared to come to a new land on their own, without the usual intermediaries (238–40):

How you fearlessly dared to come to the country
without heralds or *proxenoi* or leaders—
this is astonishing.

ὅπως δὲ χώραν οὔτε κηρύκων ὕπο
ἀπρόξενοί τε νόσφιν ἡγητῶν μολεῖν
ἔτλητ᾽ ἀτρέστως, τοῦτο θαυμαστὸν πέλει.

The Danaids' two main movements in the play so far are ontologically significant.[90] They show that the women are potentially sacrilegious boundary-crossers and that they are largely unfamiliar with Greek poleis and their customs.[91]

The Danaids' choice of which border to cross is not happenstance: they claim descent from an Argive woman and see themselves as exiles returning to their ancestral home.[92] Desired by Zeus, hated by Hera, and pursued by a gadfly, their foremother Io fled through much of Asia before coming to rest in Egypt. There she gave birth to Epaphus, from whom Danaus and his brother Aegyptus trace their line. In a sense the Danaids have reversed Io's progress, migrating back from Egypt to Argos.[93] And their ability to recount the particulars of her journey and to list her subsequent descendants convinces Pelasgus they are telling the truth.[94] At lines 325–26 the Argive leader acknowledges their ancient kinship: "you seem to me to share in this land from long ago" (δοκεῖτε ⟨μέν⟩ μοι τῆσδε κοινωνεῖν χθονός / τἀρχαῖον).

Vincent Farenga has argued that this cross-examination of the Danaids by Pelasgus resembles the ritual scrutiny (*dokimasia*) young Athenian men underwent at eighteen to make sure they were qualified for membership in the citizen body.[95] In the first stage of the process, phratry and deme assemblies reviewed the candidates and voted on whether they were of age and born of Athenian parents married to one another. Those passing the initial scrutiny were subsequently presented to the council (*boule*) as well, which upheld or overturned the local assemblies' judgments.[96] Farenga's claim is attractive in some regards. In its account of the *dokimasiai* of would-be citizens, the Aristotelian *AthPol* uses the verb δοκέω ("to seem") four times.[97] The deme assemblies vote εἰ δοκοῦσι γεγονέναι τὴν ἡλικίαν τὴν ἐκ τοῦ νόμου ("whether [the young men] *seem* to be the legal age"), while the council decides κἄν τις δόξῃ νεώτερος ὀκτωκαίδεκ' ἐτῶν εἶναι ("if anyone *seems* to be younger than eighteen years").[98] When the Danaids seek inclusion in the community by recounting Io's story, Pelasgus uses the same verb (δοκεῖτέ ⟨τοί⟩ μοι . . .) in accepting their claim to Argive descent. Moreover, the political bodies involved in Athenian *dokimasiai* likely posed a series of questions to candidates before arriving at a decision. While no precise description of a *dokimasia* of candidates for citizenship survives,[99] the candidates for Athenian magistracies underwent a similar process likewise referred to as a *dokimasia*. These latter occasions "began with a series of questions that the candidate had to answer, with support from witnesses."[100] And Farenga notes that at lines 291–324 the Danaids attempt to prove the ancestry of their mother "through question and answer, with Pelasgus asking all the questions and the Danaid chorus leader providing all the answers."[101]

Yet upon further examination Farenga's claim reveals its own limitations. First of all, stichomythia (the type of dialogue in Greek tragedy where two characters take turns uttering single lines in a rapid back-and-forth exchange) is a frequent and formal element of the genre. Stichomythia occurs in almost every surviving play, and in contexts having nothing to do with *dokimasiai*. We therefore need to be careful not to read too much into the short question-and-answer format of *Suppliant Women* 291–324. Moreover, as M. L. West notes in his critical apparatus, at lines 291–335 "indications of speakers are lacking; the distribution of lines 298–307 among chorus and king is less certain."[102] Put differently, we cannot be sure that it is always the king who asks the questions and the Danaids who respond.[103] Nor is Pelasgus's interest in the women's genealogy unusual. From Homer onward, Greek literature is replete with instances in which individuals meeting for the first time recount their ancestries at length in search of a common connection.[104] Still more harmful to Farenga's argument is the fact that the Danaids are young women, not young men. While Athenian women did possess citizenship (albeit of a somewhat different sort than men),[105] they were never subjected to anything like the public scrutiny the ephebes underwent at their *dokimasia*. Indeed, the Athenians were careful to shield their wives, daughters, and sisters from the inquiring gaze of other men.[106]

Yet the greatest objection to Farenga's claim is not the Danaids' gender, but the civic status they ultimately receive at Argos. According to *AthPol*, when young men presented themselves for citizenship, two main outcomes were possible. If they were approved, they were inscribed into the citizen body (ἐγγράφεσθαι, 42.1), apparently via the deme registers.[107] If, on the other hand, they were rejected as unfree and lost their appeal, they were sold into slavery (πωλεῖ τοῦτον ἡ πόλις, 42.1). Yet in the play the Danaids receive the in-between status of metics, and so undermine the argument that their interchange with Pelasgus resembles a *dokimasia*.[108]

Although he accepts the women's claim to Argive ancestry, Pelasgus does not admit them as citizens: distant descent was ordinarily insufficient for citizenship, at Athens or elsewhere. The Danaids remain foreigners in important ways, and Pelasgus's language consistently reflects this fact. His preferred word to describe his fellow Argives is ἀστοί.[109] Not once but twice in *Suppliant Women* he refers to the citizen body as ἀστοὶ πάντες in a way that clearly excludes the newcomers (369, 964).[110] His term for the Danaids is at first an oxymoron (ἀστόξενοι, 356) that means something like "citizen-strangers."[111] The women's juridical locale thus mirrors their geographical one: they are stuck in the *methoria*, the vaguely defined border region lying between one set of people and another.[112] They are neither citizens (ἀστοί) nor foreigners (ξένοι), but both at once: ἀστόξενοι.

The Argive Assembly's Grant of Metoikia

In the face of Pelasgus's hesitation to accept them, the Danaids emphasize their suppliant status. Although they have laid their olive branches on the altar of the city's gods and seated themselves in a sanctuary, Pelasgus fears to honor their suit. As Zeitlin notes, within the conventions of Greek tragedy the act of supplication is not a simple phenomenon. On the contrary, it serves as "a staging ground for opposing claims between different practical and moral imperatives that have to be played out in the political arena."[113] In thinking about whether and how to receive the Danaids, Pelasgus must weigh religious and moral, political and practical concerns all at once. Daunted by the consequences, he temporizes. The Danaids may think their supplication is straightforward, like that of, for example, Odysseus on Scheria, who enters the household of a powerful ruler and sits at the hearth seeking refuge.[114] But Pelasgus points out that their circumstances are quite different (365–69):

You are not seated at the hearths of my house.
If the city is (to be) polluted in common,
let the people join in working out remedies.
I will make no promise before
communicating with all the citizens about these matters.

οὔτοι κάθησθε δωμάτων ἐφέστιοι
ἐμῶν. τὸ κοινὸν δ' εἰ μιαίνεται πόλις,
ξυνῆι μελέσθω λαὸς ἐκπονεῖν ἄκη.
ἐγὼ δ' ἂν οὐ κραίνοιμ' ὑπόσχεσιν πάρος,
ἀστοῖς δὲ πᾶσι τῶνδε κοινώσας πέρι.

The women have taken refuge in a public sanctuary, not a private home.[115] Their request affects the community as a whole (τὸ κοινόν, πόλις), and so all the citizens (λαός, ἀστοῖς δὲ πᾶσι) must be involved in finding a solution.

Pelasgus resolves his dilemma by turning it over to his fellow citizens, convening an assembly (described in detail at lines 600–624) with recognizably Athenian features.[116] The adverb πανδημίαι at line 607 indicates that the session is not just a deme assembly, but rather open to all the citizens.[117] The meeting is an unscheduled one, convened by the city's top general with the customary verb ξυγκαλέω (517).[118] It has a herald who closes debate and puts matters to a vote (622).[119] The proposal to give the Danaids sanctuary is ratified by a show of hands (periphrasis of χειροτονία, 607–8).[120] The verb κυρόω describes the assembly's action (603);[121] the result is called a ψήφισμα (601). And Danaus's account of the decree proper begins with an evocative, quintessentially democratic phrase: ἔδοξεν Ἀργείοισιν ("it seemed good to the Argives," 605).[122]

The specific measure enacted is introduced with a deictic article and noun (τόνδε . . . λόγον, 608) that seem a periphrasis of the traditional "so-and-so spoke" (. . . εἶπε) formula used in Athenian decrees.[123] The proposal itself has the ordinary pattern of accusative and infinitive constructions in indirect statement, with the lone finite verb coming in the protasis of a conditional (609–14):

For us[124] to be metics of this land, free
and inviolable, with protection from mortals,
and for no one, whether local or foreign,
to lead us away. And if [someone] uses force,

whoever of these landholders does not help
loses his rights and is sentenced to exile by the people.

ἡμᾶς μετοικεῖν τῆσδε γῆς ἐλευθέρους
κἀρ⟨ρ⟩υσιάστους ξύν τ᾽ ἀσυλίαι βροτῶν·
καὶ μήτ᾽ ἐνοίκων μήτ᾽ ἐπηλύδων τινά
ἄγειν· ἐὰν δὲ προστιθῆι τὸ καρτερόν,
τὸν μὴ βοηθήσαντα τῶνδε γαμόρων
ἄτιμον εἶναι ξὺν φυγῆι δημηλάτωι.

The first four words of the decree, ἡμᾶς μετοικεῖν τῆσδε γῆς, give its essence: the Danaids are to be metics at Argos. As such they will not be slaves, but free persons (ἐλευθέρους, 609). They further receive a cluster of rights protecting themselves and their movable property.[125] They are to be ἀρρυσίαστοι (610), enjoy ἀσυλία (610), and be exempt from the process of ἄγειν (612).[126] The first of these terms means that Danaus and his daughters are not subject to ῥυσιάζειν—that is, they may not be seized as surety for any outstanding obligation.[127] The second term, ἀσυλία, denotes the "inviolability of both person and property"[128] and extends the protection afforded the Danaids beyond the confines of the sanctuary itself.[129] Finally, the newcomers are not subject to the process of φέρειν καὶ ἄγειν, of which the text's ἄγειν is an abbreviated form;[130] they may not be claimed as runaway slaves and carried off by anyone, whether local (ἐνοίκων) or foreign (ἐπηλύδων).[131] Lines 612–14 constitute an enforcement clause. If any of the citizens (γαμόρων) fails to assist them against such violence, he is to be punished with loss of civic rights (ἄτιμον εἶναι) and exile.[132]

These lines provide the most extensive legal description of metoikia surviving from the mid-fifth century. At first glance, they seem more at home in a political treatise like *AthPol* than in Aeschylus. But their position here in a tragedy has ample dramatic motivation. The Danaids are manifestly un-Greek, and so the Argive assembly seeks to clarify for them just what sort of protection they will receive.[133] Moreover, the passage is historically motivated. As we saw earlier, metoikia was an extremely recent legal development at Athens, and one of the play's functions may have been to educate the audience about what exactly this new civic status entailed.[134] In short, *Suppliant Women* offers a mythological *aition* to explain a complex process of historical development. In earlier times, requests for sanctuary had been essentially private in nature and often framed in terms of guest-friendship (ξενία), at both individual and familial levels.[135] But changing circumstances called for a new approach. *Suppliant Women* shows a democratic city taking over and supervising an aristocratic custom. By drawing a link between metoikia and the older practice of supplication, Aeschylus presented "a sophisticated, 'political' version of a primitive and ancient social institution."[136]

Into Argos

The assembly's commitment to the Danaids is soon put to the test. After an intervening choral ode blessing Argos, Danaus again climbs to his lookout, gazes in the opposite direction, and spots the approaching ships of the pursuing Aegyptids.[137] He quickly reassures his daughters and departs for town seeking help. In his absence the Egyptian herald arrives to reclaim the women. After a substantial interlude (whose particulars are unrecoverable because of the corrupt and damaged state of the text),[138] Pelasgus and his attendants enter and intercede; the herald departs with a threat of war. The king's next move is to send the women into the city for safety (954–56):

And you all, together with your attendants,[139]
take heart and proceed into the well-fenced city
closed about with deep device of towers.

ὑμεῖς δὲ πᾶσαι ξὺν φίλοις ὀπάοσιν
θράσος λαβοῦσαι στείχετ' εὐερκῆ πόλιν
πύργων βαθείαι μηχανῆι κεκλῃιμένην.

The walls and towers do more than provide protection; they indicate that the women are headed to the *asty* proper, the city center. Aeschylus's audience would likely have understood this area as analogous to the five urban demes contained within Athens's own city walls prior to the construction of the Phaleric and Long Walls: Coile, Collytus, Cydathenaion, Melite, and Scambonidae.[140] In Athenian parlance, the women's destination is a part of town with strong metic associations. According to the epigraphical evidence, four of these five demes (excepting only Coile) were among the six demes with the largest total number of metics.[141] The Danaids would have found plenty of immigrant company within the walls; Whitehead's figures suggest that almost half (over 48 percent) of all metics with known domiciles lived in the Athenian *asty*.

As the newcomers prepare to enter Argos, the play reaches its end. Taplin comments that "the final clearing of the stage is not merely an unavoidable and mechanical stage movement. The willing and unmolested departure of the chorus from the sanctuary represents in visual stage terms the achievement and ratification of its safety."[142] But the Danaids' departure has an unmistakable political dimension as well. For the Danaids do not exit by themselves: they are attended by another, secondary chorus consisting of Argive men.[143] These citizens had likely attended the assembly and voted to make the Danaids metics; their appearance at line 985 is thus the visible fulfillment of their promise to protect the newcomers against aggression. As the final procession gets underway, the spectators see before them a representation of successful metoikia.[144] Metics and citizens, each group marked by its distinctive garb, exchange song and dance their way out the *eisodos* toward the city that will house them both.[145] For their part, the newcomers praise their hosts and declare firmly (1024–29):

Let us no longer honor
with hymns the mouthings of the Nile,
but rather the life-giving rivers which through the land
tip a tranquil draught,
soothing this country [i.e. Argos]
with fertile pourings of earth.

μηδ' ἔτι Νείλου
προχοὰς σέβωμεν ὕμνοις,
ποταμοὺς δ' οἳ διὰ χώρας
θελεμὸν πῶμα χέουσιν
πολύτεκνοι, λιπαροῖς χεύμασι γαίας
τόδε με⟨ι⟩λίσσοντες οὖδας.

This declaration is extra-religious in nature. By shifting their worship from the mighty Nile to the rivulets of Inachus, the Danaids are in effect shifting their allegiance from Egypt to Argos.[146] And like their adopted streams, they have the potential to benefit the land that takes them in.

2

Spoken Like a Metic

The Argive decision to accept the Danaids is one of the focal points of *Suppliant Women*. The welcome the newcomers receive is only partial, however: they are offered metoikia rather than citizenship. The play gives no explicit rationale for the motion adopted by the Argive assemblymen. Their meeting occurs off-stage, and the audience hears only a summary account of the proceedings from an interested party. Yet the Argives may act as they do because of their fears about the potential impact of the newcomers. This chapter traces the political lineaments of their unease, arguing that the play posits important connections between civic status and speech norms. In their foreign speech, antidemocratic inclinations, and willingness to put their own interests ahead of the city's, the Danaid women constitute a threat to Argos. And their father proves worse. Although he encourages his daughters to mind their tongues and manners, his guile matches and indeed surpasses their violence. His unprepossessing request for Argive bodyguards conceals something more sinister: coup d'état and tyranny. In contrast to the newcomers, Pelasgus exemplifies virtuous principles of citizen speech. His free-speaking, forthright ways embody the *isegoria* and *peitho* upon which democracy depends.

The fears *Suppliant Women* evokes about metic speech are consonant with Pericles's citizenship law of 451/50 limiting membership in the city to those born of two Athenian parents. Some scholars have understood the law as an attempt to regulate the number of citizens. While this view has some merits, other scholars have shown that the law can simultaneously be read as an attempt to regulate the caliber of the citizen body and craft an Athenian civic identity. One way it does so is by restricting metic political activity. Because non-citizens could not be trusted to subordinate their own interests to those of Athens, they were given no opportunity to serve on the deliberative bodies governing its democracy. In short, they were barred from participating in the assembly (*ekklesia*), council (*boule*), and law courts (*dikasteria*) because they could not be trusted to speak and listen like citizens. Like their real-life counterparts, Danaus and his daughters seemed insufficiently committed to persuasion (πειθώ). Preferring bold speech (θρασυστομεῖν) and guile to free speech (ἐλευθεροστομεῖν) and truth, they could never be safely assimilated into the polis.

The Danaids: Metic Speech and *Bia*

The newcomers from Egypt are a linguistic anomaly at Argos. At lines 118–19, and again at 129–30, the chorus address the soil on which they now stand: ἱλεῶμαι[1] μὲν Ἀπίαν βοῦνιν— / καρβᾶνα δ' αὐδὰν εὖ γᾶ κοννεῖς—. Their first clause is straightforward: "I propitiate the Apian territory"; the second, however, admits of multiple meanings. Its verb κοννέω is unusual, glossed by Hesychius as equivalent to συνίημι, ἐπίσταμαι, and γινώσκω.[2] On one interpretation, the accusative καρβᾶνα δ' αὐδάν functions as its direct object: "land, well you know my foreign tongue." But as a verb of knowing or understanding, κοννεῖς can also (like those mentioned by Hesychius) introduce indirect statement. Understood with an omitted participle or infinitive, the clause might then mean: "land, well you know *that* my speech is foreign." One reading suggests previous acquaintance, the other a first encounter: which is to be preferred? The chorus's words are Greek, and their use of the adjective Ἀπίαν suggests that these descendants of Io may already know some version of the story Pelasgus will later recount at lines 268–70.[3] On this understanding, the arrivals and the land recognize one another despite the passage of time and supervening changes.[4] Yet the Danaids' use of Greek requires little or no explanation, since "it is the established convention of tragedy to disregard [differences of language] . . . unless their mention serves some special purpose."[5] Of greater interest is the Danaids' vocabulary: in addition to the rare κοννέω, they employ an unusual word for "foreign" (καρβάν, κάρβανος).[6] In some ways, then, the women's speech parallels their exotic appearance. As Sandin puts it, "the language [of the first ode] is peculiar at times even by Aeschylean standards . . . [and] perhaps a deliberate means to depict . . . the foreignness of the Danaids."[7] The newcomers' strange speech works to isolate them from the natives they will soon encounter.[8] Friis Johansen and Whittle conclude that "their language is intelligible to the land from which they draw their origin . . . but not . . . to any other human beings in it than themselves."[9]

The Danaids' political sentiments are as alien to the Argives as the words they utter. When, after a long exchange, Pelasgus rejects their request for sanctuary by saying he must consult with all the citizens, the women respond with an impassioned outburst (370–75):

You *are* the city, you the people:
you, head of the council, subject to no judge,
administer the altar, the hearth of the land
with your single-voted nods,
and on your single-sceptered thrones
you arrange every matter. Steer clear of pollution.

σύ τοι πόλις, σὺ δὲ τὸ δήμιον[10]
πρύτανις ἄκριτος ὢν
κρατύνεις βωμόν, ἑστίαν χθονός,
μονοψήφοισι νεύμασιν σέθεν,
μονοσκήπτροισι δ' ἐν θρόνοις χρέος
πᾶν ἐπικραίνεις· ἄγος φυλάσσου.

The women's veiled threat to pollute the land provides a fitting cap to their outspoken tone. Yet their remarks are even more inappropriate than scholars have hitherto recognized. Patricia Easterling has argued that these lines combine "the language of monarchy (thrones, nods) and the language of Athenian democratic institutions."[11] The passage is not, however, a neutral mélange of political terminology borrowed from various types of regime. On the contrary, its many incongruities are deliberate and reveal the Danaids' fundamental antipathy to democracy.[12]

Although the chorus evoke important features of political life familiar from historical Athens, they consistently do so in negative ways. According to the women, Pelasgus is not an individual representing the city and carrying out its wishes; rather, he *is* the city (πόλις) and its sovereign people (τὸ δήμιον) rolled into one. They further describe him as πρύτανις (*prytanis*), a word sometimes found in lyric poetry with the meaning "ruler, lord."[13] But to the Athenian spectators, the term denoted above all a "member of the tribe presiding in βουλή or ἐκκλησία."[14] Put differently, the women compare Pelasgus to a member of the influential group directing the government of Athens. Like real-life πρυτάνεις, the fictive Pelasgus receives foreigners, sets the agenda for and summons an assembly, and manages his city's response to a crisis.[15] There are, however, crucial differences. To begin with, *prytaneis* of the council ordinarily numbered fifty at any given moment, while Pelasgus is the sole occupant of the office. Moreover, the Danaids describe Pelasgus as a πρύτανις ἄκριτος. LSJ translate the adjective here as "subject to no judge."[16] As Easterling notes, this is tantamount to saying that he is οὐχ ὑπεύθυνος—politically unaccountable.[17] Yet it was a fundamental feature of Athenian life that all the city's magistrates were subordinate to and scrutinized by the *demos*.[18] The Danaids thus invert the ordinary Athenian political relationships whereby *prytanis* is subject to *boule* and *boule* to *ekklesia*: on their view the Argive people take their marching orders from Pelasgus and not vice versa. A second meaning of ἄκριτος perhaps applies here as well. According to LSJ, the word can also mean "continual, unceasing."[19] But one of the most important aspects of the council presidency (πρυτανεία) was that it rotated continuously, with each tribe's representatives holding it for precisely one lunar month.[20] Given that council members were chosen by lot, and that each man could serve only twice in his lifetime,[21] the individual *prytaneis* who presided over meetings of the *boule* were constantly changing.[22] In describing Pelasgus with the oxymoronic phrase πρύτανις ἄκριτος, the Danaids are not so much employing democratic terminology as subverting it. The Argive's role in directing his state is alleged to be continual and free from popular scrutiny; as such it would run counter to the democratic norms cherished by the play's spectators.

The Danaids endow Pelasgus with other problematic attributes as well. Some of his powers are religious. His administration of the city's altar (κρατύνεις βωμόν) resembles that of a hereditary priest, and his manner in discharging his duties is peremptory. Like Zeus he accomplishes things with a nod here and there (νεύμασιν).[23] The motions of his chin are μονοψήφοισι ("single-voting")—that is to say, sovereign; as such they contrast with the many individual votes repeatedly tallied in Athenian courts and assemblies.[24] And with the phrase χρέος / πᾶν ἐπικραίνεις the Danaids assign him direction of all Argos's financial affairs. Although LSJ give the noun χρέος the more general meaning of "business, affair, matter" in this passage, Friis Johansen and Whittle note that it likely has the particular connotation of "debt" as well.[25] Yet at Athens spending authority was often vested in boards; those men empowered to disburse the city's funds on their own[26] were subject to annual financial audits conducted by teams of magistrates called *euthunoi* and *logistai*. By contrast Pelasgus is said to control things individually from on high, μονοσκήπτροισι δ' ἐν θρόνοις ("on his single-sceptered thrones"); the metaphorical scepter he wields represents the traditional Greek symbol of monarchical authority.[27] In short, although the Danaids employ apparently democratic terminology to describe Pelasgus's position, they do so in an outspoken way that calls into question both their understanding of democracy and their support for it.[28]

Pelasgus immediately recoils, appalled by the women's remarks. Yet their cavalier threat of ritual pollution causes him to avoid an immediate confrontation. He instead stalls, pressing the women for details about why they reject their cousins' suit (387–91):

If the sons of Aegyptus have power over you
by law of the city, claiming to be nearest of kin,
who would wish to oppose them?
It is necessary for you to defend yourselves according to your laws
from home,
that [the men] have no authority over you.

εἴ τοι κρατοῦσι παῖδες Αἰγύπτου σέθεν
νόμωι πόλεως, φάσκοντες ἐγγύτατα γένους
εἶναι, τίς ἂν τοῖς ἀντιωθῆναι θέλοι;
δεῖ τοί σε φεύγειν κατὰ νόμους τοὺς οἴκοθεν,
ὡς οὐκ ἔχουσιν κῦρος οὐδὲν ἀμφὶ σοῦ.

The Danaids avoid his questions entirely, taking refuge in a blanket rejection of servitude: "May I never be in any way subject to the rule of men" (μή τί ποτ' οὖν γενοίμαν ὑποχε⟨ί⟩ριος / κράτεσιν ἀρσένων, 392–93). As several scholars have noted, their failure to even mention the laws of Egypt tacitly endorses the suitors' claim to them. Their remark seems intended as a red herring to divert Pelasgus, for what they perhaps dare not say is that they are following their father's lead in seeking to outsmart an oracle.[29]

When Pelasgus continues to temporize,[30] the women make explicit their earlier, latent threat (455–66):

Danaids: Hear the end of our many reverential words.
Pelasgus: I am listening, and you may speak. They will not escape me.
D: We have upper and lower girdles[31] that gather our *peploi*.
P: These items are perhaps appropriate to women.
D: They possess a marvelous trick, you know.
P: What do you mean by this remark?
D: If you will not lend some reliable help to our expedition—
P: What does your girdle-trick accomplish?
D: To decorate these images with new tablets.

P: This is enigmatic talk: tell me straight out.
D: To hang ourselves from these gods as swiftly as possible.
P: Your speech lashes my heart.

Χο.: πολλῶν ἄκουσον τέρματ' αἰδοίων λόγων.
Βα.: ἤκουσα, καὶ λέγοις ἄν· οὔ με φεύξεται.
Χο.: ἔχω στρόφους ζώνας τε, συλλαβὰς πέπλων.
Βα.: τάχ' ἂν γυναικῶν ταῦτα συμπρεπῆ πέλοι.
Χο.: ἐκ τῶνδε τοίνυν, ἴσθι, μηχανὴ καλή.
Βα.: λέξον τίν' αὐδὴν τήνδε γηρυθεῖς' ἔσηι.
Χο.: εἰ μή τι πιστὸν τῶιδ' ὑποστήσηι στόλωι—
Βα.: τί σοι περαίνει μηχανὴ ξυζωμάτων;
Χο.: νέοις πίναξιν βρέτεα κοσμῆσαι τάδε.
Βα.: αἰνιγματῶδες τοὔπος· ἀλλ' ἁπ⟨λ⟩ῶς φράσον.
Χο.: ἐκ τῶνδ' ὅπως τάχιστ' ἀπάγξασθαι θεῶν.
Βα.: ἤκουσα μαστικτῆρα καρδίας λόγον.

This stichomythia reveals much of the Danaids' *modus operandi*.[32] Conceptually, the Greeks often conceived of the opposition to *peitho* ("persuasion") as twofold, with *dolos* ("cunning") representing one end of the spectrum and *bia* ("force") the other. The first of these was ordinarily gendered female, the second male.[33] As elsewhere in the play, however, here too there is a strong element of gender reversal, with the Danaids linked to violence.[34] Zeitlin has tried to minimize the coercive nature of the women's speech, arguing that "pure Persuasion is only an ideal, not a reality. The opposition between *Peitho* and *Bia* is not a mutually exclusive dichotomy but rather a hierarchy of values."[35] Yet her contention does not take sufficient account of the way the Danaids toy with Pelasgus,[36] progressing from hint to riddle before ending with euphemism and threat.[37] Pelasgus's final metaphor lays bare the violence embodied by their plan.[38] Although he hears words (ἤκουσα . . . λόγον), he experiences something far more visceral: the scourging of his heart.[39] The Danaids have the whip hand in the exchange, resembling foreign despots like Xerxes who routinely have their subordinates flogged.[40] With their violent ways and willingness to pollute the city, the Danaids resemble nothing so much as the serpents that earlier plagued "Apian" Argos—that is, the city when it was governed by Apis.[41] At line 267 Pelasgus described those creatures as a "hostile colony of snakes" (δρακονθόμιλον δυσμενῆ ξυνοικίαν). Each of these three terms has an analogue in the women. When Pelasgus originally sees them, his first words are ποδαπὸν <u>ὅμιλον</u> . . . προσφωνοῦμεν; ("What sort of band do I address?" 234). The ξυνοικίαν of the snakes calls to mind the μετοικία awarded the

Danaids.[42] And as their threat shows, the women have just as much potential to be δυσμενεῖς to Argos and its inhabitants.

Danaus: Metic Speech and *Dolos*

Danaus constitutes a different sort of threat to Argos. More polished than his daughters, he has a different sense of how to achieve their ends. As soon as he spots the dust raised by the approaching Argives, he offers his daughters extensive elocutionary advice (191–203):

Move as quickly as possible.
Reverently holding in your left hands
the white-wound suppliant boughs,
ornaments of Zeus Aidoios,
answer the strangers clearly with
humble, pitiful, needy words,
as befits newcomers, saying that
your exile involves no bloodshed.
Let no effrontery accompany your speech,
nor idle talk from † †
Speak with a tranquil countenance.
Be neither quick nor slow to speak.
The folk here are especially suspicious of that.
Remember to yield: you are needy foreigners in exile.
Speaking boldly does not become those who are weak.

ἀλλ' ὡς τάχιστα βᾶτε καὶ λευκοστεφεῖς
ἱκετηρίας, ἀγάλματ' αἰδοίου Διός,
σεμνῶς ἔχουσαι διὰ χερῶν εὐωνύμων
αἰδοῖα καὶ γοεδνὰ καὶ ζαχρεῖ' ἔπη
ξένους ἀμείβεσθ', ὡς ἐπήλυδας πρέπει,
τορῶς λέγουσαι τάσδ' ἀναιμάκτους φυγάς.
φθογγῆι δ' ἑπέσθω πρῶτα μὲν τὸ μὴ θρασύ,
τὸ μὴ μάταιον δ' ἐκ †μετώπω† σωφρονῶν[43]
ἴτω προσώπων ὄμματος παρ' ἡσύχου.
καὶ μὴ πρόλεσχος μηδ' ἐφολκὸς ἐν λόγωι
γένηι· τὸ τῆιδε κάρτ' ἐπίφθονον γένος.
μέμνησο δ' εἴκειν· χρεῖος εἶ ξένη[44] φυγάς·
θρασυστομεῖν γὰρ οὐ πρέπει τοὺς ἥσσονας.

Danaus matches his daughters' movements to their speech. Their suppliant boughs and presence at the altar offer a visual representation of their suit. Their words must underscore their humility, neediness, and claim to protection. The women should hold the boughs reverentially (σεμνῶς, 193) with the left hand (διὰ χερῶν εὐωνύμων, 193), leaving the right hand free to grip the altar. They must speak distinctly (τορῶς, 196) and calmly (ὄμματος παρ' ἡσύχου, 199). Danaus's imperative ἀμείβεσθ' (195) implies that they should not speak first, but wait until spoken to. Their answers should neither interrupt nor require prompting (μὴ πρόλεσχος μηδ' ἐφολκὸς ἐν λόγωι / γένηι, 200–201). They should not argue but yield (μέμνησο δ' εἴκειν, 202). Above all, they must remember their inferior position and avoid any sort of bold speech (θρασυστομεῖν γὰρ οὐ πρέπει τοὺς ἥσσονας, 203).[45]

Danaus's coaching is carefully calculated.[46] Like the best logographers later in the fifth century, he tailors the Danaids' speech to fit them and their circumstances (ἠθοποιία): their language must reflect their status as suppliants. Susanne Gödde has argued that in tragedy, suppliant ritual "establishes a specific manner of speech, whereby the suppliant presents his case and seeks to bring about his acceptance."[47] According to her, such speech is characterized by the suppliant's awareness of the fragility of his situation and by the proximity of death.[48] This is certainly true of the Danaids, who throughout the play stress their flight, the persecution they face, and their willingness to die.[49]

Yet additional features of his remarks require comment. There were in ancient Greece several types of suppliants; the women are to differentiate themselves from these others by emphasizing their unpolluted state (τάσδ' ἀναιμάκτους φυγάς).[50] Moreover, suppliants might come from all over, including within the polis.[51] But Danaus emphasizes the women's status as *foreign* suppliants: they must speak as befits newcomers, ὡς ἐπήλυδας πρέπει. The noun ἔπηλυς should here be given the full force of its primary definition in LSJ: "*one who comes to* a place."[52]

An equally important aspect of Danaus's instructions is what he omits: nowhere does he mention gender. Yet Laura McClure has noted that "Attic drama more commonly depicts women's speech, even when it takes a ritual form, as disruptive and subversive of social stability."[53] One might therefore expect Danaus to caution his daughters that they are women, and as such should defer to their male interlocutors. Elsewhere in the play (e.g. 996–1005) he certainly tells his daughters to mind their gender. The overall effect of the earlier passage is therefore to imply that although the Danaids operate under a number of linguistic constraints at Argos, the most important is their status as newcomers.[54] Their father recognizes how important it is for them to conform to Argive expectations about how foreigners should talk.[55] If they wish to succeed, they must above all avoid every sort of bold speech (θρασυστομεῖν).

Danaus's soft-spoken exterior conceals a more insidious and greater danger to Argos. After Pelasgus, reluctantly and under duress, decides to consult his fellow Argives, he tells Danaus to gather up the women's suppliant branches, and prepares to send him off to the city. But before departing, Danaus makes an unusual request of his own (492–99):

Send with me bodyguards and local guides
so that we may find
the altars of the city's tutelary gods,
and the †tutelary† seats before the temples,
and so that we may safely move throughout the town.
My appearance is not the same as yours.
The Nile does not raise a race like that of the Inachus.
Be careful lest boldness beget fear.
In the past people have killed their friends out of ignorance, you know.

ὀπάονας δὲ φράστοράς τ᾽ ἐγχωρίων
ξύμπεμψον, ὡς ἂν τῶν πολισσούχων θεῶν
βωμοὺς προνάους καὶ †πολισσούχων† ἕδρας
εὕρωμεν, ἀσφάλεια δ᾽ ἧι δι᾽ ἄστεως
στείχουσι. μορφῆς δ᾽ οὐχ ὁμόστολος φύσις·
Νεῖλος γὰρ οὐχ ὅμοιον Ἰνάχωι γένος
τρέφει. φύλαξαι μὴ θράσος τέκηι φόβον·
καὶ δὴ φίλον τις ἔκταν᾽ ἀγνοίας ὕπο.

At first glance, Danaus's request for a bodyguard to help him move safely to the city's altars seems unobjectionable, even prudent. He does not look like an Argive and could attract hostile attention. Yet his justification contains a troubling echo of events that had occurred in Athens nearly a century before the play's production. In 561/60 Peisistratus claimed he had been attacked by his enemies and requested a citizen bodyguard; with these armed attendants he promptly took control of the Acropolis and its sanctuaries and established a tyranny.[56]

Suppliant Women's initial depiction of Danaus assumes added significance in light of this later request for a bodyguard.[57] As they enter the orchestra at the start of the play, the women identify their father as the brains behind their flight (11–15):

Danaus, our father and councilor and leader,
moving these pawns brought it about as the most honorable of ills

for us to flee pell-mell through the sea's wave
and come to the land of Argos . . .

Δαναὸς δέ, πατὴρ καὶ βούλαρχος καὶ στασίαρχος,
τάδε πεσσονομῶν κύδιστ' ἀχέων ἐπέκρανεν,
φεύγειν ἀνέδην διὰ κῦμ' ἅλιον,
κέλσαι δ' Ἄργους γαῖαν . . .

Danaus is here described with three uncommon terms: βούλαρχος, στασίαρχος, and πεσσονομῶν; each makes its first recorded appearance in the present passage. LSJ translate the first two words as "adviser of a plan" and "chief of a band or company"; these nouns clearly relate to the play's background.[58] As their leader, Danaus has literally orchestrated his family's flight to Argos. The participle πεσσονομῶν comments on the way he has done so.[59] The verb from which it is formed appears in only one other place in Greek literature,[60] with the primary meaning of "set the πεσσοί in order for playing; play at πεσσοί."[61] Danaus resembles someone playing a board game, and his ability to outwit his Egyptian opponents under difficult circumstances is a testament to his strategic vision and tactical abilities.[62]

Yet as scholars have noted, these same three terms operate in multiple registers. Friis Johansen and Whittle see βούλαρχος καὶ στασίαρχος as a hendiadys with sinister accents; "Danaus' βουλαρχία, the more general term, amounts in fact to a στασιαρχία, a leadership of sedition."[63] The surrounding context suggests that both nouns look backward in time to Danaus's quarrel with his brother about who should rule Egypt.[64] But Sommerstein rightly argues that the description is also proleptic: the meaning of *boularchos* here encompasses "one who desires to rule."[65] Moreover, the term *boularchos* does more than point out Danaus's objective; it is suggestive about the ways he seeks to acquire and maintain power.[66] The first part of the compound (βουλ-) hints at a link to βούλευσις, the intentional killing of another by means of an agent, and thus to the Danaids' impending murder of the Aegyptids.[67]

The term *stasiarchos* is likewise multifaceted. Wilson notes that "in choreographic terms, *stasis* was one's 'position' within the choral unit,"[68] and Danaus directs the chorus's initial entrance. But in tragedy, music in general and choral activity in particular often have important political implications.[69] In the *Oresteia*, for instance, the Erinyes form a chorus, at first figurative and later literal, which is repeatedly linked to political strife—that is, *stasis*.[70] And Sommerstein correctly notes that in

Suppliant Women stasiarchos has the added meaning of "one who begins civil strife."[71] The play's presentation of a *stasiarchos* explicitly asking for an escort is therefore ominous, not innocuous.[72]

Danaus's description as βούλαρχος καὶ στασίαρχος is in fact programmatic for the subsequent trilogy.[73] The image of him as πεσσονομῶν builds on the implications of the first two terms. Ancient evidence for play with *pessoi* extends as far back as the *Odyssey* (1.107), where the term seems to refer to an unspecified sort of board game.[74] Yet game playing is not just a recreational activity; it can also be politically charged.[75] And while the noun πεσσός ("stone," "piece") does not appear in *Suppliant Women*, its semantic cousin ψῆφος does so repeatedly, and in political contexts.[76] According to Leslie Kurke, two distinct types of political *pessoi* games emerged during the archaic period. The first, called *polis*, was a "battle game" whose objective was to keep one's own forces together and use them to disperse and then capture the enemy. The second, a more enigmatic one known as "five lines" (*pente grammai*), involved a king-piece (βασιλεύς) and "movement from a holy line" (ἱερὰ καλουμένη γραμμή). A fragment of Heraclitus implies that the object of the game was to capture the kingship.[77] Now, many of the fifth-century spectators watching *Suppliant Women* were doubtless gamers themselves.[78] And so Aeschylus's audience might naturally have wondered which type of *pessoi* game Danaus was playing. The appearance of the participle πεσσονομῶν early in the play, together with the subsequent uses of ψῆφοι, permits us to interpret the action of the trilogy as game-playing on a grand scale. Kurke has claimed that of the two *pessoi* games, "*polis* analogizes the democratic city . . . [and] is played with many pieces, all of equal status, on an undifferentiated gameboard."[79] Pelasgus's confrontation with the Egyptian herald is suggestive in this regard: the Argive casts himself as a nameless, ordinary citizen of a homogeneous city without political hierarchy or differentiation.[80] When the Egyptian herald departs, Pelasgus awaits a battle proper in which he must seek to outmaneuver his foes and drive them from the field.[81]

By contrast, the second *pessoi* game, *pente grammai*, "mimes the form of oligarchy . . . [and is played with] pieces in competition for supreme status, on a board whose space is itself differentiated and hierarchized."[82] As their κύριος (legal guardian), Danaus outranks his daughters and directs their movements throughout the play.[83] With his move to the altars in the center of the city (βωμοὺς ἀστικούς θεῶν ⟨θ'⟩ ἕδρας, 501), he assumes a position on the "holy line."[84] And he subsequently ventures forth alone in a bold[85] and ultimately successful[86] effort to gain dominion at

Argos. It seems that everyone in *Suppliant Women* is playing *pessoi*. But while Pelasgus and the other Argives are busy losing to the Egyptian suitors at *polis*, crafty Danaus proves a champion at *pente grammai*.[87]

Pelasgus: Citizen Speech and *Peitho*

In contrast to the threats of the Danaids and the deceptions of Danaus, the speech of Pelasgus is free and forthright. Early in the play, the Danaids ask who he is (247–49). He responds with a proud assertion of his ancestry: "I am Pelasgus, son of the earth-born Palaichthon" (τοῦ γηγενοῦς γάρ εἰμ' ἐγὼ Παλαίχθονος / ἶνις Πελασγός, 250–51). Yet when the Egyptian herald asks substantially the same question at lines 938–39, Pelasgus's response is markedly different:[88] "Why should I tell you my name? You will learn it in time . . . (τί σοὶ λέγειν χρὴ τοὔνομ'; ἐν χρόνωι μαθὼν / εἴσηι ⟨σύ⟩ τ' αὐτός). Following this bit of bravado, he elaborates. The decision to accept the Danaids is the act not of a royal scion, but of a democratic city: "a united vote of the people acting in concert has authorized [the women's metoikia]" (τοιάδε δημόπρακτος ἐκ πόλεως μία / ψῆφος κέκρανται, 942–43). Pelasgus here links his authority to his status as an Argive citizen.[89] He explicitly alludes to the primary venue for democratic political speech, the assembly, and to a specific motion voiced and approved there.[90] His words δημόπρακτος ἐκ πόλεως recall the δήμου κρατοῦσα χείρ of line 604; his phrase μία / ψῆφος reminds us that the Argives voted οὐ διχορρόπως (605); and the perfect indicative κέκρανται comes from the same verb as the participle describing the assemblymen's actions (κραινόντων, 608).[91]

Shortly thereafter he sums things up by describing himself as a "free-mouthed tongue" (σαφῆ δ' ἀκούεις ἐξ ἐλευθεροστόμου / γλώσσης, 948–49). His main point here is that his identity as an individual is in some senses irrelevant, for his voice and the city's are identical. But his description of himself as an ἐλευθεροστόμου / γλώσσης has other ramifications: it alludes not just to his participation in the democratic assembly, but to the principles guiding that body's deliberations as well.[92] Kurt Raaflaub has argued that in Aeschylus locutions such as ἐλεύθερον λέγειν and ἐλευθεροστομεῖν denote a general "ability to express one's opinion"[93] deriving from the binary oppositions Greek/barbarian and free/slave already operative by the end of the sixth century. He further claims that while the *context* of Pelasgus's remark is political, "its meaning is entirely unpolitical: the word of a free man is true and reliable."[94] Yet this view does not take full account of the passage's particulars. After all, the Egyptian messenger is a barbarian and an underling, yet in time his threats of war and Argive defeat (934–37, 950–51) prove just as true and reliable as Pelasgus's remarks, if not more so.[95] Moreover, Raaflaub himself has argued that the concept of *isegoria* first emerged under the Peisistratids in the context of power struggles among the Athenian nobility.[96] Etymologically linked to the words ἰσός ("equal") and ἀγορεύω ("address, announce"), the noun originally denoted the equal opportunity for aristocratic citizens to speak in public gatherings.[97] Cleisthenes's reforms of 508/7 extended this possibility to citizens of more moderate means (i.e. zeugite status) as well. By the time of *Suppliant Women*'s performance in the 460s, the broad middle stratum of Athenian citizens had had four decades to practice speaking in a variety of democratic bodies, including the reconstituted *boule*, the local deme assemblies, and the *ekklesia* itself.[98] Given this history, Pelasgus's portrayal of himself as a free-speaking, nameless "everyman" who participates in and takes responsibility for his community's decisions has particular resonance.[99] His habit of free speech stands as a counterpoint to the words and ways of the play's new metics. While he exercises his right as an Argive citizen to ἐλευθεροστομεῖν, the Danaids engage in θρασυστομεῖν.

Although Pelasgus is the leader of Argos, he does not rule the city by fiat. We saw earlier that he initially refuses to accept the Danaids' supplication without involving all the citizens in the decision. When the women protest, he again insists (398–401):

As I said earlier, I would not do this
without the *demos*, though I might,
lest the people sometime say, if something somehow goes wrong,
that "honoring newcomers you destroyed the city."[100]

εἶπον δὲ καὶ πρίν, οὐκ ἄνευ δήμου τάδε
πράξαιμ' ἄν, οὐδέ περ κρατῶν, μὴ καί ποτε
εἴπηι λεώς, εἴ πού τι μὴ τοῖον[101] τύχοι,
'ἐπήλυδας τιμῶν ἀπώλεσας πόλιν.'

Crucial to the passage are the words οὐδέ περ κρατῶν, which Friis Johansen and Whittle expansively translate as "even though I am ruler (and so could act without consulting the people, if I wanted to)."[102] Peter Burian makes much of the phrase, arguing that Pelasgus's voluntary transfer of jurisdiction produces much of the play's tragic power.[103] The historical context and dramatic particulars support a more nuanced reading, however. Pelasgus's ancestry, accomplishments, and military credentials certainly establish him as the preeminent man in Argos. At lines 251–52, for instance, he refers to himself as both ἀρχηγέτης and ἄναξ. Yet in important ways he is more like an Athenian *strategos*: he is ultimately subordinate to the citizenry, and not vice versa.[104] As he goes to convene the Argive assembly, he utters a parting remark: "May persuasion follow, and practical good fortune" (πειθὼ δ' ἕποιτο καὶ τύχη πρακτήριος, 523). His implication is that those in attendance will be rhetorically sophisticated, and that even his considerable authority will only go so far: persuasion will be required. Not for nothing is his grammatical construction an optative of wish.

Pelasgus's desire to involve the Argive *demos* seems less the magnanimity of an unfettered monarch than the habit of someone accustomed to looking over his shoulder.[105] His fear of blame from the λεώς perhaps reminded spectators of the treatment the sovereign people had meted out to Athenian leaders during the previous decades. Prior to the reforms of Ephialtes in 462/61 "the *demos* had already assumed authority in trials for treason and conspiracy and in prosecutions for official misconduct."[106] In 489, for instance, Miltiades was led before the *demos* (ὑπὸ τὸν δῆμον) on a charge of attempting to deceive the Athenians (τῆς Ἀθηναίων ἀπάτης εἵνεκεν).[107] Pelasgus demonstrates a caution that would have behooved real-life Athenian politicians: when it came to making important decisions, close collaboration with the *demos* was advisable.

The precise accusation Pelasgus fears (ἐπήλυδας τιμῶν ἀπώλεσας πόλιν) points in the direction of bribery. In the Greek world, honor was generally bestowed in recognition of benefactions made or services rendered. If Pelasgus were not careful, his fellow Argives might imagine he had used his relative independence as commander to arrange with the Danaids some type of aristocratic understanding, a private *quid pro quo* endangering the whole city.[108] This anxiety apparently motivates his instructions to Danaus to gather and move the suppliants' branches. His purpose is (483–85):

> . . . so that all the citizens may see a proof
> of this arrival, and I may not be accused:
> for the people like to find fault with their magistrates.

> . . . ὡς ἴδωσι τῆσδ' ἀφίξεως τέκμαρ
> πάντες πολῖται, μηδ' ἀπορριφθῆι λόγος
> ἐμοῦ κάτ'· ἀρχῆς γὰρ φιλαίτιος λεώς.

Pelasgus's claim that ἀρχῆς . . . φιλαίτιος λεώς implies that the Argives have become used to criticizing their leaders publicly and holding them to account.[109] In this regard they resemble the Athenians, who sometime in the fifth century implemented the annual accountability proceedings known as *euthunai*.[110] Knowing that he would come under such scrutiny, a prudent democratic leader like Pelasgus could minimize his risk by emphasizing the external constraints under which he operated, and by involving as closely as possible the citizens who might ultimately judge him.[111]

How Pelasgus consults with the Argive *demos* is as important as the fact that he does so. Some scholars have claimed that he deceives his fellow citizens and thus manipulates the assembly's deliberations.[112] Their argument is essentially twofold. First, they say he withholds crucial information. Although he claims that ritual pollution and hostility from Zeus will ensue if the women are rejected and kill themselves, he does not mention that war with the Egyptians will follow upon their acceptance.[113] But this argument does not take into account the fact that the assembly occurs off-stage, and that the audience hears only highlights from an interested party, Danaus.[114] Even if Pelasgus was silent about war with the Egyptians, that does not prove deception. He might have thought the women's threat of suicide clear, and the ensuing pollution inescapable.[115] War, by contrast, might have seemed more remote and less frightening. If worse came to worst, the bravery of his Argives would doubtless prevail against a small band of effeminate barley-drinkers far from home.[116]

The second argument for a deceptive Pelasgus derives from Danaus's summary of the meeting. According to him, "the Pelasgian people heeded [Pelasgus's] rhetorical turns, and Zeus brought about the result" (δημηγόρους δ' ἤκουσεν εὐπειθὴς στροφάς / δῆμος Πελασγῶν· Ζεὺς δ' ἐπέκρανεν τέλος, 623–24).[117] The phrase δημηγόρους . . . στροφάς requires analysis here. Sommerstein construes it as pejorative, "tricks of oratory."[118] But the adjective δημηγόρους seems to derive from δῆμος ("the sovereign people") and ἀγορεύω ("to speak in the assembly"), neither of which is inherently unfavorable.[119] The preambles to fifth-century decrees routinely began with implicit praise for the judgment of the *demos* (ἔδοξε τῷ δήμῳ, "it seemed good to the people"). And a herald traditionally started assemblies by asking τίς ἀγορεύειν βούλεται; ("Who wishes to speak?").[120] Friis Johansen and Whittle have likewise argued for a negative cast to the noun στροφάς, translating it as "turnings." They contend that it generally means clear changes in direction and so "cannot denote 'turnings' of the people by Pelasgus. . . . It must therefore denote Pelasgus' 'turnings' of himself, i.e. rhetorical twistings and tricks."[121] For his part Farenga translates στροφάς as "moves," expanding its semantic range to include the "virtuoso performance[s]"[122] of athletes and entertainers. Now στροφάς does seem to describe the movements of Pelasgus, and he is indeed an able speaker. Even so, these scholars read too much into the term. Christopher Johnstone has recently called attention to the numerous practical difficulties involved in speaking to open-air assemblies.[123] In the mid-fifth century Pnyx, for instance, "under the *best possible* conditions, perhaps one fifth of the audience could not have heard well enough to have understood more than about 85 percent of what was said."[124] He concludes that "vocal strength and formal oratorical training were significant factors in the influence a citizen-orator could exercise at meetings of the assembly."[125] Understood in this context, Pelasgus's δημηγόρους . . . στροφάς may denote nothing more than techniques orators commonly used to make themselves heard.[126] Far from being a slippery speaker. Pelasgus may simply turn in different directions to address the assembled Argive *demos*.[127]

Also at issue is the meaning of the adjective εὐπειϵής.[128] According to LSJ the adjective can mean either "ready to obey, obedient," or "persuasive."[129] Friis Johansen and Whittle note that in this context, however, "it is the positive response of the Argive people that requires emphasis, not the persuasive powers . . . of Pelasgus."[130] Significantly, the Danaids offer thanks to the Argives as a whole immediately after they hear Danaus's summary of the assembly: "Come, let us pray good things upon the Argives in return for the good they have done us" (ἄγε δή, λέξωμεν ἐπ᾽ Ἀργείοις / εὐχὰς ἀγαθάς, ἀγαθῶν ποινάς, 625–26). In fine, Pelasgus's interactions with the Argive assembly are not deceptive, but rather the epitome of democratic speech. He is a leading citizen who uses his right of *isegoria* to tell the Argives what he thinks. He does so to the best of his ability. And his peers listen attentively, giving their approval to a decree that carries behind it the weight of the entire citizen community.

Speech Norms, Citizenship, and Pericles's Law

Suppliant Women presents the Danaids and Danaus on the one hand, and Pelasgus on the other, as having distinct speech habits related to their civic status. In this regard the play illustrates John Heath's contention that in classical Greece the power of speech was crucially linked to political hierarchies. It not only separated people from animals, but also marked out human hierarchies. According to him, "the less we are able to articulate our thoughts, the less morally and politically significant we appear. In what becomes a convenient and nearly irreversible cycle, second-class moral and political status can be explained, justified, and maintained by carefully monitoring the opportunity to speak. In ancient Hellas, you are what you can say."[131] *Suppliant Women* depicts the Argive citizen Pelasgus as speaking more fairly and forthrightly than the strangers his city accepts as metics. The speech norms sketched by the play are also explicable within a more precise political context—namely, the run-up to Pericles's famous citizenship law. The dangers attached to metic speech help to account for why the Athenians chose to restrict their citizenship a decade or so after the play's performance.

All ancient Greek poleis accepting immigrants had to decide on the extent to which they would include newcomers in their political life.[132] Cynthia Patterson notes that "the formulation of a distinct status for the resident foreigner, with rights (to the protection of law) and responsibilities . . . could only have emerged as the status of citizen became likewise distinct."[133] As the Athenians thought about who should and should not belong to their city, and in what ways, they experienced unprecedented levels of immigration, as well as political turmoil culminating in assassination and reform. In the archonship of Antidotus (451/50), they reached a communal agreement that "whoever is not born from two citizens (ἀστοί) shall have no share in the polis" (μὴ μετέχειν τῆς πόλεως ὃς ἂν μὴ ἐξ ἀμφοῖν ἀστοῖν ᾖ γεγονώς).[134] At mid-century, the Athenians were thus busy distinguishing two separate phenomena: μετέχειν τῆς πόλεως and μετοικεῖν τῆσδε γῆς (*Suppliant Women* 609). Although the infinitives μετέχειν and μετοικεῖν are similar in sound, they have very different meanings. And the genitive noun phrases they respectively govern, the city-state (τῆς πόλεως) and the land (τῆσδε γῆς), are likewise far from identical. "Having a share in the city" is not the same as "living together in the land."

Despite the seminal importance of Pericles's law, surprisingly much about it remains in dispute.[135] Arguably the greatest difficulty concerns its motivation. Only two statements about its possible purpose survive from antiquity. The author of *AthPol* says that the measure arose "on account of the multitude of citizens" (διὰ τὸ πλῆθος τῶν πολιτῶν, 26.4),[136] while Plutarch describes the measure as concerned with "bastards" (νόθοι).[137] Of these remarks, the first is perhaps the more reliable, given that Plutarch's reference comes several centuries later, occurs in a digression, and reflects the interests of a biographer rather than a historian.[138] Nevertheless, the phrase from *AthPol* is itself enigmatic, giving rise to a number of interpretations. Scholars have often sought to isolate the practical effects of the measure and work backward toward its presumed intent. This approach is not without methodological difficulties. In addition, Pericles's reason for proposing the law does not necessarily coincide with why the assembly approved it. In all likelihood, those voting to approve did so for a variety of reasons.[139]

AthPol nevertheless remains the best starting point. The primary meaning for πλῆθος is "great number, multitude,"[140] and a logical inference has been that the measure sought to limit, or perhaps reduce, the number of citizens. But what about a large or increasing number of πολῖται was worrisome? One possibility is that the Athenians hoped to keep the perquisites of their citizenship from being spread too thin. Alan Boegehold, for instance, has linked the measure to widespread concern about inheritance.[141] With growth in the city's population came increased pressure on its most finite and valuable asset, the Attic soil. As offspring of various types of unions sought to inherit their families' holdings, the jurors staffing the popular courts faced the need to rank competing claims, and arrived at a rule of thumb: litigants with two Athenian parents took precedence over those with one or even none.[142] Nor were fertile acres the only possible point of contention; their produce was also important. As the population grew, food supplies may well have tightened.[143] In 445/44, the gift of a vast quantity of grain from the Egyptian prince Psammetichus led the Athenians to scrutinize their own ranks.[144] If the ancient sources are to be believed, this process led to the disfranchisement of 4,760 spurious citizens[145] and was primarily an effort to ensure that shares would go to citizens in good standing. Its disputed historicity notwithstanding,[146] the scrutiny (διαψηφισμός) of 445/44 is emblematic of other, better-attested attempts to channel tangible benefits to Athenians. During the *Pentecontaetea* (the fifty-year stretch between the Persian and Peloponnesian Wars), the material advantages to being a citizen grew considerably. The economic boom caused by building and rebuilding at Athens, the growth of trade through the Piraeus, and the development of a tribute-producing empire all made new resources available for redistribution. In particular, the decade and a half prior to the production of *Suppliant Women* saw a number of significant financial innovations. Many of these were attempts to compensate Athenian citizens for the hazards of the increased military service required of them during this time.[147] With longer, more remote, fleet-based campaigns supplanting the shorter, more local hoplite affairs characteristic of previous eras, the city instituted the πάτριος νόμος, the "ancestral custom" providing citizens who fell in battle with a sumptuous funeral, stirring public eulogy, prominent interment, and heroic memorialization via inscribed casualty list.[148] Perhaps as part of the same process, the city also began to provide financial support for the citizen sons of its dead warriors.[149]

At approximately the same time, the city began paying a *per diem* military wage to its sailors and hoplites. *AthPol* attributes the practice to Aristides, who apparently died in the early to mid-460s.[150] Ulpian, by contrast, ascribes the innovation to Pericles,[151] whose political debut likely dates to the late 470s.[152] Surveying the evidence, W. K. Pritchett concluded that military wages dated to the 460s or 450s; P. J. Rhodes and William Loomis agree but prefer an earlier date within that range.[153] In any event, by the time of *Suppliant Women*'s performance, Athens had taken a number of steps toward becoming an ἔνμισθος πόλις,[154] a city paying wages to its citizens.

Shortly thereafter, Athens began compensating its citizens for political tasks as well. *AthPol* (27.3) and Aristotle (*Politics* 1274a8–9) claim that Pericles, acting from demagogic motives, first instituted pay for jurors (dicasts) in the popular law courts. Of these two sources, the first adds that Pericles hoped to counter the effects of Cimon's wealth, while the second associates the move with Ephialtes's attack on the powers of the Areopagus in 462/61. Hansen concludes that the start of pay for dicasts helped pave the way for the citizenship law of 451/50: "once citizens had got an advantage out of political activity, they were glad not to have too many others to share it with."[155] This dynamic, whereby citizens looked to their own financial interests, would only have intensified as Athens subsequently instituted pay for the numerous magistracies filled by lot, including seats on the *boule* and the archonships.[156]

Athenian attempts to extend the material benefits of citizenship were hampered by significant growth in the population of Attica during the period after the Persian Wars. Precious little information on citizen numbers survives from the fifth century, and it is invariably problematic. The most commonly cited figures derive in one way or another from the account by Thucydides of Pericles's attempt to encourage the Athenians on the eve of the Peloponnesian War in 431. According to the statesman (2.13.6–7), the manpower at the city's disposal included: (a) a field army of 13,000 citizen hoplites; and (b) a garrison force of 16,000 drawn from the oldest and youngest citizens, as well as the metic hoplites.[157] There is a venerable tradition, beginning with Karl Beloch, of attempting to extrapolate from this passage figures for the Athenian population more generally.[158] More recently, scholars have turned to demographic age tables for developing modern nations in order to arrive at approximate values. All these approaches, applied *faute de mieux*, are heavily fraught with difficulties.[159] Not until the last quarter of the fourth century do we get anything remotely approaching reliable numbers for the population of Athens,[160] and even these are disputed.

All is not hopeless, however: Patterson has applied a safer, if less precise, approach to the question for the first half of the fifth century. She notes that just prior to the battle of Salamis, a time of maximum mobilization, the city could outfit only 180 triremes and therefore lent another 20 of its ships to Chalcis for their use in the pan-Hellenic effort. Moreover, even these 180 ships could be manned only with the help of non-citizens.[161] Then, in the following year, Athens sent but 8,000 hoplites to the crucial battle in nearby Plataea.[162] Patterson therefore suggests that these figures represent roughly the maximum naval and hoplite forces at the city's disposal in 480. Yet Athens's frequent military expeditions in the 460s and 450s, combined with the fact that the allies were decreasing their contributions of ships and men to the Delian League, meant that by the time of the citizenship law, the city could staff 200 triremes by itself when necessary.[163] Based on these facts, Patterson concludes that "the citizen population of Athens may have grown by as much as 50% in the course of about 20 years, from 25–30,000 in 480 to some 40,000 in the early 450s."[164]

In addition to staking out rough parameters for the population increase during the years surrounding the production of *Suppliant Women*, Patterson has convincingly identified its main source: immigration.[165] In all likelihood, life expectancy at Athens was short, twenty-five years or so, with a low "natural" population increase on the order of 0.3 percent per annum.[166] On her reading, the explosive growth suggested by Athens's pursuit of an aggressive foreign policy in the decades following 480 is most plausibly explained by an upsurge of foreigners who came to Athens, intermarried with the locals, and enrolled themselves (and their children) as citizens. Prior to 451/50, becoming an Athenian citizen was primarily a local process overseen by the numerous individual phratries and demes throughout Attica.[167] In the urban demes especially, whose populations tended to be more fluid and which were preferred by metics, residents knew each other less well; newcomers consequently had an easier time passing as citizens.[168] On Patterson's interpretation, the Periclean law of 451/50 was thus an attempt to exert centralized, polis-wide control over the definition and scrutiny of the

Athenian citizen body, and excluded those not born from two Athenian parents.[169] Thucydides's military figures provide some limited confirmation of Patterson's claim about a surge in immigration to Athens during the earlier part of the fifth century. Regardless of the size of the Athenian population overall, the number of citizen hoplites in the prime of life allows scholars to estimate (via age tables) the size of the citizen hoplite population. If, for instance, we assume with R. P. Duncan-Jones that the 13,000 citizen hoplites ranged in age from 20 to 49, and that the 16,000 men in reserve included the citizen hoplites aged 18 to 19 and 50 to 59, of the total hoplite population only 57–58 percent will have been citizens: some 42–43 percent will have been metics.[170] Put differently, metics will have comprised some 12,000 of the 29,000 hoplites at the city's disposal. And as Duncan-Jones further notes, if metics formed such a large percentage of the hoplite contingent, "lower down the social scale the metic element could be larger."[171] On his reckoning metics may have accounted for up to half the free population living in Attica.[172]

Thus far we have considered the quantitative backdrop to Pericles's citizenship law, analyzing the measure in light of a decreasing citizen-to-newcomer ratio in the decades preceding 451/50. At the same time, other scholars have argued that the law had a primarily qualitative dimension, affecting the caliber of Athens's citizenry. Rhodes, for instance, has claimed that its primary effect was to exclude *metroxenoi* (children born of Athenian fathers and foreign mothers) and that such offspring had previously been considered citizens. Moreover, since *nothoi* (children born out of wedlock) were already barred from citizenship and the measure was not retrospective, it would have had a minimal impact on citizen numbers.[173] He concludes that "Pericles must have been concerned with the quality of the citizen body, not with its size."[174] Daniel Ogden and others have offered related claims. On their view, the measure addressed the issue of citizen quality by focusing on the concept of "autochthonous pride."[175] By requiring two Athenian parents for citizenship, the measure sought in equal measures to craft and preserve a distinctly Athenian identity.[176]

The idea that Pericles's citizenship law proceeded from qualitative as well as quantitative concerns has merit. But an important aspect of the argument has to date been largely neglected. Let us return to *AthPol*'s formulation of the measure: μὴ μετέχειν τῆς πόλεως ὃς ἂν μὴ ἐξ ἀμφοῖν ἀστοῖν ᾖ γεγονώς. Historically, scholars have tended to focus more on the two-ἀστοί clause than the phrase μὴ μετέχειν τῆς πόλεως. Yet what did it mean to "share in the city"? Aristotle held (*Politics* 1275a22–23) that the citizen was defined above all by his ability "to share in judgment and in rule" (πολίτης δ' ἁπλῶς οὐδενὶ τῶν ἄλλων ὁρίζεται μᾶλλον ἢ τῷ μετέχειν κρίσεως καὶ ἀρχῆς). It is significant that he uses the same infinitive contained in *AthPol*'s paraphrase of Pericles's law, μετέχειν.[177] And how might a citizen exercise this capacity under the Athenian democracy of 451/50? He did so primarily by being a juryman (δικαστής) and an assemblyman (ἐκκλησιαστής).

The importance of these two political roles is difficult to overstate. In emphasizing them, Aristotle includes the interruption of an imaginary interlocutor: "Someone might swiftly claim that these individuals are not engaged in ruling, nor sharing in authority through their activities" (τάχα μὲν οὖν ἂν φαίη τις οὐδ' ἄρχοντας εἶναι τοὺς τοιούτους, οὐδὲ μετέχειν διὰ ταῦτ' ἀρχῆς, *Politics* 1275a26–28). Yet he immediately dismisses the objection as ludicrous (γελοῖον), claiming that jury- and assemblymen are in fact the most powerful political figures of all (τοὺς κυριωτάτους).

The two chief political institutions of fifth-century Athens were the assembly and the law courts. Staffed by citizens who were eventually paid for their service, these composite bodies depended on the principles and practices of democratic speech. The very health of the polis rested on the ability of large numbers of its citizens to listen attentively to others, to assess the arguments and opinions they heard, and to articulate their own views convincingly. All these activities in turn required a devotion to "persuasion," an abstraction that was personified as the goddess Peitho and worshiped at the foot of the Athenian Acropolis.[178] The end result was the development of a specific rhetorical ethos at Athens in which all citizens shared, while foreigners did not and could not.[179]

The interpretation of Pericles's citizenship law offered here finds further support in evidence drawn from later in the fifth and early fourth centuries. As we have seen, Athenians were interested in several factors when they sought to regulate the number and caliber of their fellow citizens. One of the most important was whether individuals were ready to subordinate their own interests to those of the polis.[180] A crucial litmus test in this regard was whether one was willing to obey the laws. This notion is made explicit in Plato's *Crito* (51D–E), where the personified *Nomoi* inform Socrates that "they offer all Athenians a clear choice upon coming of age: take their property and emigrate elsewhere (μετοικεῖν), or remain in Athens and obey the laws." To choose departure was to suggest that one was *ipso facto* unworthy of citizenship.

In a speech of Lysias, for instance, the prosecutor attacks the Athenian

Philon at his *dokimasia* for preferring comfort and safety in Oropos to danger in his native city (31.7):[181] "I will show that this man Philon thought his private safety more important than the common danger faced by the city, and considered it better to lead his life without danger than to save the city by running risks with the other citizens" (ἐγὼ τοίνυν ἀποφανῶ Φίλωνα τουτονὶ περὶ πλείονος ποιησάμενον τὴν ἰδίαν ἀσφάλειαν ἢ τὸν κοινὸν τῆς πόλεως κίνδυνον, καὶ ἡγησάμενον κρεῖττον εἶναι αὐτὸν ἀκινδύνως τὸν βίον διάγειν ἢ τὴν πόλιν σῴζειν ὁμοίως τοῖς ἄλλοις πολίταις κινδυνεύοντα). The participial constructions περὶ πλείονος ποιησάμενον and ἡγησάμενον κρεῖττον εἶναι imply rational calculation on Philon's part. A few moments later the prosecutor notes that, far from acting impulsively, the defendant had taken pains to lay his plans in advance: συσκευασάμενος γὰρ τὰ ἑαυτοῦ ἐνθένδε εἰς τὴν ὑπερορίαν ἐξῴκησε (31.9). The prosecutor's disdain for this craven arithmetic is clear: Philon would rather be a metic among "them" than a citizen among "us" (βουληθεὶς παρ' ἐκείνοις μετοικεῖν μᾶλλον ἢ μεθ' ἡμῶν πολίτης εἶναι).[182] Voluntary emigration from the city reflected individual ontology and could only be fully explained by the aggressive pursuit of self-interest.

While emigration *from* Athens made one less than a citizen, the converse was nevertheless not true: immigration *to* Athens did not qualify one for citizenship. Despite the implicit compliment to the city, the motives of those arriving to stay were suspect. In another of Lysias's speeches (*Against the Grain Dealers*), a citizen accuser questions a metic grain dealer who has been charged with profiteering (22.5):[183]

Tell me, are you a metic?
Yes.
And do you live here as a metic to obey the laws of the city, or to do whatever you want?
To obey the laws of the city.

Εἰπὲ σὺ ἐμοί, μέτοικος εἶ;
Ναί.
Μετοικεῖς δὲ πότερον ὡς πεισόμενος τοῖς νόμοις τοῖς τῆς πόλεως, ἢ ὡς ποιήσων ὅ τι ἂν βούλῃ;
Ὡς πεισόμενος.

The dichotomy the prosecutor presents is straightforward: individuals either obey the laws or do what they please. Here the prosecutor uses it to back the defendant into a corner. Naturally the metic's answer must be that he lives in Athens to obey the laws. But as *Crito* suggests, this disposition was presumptively linked to citizenship. The prosecutor's introductory question—Εἰπὲ σὺ ἐμοί, μέτοικος εἶ;—was therefore a disingenuous attempt to discredit the forthcoming response. Many of the citizen jurors doubtless believed that a metic was someone who put his own interests ahead of those of the city, which were in turn represented by its laws; by denying the charge, the defendant merely appeared untruthful as well.

The perceived tendency of metics to look out for themselves created nearly insurmountable obstacles to their political incorporation. As we saw above, *isegoria* was a cornerstone of the Athenian democracy, and yet it could not guarantee that sound policies would emerge from Athenian assemblies. Each citizen rising to speak in the Pnyx might be motivated by any number of concerns; the greatest threat to the public interest was arguably "manipulative and deceptive oratory in the service of a speaker's personal ambitions."[184] As time went on, the civic virtue of παρρησία ("frank speech") emerged as a necessary complement to *isegoria*. Individuals offering salutary criticisms of officials and of the *demos* itself learned to couch their words in particular ways. As Sara Monoson notes, "When one spoke out in the Assembly, one risked being disliked, shouted down, humiliated, fined or brought up on any one of a variety of charges, some of which could carry stiff penalties. The climate of personal risk was, in fact, emphasized by the orators. The presence of the risks made more credible the orator's claim to be saying what he thinks is true and right, that is, what he thinks is in the best interest of the polis in contrast to what might benefit him personally."[185]

By the very act of leaving their homelands, metics had offered concrete evidence that they put their own interests ahead of their communities; as such, they seemed constitutionally incapable of *parrhesia*. And so the Athenians took care that they had no opportunity to speak politically. To Athenian minds, one of the enduring benefits of Pericles's measure must have been that it banned metics from deliberating in assemblies,[186] from belonging to the *boule*, and from serving on juries.

Conclusion

Zeitlin has argued that one of *Suppliant Women*'s main themes is the acculturation of the Danaids to life at Argos. For her the play depicts "the beginning of their education into the rules of this 'civilized' society into which they will be incorporated."[187] Yet on any reading, the newcomers' education is at best partial and their incorporation imperfect. Their disregard for democratic institutions and practices, and for the civic *peitho* on which these depend, makes their political assimilation impossible. The Danaids' presence leads to turmoil and violence at Argos; war comes; the democracy is overthrown; Danaus and his daughters assume control. If *Suppliant Women* demonstrates anything about the "education" and "incorporation" of foreigners, it is how delicate and dangerous the process is, especially for democratic cities like Athens.

In its sensitivity to the political challenges posed by metoikia, Aeschylus's play accords well with the thinking that helped produce the citizenship law of 451/50. The tragedy suggests that by the second half of the 460s, the Athenians had begun to separate the notion of living in the land (μετοικεῖν τῆσδε γῆς) from that of sharing in the political affairs of the city (μετέχειν τῆς πόλεως). On an expansive reading, Pericles's measure embodied the judgment that only those born of two citizen parents were capable of fully subordinating their private interests to the public good.

With some notable exceptions, most citizens were also residents of Attica. For those Athenians living abroad, such as colonists and cleruchs, practical obstacles complicated both the short-term exercise and the long-term maintenance of citizenship. Given the inherent difficulties involved in proving the identity of oneself and one's children over time,[188] Athenian citizenship tended to develop an implicit geographical requirement alongside its explicit genealogical one. The city had historically understood itself as a place of refuge welcoming and incorporating those from elsewhere.[189] But in the fifth century, the number of newcomers grew exponentially, with many reversing the journey of Io and pouring in from Pontus, Lydia, Phrygia, Pamphilia, Egypt, and elsewhere.[190] Aeschylus's *Suppliant Women* suggests that immigrant ἀλλοθροοί were seen as the conceptual opposite of native-born ἐλευθεροστομοὶ γλῶσσαι. Devoted to their own self-interest, the newcomers were prone to θρασυστομεῖν. Consequently their tongues, versed in neither the principles nor the practices of democratic speech, had to be held.[191]

3

The Cypriote Stamp

The preceding chapter addressed the political difficulties involved in the incorporation of metics. But as Grethlein notes, in *Suppliant Women* "the problem of the integration of strangers is made yet more difficult by the position of women whose place in the polis is not fixed by marriage."[1] The Danaids' rootlessness is not an incidental matter: the attempt to avoid their cousins' suit is what brings them to Argos. Despite the importance of the question, the reason for their refusal remains opaque. Over the years scholars have proposed a wide range of ingenious solutions; most see the women's stance as anomalous and requiring explanation.[2] Wilamowitz, for instance, famously argued that the women act "out of an inborn hostility to men."[3] Others consider the women opposed to the Aegyptids in particular, not men in general. Of these, one subset link the women's hostility to the *hybris* of their pursuers.[4] Another subset claim that the men's status as first cousins renders them objectionable.[5] G. D. Thomson sees a broader principle at stake in the family relationships, arguing that the Aegyptids represent the principle of endogamy over exogamy.[6] The Danaids' relationship with their father may also be germane.[7]

Feminist scholarship has, however, begun to shift the interpretive focus, calling attention to tragedy's interest in (and sympathy for) "female experience and female subjectivity."[8] Seaford, for instance, has claimed that the Danaids' reluctance to marry the Aegyptids is not so much an anomaly requiring explanation as an intensification of everyday reality. The women's misgivings about marriage "[resemble] in several respects the attitude associated with the Greek bride or her female companions, but taken to an exotic extreme."[9] In their devotion to their father, their anxiety about separation from their natal *oikos*, and their fear of violent male sexuality as embodied by their suitors, the Danaids have much in common with real-life women. Zeitlin accordingly reads the play as an exploration of the mixed feelings that both women and the polis have about marriage. For her, *Suppliant Women* revolves around the civic education needed to transform fearful *parthenoi* into responsible *gunaikes*. She also reconstructs the Danaid trilogy to provide a historical *aition*: after the Danaids slaughter their cousins and become reconciled to marriage, they import from Egypt the celebration of the Thesmophoria.[10] In these rites "marriage itself as an institution is given a place of honor in the city's ideology and is elevated from a relation the Danaids view as enslavement and degradation to a microcosmic reflection of the *hieros gamos*."[11] Although Zeitlin's reconstruction has considerable appeal, it suffers from several important difficulties. First, there is no Aeschylean evidence linking the Danaids with the Thesmophoria; Herodotus (2.171) is our only source for the association. Second, the festival emphasized the kinship between daughter and mother, not daughter and father.[12] Yet *Suppliant Women* is strictly patrilineal, eliding all mention of mothers other than Io.[13] Simply put, there is no one with whom the Danaids could appropriately celebrate the festival. Finally, the Thesmophoria celebrates fertility, not marriage per se.[14]

According to Zeitlin, the trilogy depicts stages in the successful integration of the Danaids into the polis: from suppliant *astoxenoi* the women become *metoikoi* and ultimately "citizen wi[ves] of the Thesmophoria."[15] Yet she does not give sufficient weight to the distinctions the play draws between these various statuses. It takes a decree of the assembly to turn the women into *metoikoi*, and nowhere in *Suppliant Women* are they further transformed into ἀσταί.[16] Evidence from the rest of the trilogy is equally thin in this regard. Little but the title remains from *Sons of Aegyptus*, and the two surviving fragments from *Danaids* are shorn of most context. Although the women do seem to marry Argive men by the end of the trilogy, there is no evidence for any change in their civic status.[17] We are therefore not justified in assuming that the trilogy had a happy ending in which the women become citizens and live happily ever after.[18] On the contrary, their sexual and marital status at Argos seems to remain every bit as problematic as their political status.

Their foreignness lends the Danaids an exotic, erotic allure. Put differently, their metic status makes them more sexually independent and available than citizen women. In their relative freedom from male control, they pose a threat to the *kyrios*-centered "family values" of the polis. In this aspect the Danaids resemble two other famous women from tragedy. Like Antigone and Medea, they defy norms imposed by citizen men to pursue goals of their own choosing.[19] They thereby undermine the concept of the citizen *oikos*, usurp the role of its *kyrios*, and damage the polis to which they have come.

Relative Independence

The very first sentence of *Suppliant Women* shows that the Danaids pose a formidable challenge to traditional Greek notions about women. The chorus enter claiming that (5, 9–10):

we flee

. . . .

because we despise marriage to the sons of Aegyptus
and their impious < >.

φεύγομεν,

. . . .

γάμον Αἰγύπτου παίδων ἀσεβῆ τ'
ὀνοταζόμεναι ⟨ ⟩.[20]

They thereby serve notice that they are rejecting the primary role prescribed for them by Greek society.[21] The identity of the speakers is crucial here; the feminine gender and plural number of the participle ὀνοταζόμεναι emphasize that it is the women themselves who object to marriage (γάμον). In addition, the verb from which ὀνοταζόμεναι is formed ("blame, abominate") lends the women a subjectivity and moral agency often denied them in historical Athens.

The passage raises indirectly an important question addressed by earlier Greek literature as well: whose consent was necessary for a woman to marry?[22] For Aeschylus's audience, the crucial figure was her male guardian (κύριος).[23] His approval was the *sine qua non*; without it, any male found engaged in sexual activity with (or even inappropriately close to) one of his female dependents could be treated as an adulterer, with thoroughly unpleasant consequences. A little later, at lines 226–29, Danaus offers what is at first glance a restatement of the traditional Greek view of marriage:

How might a bird remain holy in eating a bird?
And how might someone be holy, wedding
an unwilling woman from an unwilling father?

Not even dead and in Hades would he escape blame,
having done this.

ὄρνιθος ὄρνις πῶς ἂν ἁγνεύοι φαγών;
πῶς δ' ἂν γαμῶν ἄκουσαν ἄκοντος[24] πάρα
ἁγνὸς γένοιτ' ἄν; οὐδὲ μὴ'ν Ἅιδου θανὼν
φύγηι ματαίων αἰτίας πράξας τάδε.

Yet the father doth protest too much. That Danaus even broaches the issue suggests that his approval might be dispensed with. Moreover, the polyptoton ὄρνιθος ὄρνις that begins his claim is echoed by the ἄκουσαν ἄκοντος of the following line. The presence of the feminine adjective ἄκουσαν is important. Friis Johansen and Whittle note that "it is remarkable, by the standards of contemporary Athenian society, that the girl's reluctance is mentioned as well as her father's, and significant, in terms of the dramatic treatment of the subject, that it is accorded equal emphasis. In Attic law betrothal (ἐγγύησις) does not require the consent of the prospective bride, whose part is wholly passive."[25] Danaus's remark encourages us to consider his daughters' own views on the question of consent. In the course of the play, their suitors are frequently compared to predators from the animal realm.[26] At lines 146–50 the women pray for aid to the divine protectress of wild creatures, Artemis:

. . . with all her strength
may she, vexed at their pursuits, untamed,
keep us untamed.

. . . παντὶ δὲ σθένει
διωγμοῖς ἀσχαλῶσ' ἄδμητος ἀδμήται[27]
ῥύσιος γενέσθω.[28]

Once again polyptoton is used for emphasis; as often in Greek literature, marriage is depicted as a matter of yoking women.[29] Several lines later, the Danaids pray to escape the beds of men "unwed and unbroken" (ἄγαμον ἀδάματον, 153). Aeschylus's audience would have seen this wish as highly anomalous.[30]

The issue of the Danaids' consent is taken up anew in their textually fraught exchange with Pelasgus at lines 333–40. Here they succinctly explain to him the reason for their supplication:

Pelasgus: Why do you say you have come to these assembled gods,
holding fresh-cut, white-wrapped boughs?
Danaids: So that I might not become a servant to the clan of Aegyptus.

P: Are you speaking out of hatred or saying it's improper?
D: Who would fault those men acquiring them if the men were friendly?
P:[31] But thus [i.e. by such marriages] mortals' strength becomes greater.
Moreover, escape is easy if all does not go well.
How, therefore, from your standpoint, may I act reverently?

Βα.: τί φῄς ἱκνεῖσθαι τῶνδ' ἀγωνίων θεῶν
λευκοστεφεῖς ἔχουσα νεοδρέπτους κλάδους;
Χο.: ὡς μὴ γένωμαι δμωΐς Αἰγύπτου γένει.
Βα.: πότερα κατ' ἔχθραν, ἢ τὸ μὴ θέμις λέγεις;
Χο.: τίς δ' ἂν φίλους[32] ὄνοιτο τοὺς κεκτημένους;
Βα.: σθένος μὲν οὕτω μεῖζον αὔξεται βροτοῖς.
καὶ δυστυχο⟨ύ⟩ντων γ' εὐμαρὴς ἀπαλλαγή.
πῶς οὖν πρὸς ὑμᾶς εὐσεβὴς ἐγὼ πέλω;

The primary textual problems come in the crucial line 337: does one read the accusative plural noun φίλους or the feminine nominative singular participle φιλοῦσ'? And does one read the verb as ὤνοιτο, οἴοιτο, or ὄνοιτο?[33] No matter which readings one adopts, difficulties of sense remain. These lingering problems have traditionally been addressed by: (1) positing lacunae; (2) reassigning lines; or (3) confessing scholarly *aporia*. On my reading (i.e., φίλους[34] ὄνοιτο[35]) the spot requiring greatest explanation is the relationship between lines 336 and 337. Here the women skirt Pelasgus's question as to whether their objections to marriage stem from its impropriety or their hatred; their response suggests a little of both.[36] The verb ὄνοιτο, a present optative from ὄνομαι ("blame, find fault with") indicates at the very least a considerable dislike. And the phrase φίλους . . . τοὺς κεκτημένους implies some impropriety, with the participle κεκτημένους suggesting that the Aegyptids intend to acquire and treat them like property.[37] Moreover, the predicate position of the adjective φίλους hints that the men are acting in a way inappropriate for friends and relatives.[38] Pelasgus's answer is that even if such arranged marriages prove unhappy, they do have a silver lining—namely, the increased prosperity of the families involved. He adds by way of consolation that if things go wrong, divorce offers an out for the aggrieved parties.[39] He concludes with what is really on his mind: how he can avoid the suppliants' wrath.

The Danaids then insist on their own right to give or withhold consent, and claim that Pelasgus will not be respecting the gods if he hands them over to their suitors. After a brief interval, the king revisits the women's objection to marriage (387–91):

If the sons of Aegyptus have power over you
by law of the city, claiming to be nearest of kin,
who would wish to oppose them?
It is necessary for you to defend yourselves according to your laws
from home,
that [the men] have no authority over you.

εἴ τοι κρατοῦσι παῖδες Αἰγύπτου σέθεν
νόμωι πόλεως, φάσκοντες ἐγγύτατα γένους
εἶναι, τίς ἂν τοῖς ἀντιωθῆναι θέλοι;
δεῖ τοί σε φεύγειν κατὰ νόμους τοὺς οἴκοθεν,
ὡς οὐκ ἔχουσιν κῦρος οὐδὲν ἀμφὶ σοῦ.

Of particular interest is Pelasgus's use of the phrases νόμωι πόλεως, ἐγγύτατα γένους, and ἔχουσιν κῦρος. For all Pelasgus knows, the Danaids are the equivalent of ἐπικλῆροι—that is, independent women without male guardians to supervise their affairs.[40] When the Argive leader arrived on the scene earlier, he apparently saw only the women, for he took no notice of their father. Indeed, the fact that Danaus does not speak for another 250 lines suggests that he may have concealed himself behind the hill or altar, or, at the very least, stood silently a good distance apart.[41] Pelasgus thus addresses the women themselves without intermediary.[42] Working by analogy from the law of his own city (νόμωι πόλεως), he infers from the Danaids' remarks that their cousins are their nearest relatives on their father's side (ἐγγύτατα γένους) and should be considered their *kyrioi* on *anchisteia* grounds. If the Danaids wish to contest this, they must argue that things are done differently in Egypt (κατὰ νόμους τοὺς οἴκοθεν). Failing that, the men seem to him above reproach in seeking to marry their cousins.[43]

Tellingly, the Danaids do not offer the most obvious response. Up to this point they have made no mention of a living father; this would seem an opportune moment for Danaus to step forward, identify himself, and aver that the women are under his authority.[44] He could add that as their *kyrios* he is unalterably opposed to the Aegyptids' suit. And that would settle the question (for the Argives, at any rate). As it is, the women evade Pelasgus's thrust with a sweeping declaration (392–96):

May I never fall into the hands
of male powers. I map out starlit flight[45]
as a remedy to hostile marriage.
Taking Justice as your ally,
choose reverence toward the gods.

μή τί ποτ' οὖν γενοίμαν ὑποχε⟨ί⟩ριος
κράτεσιν ἀρσένων· ὕπαστρον δέ τοι
μῆχαρ ὁρίζομαι γάμου δύσφρονος
φυγάν. ξύμμαχον δ' ἑλόμενος Δίκαν
κρῖνε σέβας τὸ πρὸς θεῶν.

The Danaids reject marriage because they fear they will become subject to the powers of men. Their use of the adjective ὑποχείριος is significant. Later in the play, when the Egyptian herald arrives in hot pursuit, he prepares to use his hands in an attempt at "marriage by capture."[46] This type of violent courtship has been linked to other male rites of passage such as hunting. Even the "gentler" sorts of marriage practiced by more refined Greeks contained residual traces of "bride-grabbing."[47] As Ian Jenkins notes, the "hand-on-wrist" (χεὶρ ἐπὶ κάρπῳ) gesture is an obligatory element of marriage scenes in Greek vase painting. The gesture is coercive, signifying "[the bride's] surrender . . . and the subordination of her will as κτῆμα, to that of the groom as possessor."[48] The Danaids reject outright this paradigm for marriage. Before they will submit to being manhandled, they will put their own χεῖρες to work. We saw earlier that *Suppliant Women*'s stagecraft emphasizes what the women do with their hands. When the play opens, they hold suppliant boughs, which they soon deposit on an altar. One of the words Aeschylus uses to describe these boughs, ἐγχειριδίοις ("in-hand-things," 21), has the more customary meaning of "daggers."[49] And it is with such blades that the women later render the Aegyptids fatally (and ironically) ὑποχείριοι.

The Danaids' most visible rejection of marriage comes at lines 455–67, when they threaten to hang themselves. We saw above that their rhetoric constitutes a form of violence bending Pelasgus to their will. Here we follow a different thread—namely, their threat to make nooses of their clothing and hang themselves if necessary. The material they plan to use, the "upper and lower girdles that gather [their] *peploi*" (στρόφους ζώνας τε, συλλαβὰς πέπλων, 457), is sinister. As Mireille Lee has shown, "the tragic poets ascribed [to] the πέπλος a dangerous quality that did not exist in earlier literature. The malevolent character of this πέπλος is likewise associated with the feminine gender category. As a woven textile, the πέπλος is inextricably linked to women's production and therefore feminine *metis*. The tragedians evoke the Greek concept of weaving . . . to represent the ultimate expression of female craftiness and treachery."[50]

The Danaids' use of their clothing is not simply treacherous. It is also extremely revealing. For as Helen King notes, the ζώνη "reflects the stages of a Greek woman's life. The first girdle is put on at puberty and later dedicated to Artemis as part of the marriage process; a special girdle, tied with a ritual knot, is worn on the wedding night and untied by the spouse; a married woman unties her girdle in labour."[51] The Danaids' threat thus resounds on multiple levels. On the one hand, it is a clear renunciation of marriage; they will kill themselves and put an end to their sexuality before marrying their cousins. But at the same time it is sexually suggestive.[52] To carry it out, the women would have to disrobe in front of Pelasgus and his male attendants, turning the men into voyeurs gazing upon what only husbands should.[53] Read this way, the Danaids' use of their girdles sums up their approach to marriage. Rather than be passive partners, they will take matters into their own hands: decisions about if, when, and for whom to loosen their clothing are theirs and theirs alone.

The Danaids' approach to marriage clearly implies a great deal of independence from their nominal *kyrios*. At one level this is exemplified by Danaus's many absences from the stage. Taplin has argued that *Suppliant Women* is visually structured around two dramatic confrontations the women have with men at altars: first with the Argive Pelasgus and his men and later with the Egyptian herald and his. In each instance Danaus is either off-stage or inactive in the background. As Taplin notes of the latter confrontation with the Egyptians, "it is . . . somewhat awkward that Danaus should not be there for his daughters' greatest ordeal."[54] He seeks an explanation in the play's visual language: what Aeschylus is doing is showing that "the Danaids themselves should undergo their trials, and that no one else should do it for them."[55] We might put Taplin's case even more strongly. Danaus's absences do more than suggest his inability to protect his daughters; they demonstrate that the women themselves are responsible for their own relations with men who are not their kin, be they Egyptian or Argive.

The departure of the Egyptian herald following line 951 leaves the Danaids free to make their own erotic and marital choices, and Danaus knows this. As they prepare to enter the city, he worries about where his daughters will sleep. Noting their outspokenness and youthful allure, he urges them not to disgrace him (ὑμᾶς δ'ἐπαινῶ μὴ καταισχύνειν ἐμέ, 996). Shortly thereafter he launches an impassioned appeal for their continued chastity, saying (1006–9):

Let us also not suffer that for which
we toiled greatly and rowed mightily,

let us not bring shame on ourselves and pleasure
to my enemies.

πρὸς ταῦτα μὴ πάθωμεν ὧν πολὺς πόνος,
πολὺς δὲ πόντος οὕνεκ' ἠρόθη δορί,
μηδ' αἶσχος ἡμῖν, ἡδονὴν δ' ἐχθροῖς ἐμοῖς
πράξωμεν.

The implication is that unlike most Greek *kyrioi*, Danaus cannot force his daughters to obey him. His hortatory subjunctives μὴ πάθωμεν and μηδ' . . . πράξωμεν emphasize the extent to which typical gender roles have been reversed and he now depends on his daughters' voluntary cooperation. Ordinarily it would be his task to act and theirs to accept his actions; instead, he is now the passive one, and his only recourse is that typically reserved for women—namely, pleading.[56] The close of the play thus depicts nubile, foreign young women entering a Greek polis, with their nominal *kyrios* in a subordinate role and forced to countenance their sexual choices.

The Cypriote Stamp

The Danaids' independence from their father was in and of itself unsettling to the audience. Equally disconcerting were the ends to which their freedom of action might lead. We saw earlier that what Pelasgus first notices about the women is their "outlandish" appearance (234–37). And their threats of suicide link their exotic attire to their erotic nature.[57] At lines 279–89, Pelasgus expands on his initial impression of the Danaids, expressing skepticism about their claim to be of Argive descent:

You resemble Libyan women much more—
you're nothing like those from around here.
Even the Nile might nurture such a plant.[58]
The Cypriote stamp has fittingly been struck
in your female forms by male craftsmen.
Hearing [you] I would have thought you were rather
Indian nomads who ride upon the earth mounted on camels
and live next to the Ethiopians,
or husbandless, flesh-eating Amazons,
had you but bows . . .

Λιβυστικαῖς γὰρ μᾶλλον ἐμφερέστεραι
γυναιξίν ἐστε κοὐδαμῶς ἐγχωρίαις·

καὶ Νεῖλος ἂν θρέψειε τοιοῦτον φυτόν·
Κύπριος χαρακτὴρ τ' ἐν γυναικείοις τύποις
εἰκὼς πέπληκται τεκτόνων πρὸς ἀρσένων·
Ἰνδῶν τ' ἀκούω νομάδας ἱπποβάμοσιν
εἶναι καμήλοις ἀστραβιζούσας χθόνα
παρ' Αἰθίοψιν ἀστυγειτονουμένας·
καὶ τὰς ἀνάνδρους κρεοβότους ⟨δ'⟩ Ἀμάζονας,
εἰ τοξοτευχεῖς ἦστε, κάρτ' ἂν ἤικασα
ὑμᾶς.

Pelasgus's comparison of the Danaids to a host of non-Greek women is one of the play's more curious passages. Friis Johansen and Whittle claim that his catalogue of Libyans, Egyptians, Cypriotes, Indians, and Amazons "is highly organized, with a subtle play between parallelism and variation."[59] They further note that it traces a counterclockwise circuit from southwest to northeast. But they are at a loss to explain its dramatic function, contending that its embellishment progresses "from simple metaphor . . . to a wealth of patently irrelevant ethnographic detail."[60]

While Pelasgus's catalogue is indeed organized, its ethnographic details are anything but irrelevant. On the contrary, his thumbnail sketches of the women from various *ethne* are related to the plot and broader themes of the trilogy. One of the primary purposes of the passage is to highlight the Danaids' erotic independence and the dangers they consequently pose to *oikos* and to polis. For Aeschylus and his audience, geography was intimately tied to cultural practice. Let us begin as Pelasgus does, with the Libyans. The most famous Greek account of these peoples is that of Herodotus in Book 4.[61] In chapters 168–97 the historian moves inland from the shore; in several of the tribes he describes, the women play sexual roles that would have flummoxed the Athenians. For instance, a number of the tribes place no special premium on the virginity of *parthenoi* or the chastity of wives. Among the Adrymachidae the king enjoys the *ius primae noctis* with all girls about to marry (4.168). Among the polygamous Nasamonae the privilege is extended more broadly to all men attending the wedding feast (4.172). The Machlyes and Auses do not even practice marriage, instead holding their women in common and coupling like animals. And then there are the Gindanes, whose brassy women wear anklets indicating the number of lovers they have taken: "whoever has the most [anklets] is deemed to be the best, on account of having been loved by the most men" (ἣ δ' ἂν πλεῖστα ἔχῃ, αὕτη ἀρίστη δέδοκται εἶναι ὡς ὑπὸ πλείστων ἀνδρῶν φιληθεῖσα, 4.176). In short, Herodotus portrays Libyan women as frequently and flagrantly promiscuous. Far from considering this trait a vice, the Libyans make it their standard of female excellence: hence the superlative ἀρίστη.

Pelasgus's next point of comparison, the Nile, stands for Egypt by synecdoche. Herodotus is of course an invaluable source for contemporary Greek beliefs about this land as well.[62] While he does not go into great detail about Egyptian gender roles, the little that he does say in the famous chapters of Book 2 (35–36) is suggestive. Women are active in the public sphere, while men stay home and weave. Men carry loads on their heads; women, on their shoulders. Women urinate standing up; men sitting down. There are no priestesses; men are the primary servants of the deities. Women are obligated to support their parents. In all this, Egyptian women resemble Greek men, and Egyptian men, Greek women. Had Herodotus extended his analysis to sexual mores, he might well have shown Egyptian women adopting a more active, "masculine" stance in this area as well. Consider for instance the specific clause Pelasgus attaches to the Danaids at line 281, Νεῖλος ἂν θρέψειε τοιοῦτον φυτόν. The image of them as luxuriant vegetation watered by the great river brings to mind the complex associations between plant growth, *hybris*, and sexuality charted by Ann Michelini and John McMahon.[63]

Let us for the moment skip over the next two lines about the Cypriotes (282–83) and proceed to the Indian nomads. Once again Herodotus is relevant, providing evidence for Greek views of Indians close to the time of the play's production. Like the Libyans, the Indians are a heterogeneous assortment of tribes.[64] But to the Halicarnassian, their sexual mores are uniformly exotic. He says (3.101) that "the mating of all these Indians whom I mentioned occurs in public as with flocks, and they have a similar complexion, like that of the Ethiopians" (μεῖξις δὲ τούτων τῶν Ἰνδῶν τῶν κατέλεξα πάντων ἐμφανής ἐστι κατά περ τῶν προβάτων, καὶ τὸ χρῶμα φορέουσι ὅμοιον πάντες καὶ παραπλήσιον Αἰθίοψι). Several points in his description are worth noting. First, outdoor sex of the sort mentioned was generally considered shocking by Greeks and linked to prostitution. As James Davidson notes, "women who wanted to preserve a reputation for decency rarely strayed out of doors except under pressing necessity and a thick cloak . . . Women of the streets therefore lived on the wrong side of the threshold and advertised their availability by submitting to the public gaze."[65] Second, Herodotus says that this type of public intercourse is characteristic of four-footed animals (κατά περ τῶν προβάτων). As lineal descendants of Io, the Danaids owe their very existence to an earlier bovine tryst; to use the Greek language of heredity, such congress forms part of their nature (φύσις). Third, Herodotus makes a paratactic connection between skin color and sexual mores. In the theater, the Danaids' makeup and costuming establish them as swarthy foils to Greek women, whose paler complexions result from (*inter alia*) more time spent indoors.

And then there are the Amazons. The literature, both ancient and modern, about these women is voluminous. According to Athenian mythical tradition, Theseus and his followers drove the Amazons from the Areopagus in armed combat.[66] In the period after the Persian Wars, the city devoted considerable space on its public monuments to its grapplings with these invaders from abroad.[67] Yet Andrew Stewart, relying on the evidence of vase painting, argues that by the middle of the fifth century the Athenian view of Amazons had shifted somewhat, with the women now seen primarily as combining geographic liminality and female sexual potential.[68] Enticing, available, foreign: these perennial *parthenoi* set the minds of Greek men ablaze with their alternative sexual politics. In Herodotus, for instance, the Amazons reject virilocal marriages in which they would be required to tend hearth and home. More linguistically adept than their Scythian paramours, they tell them "we would not be able to live with your women, for our customs and theirs are not the same" (ἡμεῖς οὐκ ἂν δυναίμεθα οἰκέειν μετὰ τῶν ὑμετέρων γυναικῶν· οὐ γὰρ τὰ αὐτὰ νόμαια ἡμῖν τε κἀκείνῃσί ἐστι, 4.114.3). Athenian men would doubtless have agreed, as their pottery attests. In the years surrounding 450 "the number of Amazon scenes more than doubles, even though the total output of painted vases is falling."[69] Moreover, many of these scenes feature not battles, but advancing Amazons who cause "scared young Athenian women to flee to a mature man, represented not as a warrior but a bearded patriarch."[70] Stewart concludes that these Amazons function as symbolic stand-ins for the wilder foreign *parthenoi* whose arrival was hurting the marital prospects of Athenian women.[71] And so Pelasgus's comparison of the Danaids to Amazons suggests that the play's newcomers from Egypt bring with them a similarly aggressive approach to sex and marriage.[72]

With this as a general framework for understanding Pelasgus's catalogue, let us return to the passage's vexed central lines (282–83): Κύπριος χαρακτὴρ τ' ἐν γυναικείοις τύποις / εἰκὼς πέπληκται τεκτόνων πρὸς ἀρσένων. Friis Johansen and Whittle translate the lines thus: "and similar is the Cyprian impress stamped on women's forms by male artificers."[73] They take the main point of comparison to be external appearance, understanding the male τεκτόνων as fathers who have bequeathed their looks to their daughters, the γυναικείοις τύποις. They further claim that despite being an ethnically mixed entrepôt, fifth-century Cyprus had a high percentage of Greek inhabitants.[74] And they conclude that lines 282–83 should be excised, arguing that "the selection of Cypriot girls to illustrate the definitely non-Greek impression which the Danaids make on Pelasgus is therefore baffling."[75] In this they have been followed by Sandin, who adduces additional arguments.[76]

Sommerstein rightly rejects the obelus. He argues that Cyprus traditionally occupied a liminal place in the Greek world[77] and focuses on the metaphor involved in the phrase χαρακτήρ . . . ἐν . . . τύποις πέπληκται. Friis Johansen and Whittle take it as a reference to "the hammering of bronze plates on to a wooden image";[78] Sandin to an inscription carved in the exotic Cypriot script.[79] But Sommerstein is almost certainly correct that the primary metaphor is drawn from the minting of coins.[80] In inscriptions the term χαρακτήρ (282) is frequently used of a die.[81] While the noun τεκτών in line 283 commonly refers to carpenters and joiners, it can also refer to craftsmen in general, including metalworkers.[82] The basic meaning of the verb πλήττω ("strike, smite") is apropos.[83] And the noun τύπος could refer to the die involved, a symbol contained on the die, or the corresponding impression stamped on coins themselves.[84] Sommerstein accordingly concludes that Pelasgus is referring to the way "a stamp is produced by striking <coin-blanks> against dies."[85] He further claims that the metaphor is linked to sexual reproduction, with the τεκτόνων . . . ἀρσένων representing fathers and the γυναικείοις τύποις mothers; the women issuing from these erotic liaisons bear the Cypriote stamp in consequence.

But what exactly are we to make of the phrase Κύπριος χαρακτήρ? Is it simply a reference to the women's appearance, or is there more at stake?[86] In other contexts the adjective Κύπριος denotes not just the island, but its famous goddess, Aphrodite, as well.[87] Toward the end of *Suppliant Women*, a supplemental chorus composed of Argive men note (1034) the attractions of Aphrodite, referring to her as ἡ Κύπρις. They further suggest that in future she will exert her influence over ἑσμὸς ὅδε εὔφρων ("this kindly swarm"). While the choreuts do not precisely identify the swarm, the use of the demonstrative ὅδε suggests it is close at hand: they are specifying either themselves or the Danaids. Several lines later (1050–51) they are even more explicit, claiming that in the end marriage comes to most women. Pelasgus's phrase Κύπριος χαρακτήρ thus implies that the Danaids share Aphrodite's character and are prone to her ways. And the participle εἰκώς modifying the phrase assumes added importance in this regard.[88] One of the purposes of coinage was to imbue a fixed amount and grade of metal with legitimacy, marking it in a way that would resist tampering. Seen in this light, the participle suggests that Aphrodite's likeness was accurately and lastingly reproduced in the Danaids.[89] The Cypriote goddess is ineradicably part of who and what they are.

The Danaids' numismatic contours anchor them in the broader conceptual matrix of economic and sexual activity obtaining in ancient Greece, according to which women circulated among users and regulated exchange relations between men.[90] Kurke in particular has argued for a semantic link between coinage and prostitutes, claiming that both were essentially democratic phenomena that emerged against the older backdrop of aristocratic gift-exchange and mistresses (*hetaerae*).[91] Now *Suppliant Women* certainly does not depict the Danaids as common prostitutes. Nevertheless, the play is filled with reminders about their powerful sexuality and establishes them as potential partners for a variety of men. At line 997 their father compares them to fruit (ὀπώρα) possessing a beauty and ripeness (ὥραν) attractive to all.[92] Shortly after that, he says (1003–5):

Each man coming upon the shapely charms
of unmarried girls shoots them a persuasive
glance, overcome by desire.

καὶ παρθένων χλιδῆσιν εὐμόρφοις ἔπι
πᾶς τις παρελθὼν ὄμματος θελκτήριον
τόξευμ' ἔπεμψεν, ἱμέρου νικώμενος.

Here the phrase πᾶς τις underscores the universality of the Danaids' appeal; his daughters would make desirable mates for any number of men. And in the course of the trilogy the women almost certainly pass from one set of male hands to another. The image of the Cypriote die thus points toward the potential promiscuity of the Danaids; they are stamped as more foreign than Greek.[93] And the metaphorical language used to describe their minting, blows struck by men on womanly dies (ἐν γυναικείοις τύποις / εἰκὼς πέπληκται τεκτόνων πρὸς ἀρσένων), is a *double entendre* referring to their destiny as well as their conception.[94] Like the Libyans, Egyptians, Indians, and Amazons, the Danaids pose a threat to Greek men and their understanding of the world. Pelasgus's catalogue demonstrates that the Danaids' exoticism and eroticism are two sides of the same coin, and that these qualities distinguish them from citizen *astai*. Any man who would handle this currency does so at his own peril.

Reconstructing the Trilogy

The difficulties involved in reconstructing Aeschylus's Danaid trilogy are formidable. Given the paucity of remains from *Sons of Aegyptus*, *Danaids*, and *Amymone* (the accompanying satyr drama),[95] determining the order of the tragedies, let alone their content, is a daunting task.[96] Garvie has analyzed the numerous other accounts of the Danaid myth, concluding that their "most remarkable feature . . . is their lack of agreement on almost every detail of the story."[97] Yet he notes that they nevertheless do share a few common motifs: the women eventually marry their cousins; they are urged by their father to kill their husbands on their wedding night; and they all do so, with the exception of Hypermestra, who spares Lynceus.[98] Significantly, Aeschylus's version does not seem to end with the killing of the Aegyptids.

Two substantial fragments survive from the third and final tragedy, *Danaids*. The first of these, preserved in a scholion to Pindar, is as follows (fr. 43):[99]

And then, when dawn rouses the shining light
of the sun, let them befriend the bridegrooms
with songs, together with youths and maidens.

κἄπειτα δ' εὖτε λαμπρὸν ἡλίου φάος
ἕως ἐγείρῃ, πρευμενεῖς τοὺς νυμφίους
νόμοισι θέντων σὺν κόροις τε καὶ κόραις.

Garvie interprets this as an account of a ὑμέναιος διεγερτικός, a waking song to be performed by friends of the bride on the morning following a wedding.[100] Given the lack of surrounding context, several things remain unclear, however, including the speaker, the identity of the bridegrooms mentioned (τοὺς νυμφίους), and whether the passage looks backward or forward in time.[101] In any event, the play is clearly concerned with what will transpire following a marriage of the Danaids.

The second fragment (fr. 44) runs thus:[102]

Holy heaven longs to pierce the land,
and love takes hold of earth to marry.

The rain falling from the fair-flowing sky
makes pregnant the earth. She bears for mortals
food of flocks and the life-giving wheat
and the fruit of trees. From dewy marriage
is brought to perfection all that exists.
For these things I am responsible.

ἐρᾷ μὲν ἁγνὸς οὐρανὸς τρῶσαι χθόνα,
ἔρως δὲ γαῖαν λαμβάνει γάμου τυχεῖν·
ὄμβρος δ' ἀπ' εὐνάεντος οὐρανοῦ πεσὼν
ἔκυσε γαῖαν· ἡ δὲ τίκτεται βροτοῖς
μήλων τε βοσκὰς καὶ βίον Δημήτριον
δένδρων τ' ὀπώραν· ἐκ νοτίζοντος γάμου
τελεῖθ' ὅσ' ἔστι· τῶνδ' ἐγὼ παραίτιος.

Here the speaker claims credit for the erotic love joining heaven and earth, and the resulting blessings their union creates for mortals. Some of the details surrounding this passage are more certain: for instance, Athenaeus informs us that the goddess Aphrodite is the speaker. Even so, the context in which she makes these remarks remains unclear.

According to one set of interpreters, subsequent events in the trilogy must have involved a trial.[103] Pausanias states that Hypermestra was denounced by her father Danaus for disobeying his order (2.19.6):[104] "Danaus took this daughter alone to court for having disregarded his command, thinking that the salvation of Lynceus was dangerous for himself and that she, by not daring to act alongside her sisters, had increased his disgrace for plotting [the murder]. She was acquitted by judgment of the Argives and for this reason dedicated a statue to Aphrodite the Victory-Bringer (ταύτην γὰρ τῶν θυγατέρων μόνην τὸ πρόσταγμα ὑπεριδοῦσαν ὑπήγαγεν ὁ Δαναὸς ἐς δικαστήριον, τοῦ τε Λυγκέως οὐκ ἀκίνδυνον αὑτῷ τὴν σωτηρίαν ἡγούμενος καὶ ὅτι τοῦ τολμήματος οὐ μετασχοῦσα ταῖς ἀδελφαῖς καὶ τῷ βουλεύσαντι τὸ ὄνειδος ηὔξησε. κριθεῖσα δὲ ἐν τοῖς Ἀργείοις ἀποφεύγει τε καὶ Ἀφροδίτην ἐπὶ τῷδε ἀνέθηκε Νικηφόρον).

Given Pausanias's statement that Hypermestra was tried and acquitted, some scholars have argued that the second *Danaids* fragment (fr. 44) likely had Aphrodite appearing on stage to defend Hypermestra.[105] Yet there is a conspicuous hole in Pausanias's account: what could Hypermestra have been charged with? Ignoring a parent's wish, or even command, was ordinarily not a criminal offense in ancient Athens. In Greek tragedy, generational conflict was usually dealt with in-house rather than in court.[106] Moreover, the ἡγούμενος clause ascribed to Danaus contains a number of elements reflecting poorly on him and well on Hypermestra. The term used to describe Lynceus's survival, σωτηρία, has a positive valence, and the notion that one man's escape from death created danger for another was a flimsy justification for murder. By contrast, τόλμημα, the noun he employs to describe the actions of his other daughters, frequently has a negative cast.[107] The participle he uses of himself, βουλεύσαντι, implies that he is guilty of βούλευσις.[108] And the fact that Hypermestra foiled his plans and brought reproach (ὄνειδος) upon him would have created little sympathy among jurymen. In short, the ἡγούμενος clause offers a viewpoint hostile to Danaus even as it purports to describe his thinking. Put differently, it incriminates him rather than Hypermestra. Garvie's point is thus well taken: "it seems highly unlikely that when forty-nine women murder their husbands and one does not, Aeschylus should have considered that it was only the behaviour of the latter that needed to be explained and justified."[109]

Other scholars, while recognizing the incongruity of any prosecution of Hypermestra, have nevertheless sought to preserve the dramatic possibilities inherent in a trial. D. S. Robertson, for instance, argued that the climax of the trilogy must have come when Aphrodite prosecuted Danaus and all his daughters *except* Hypermestra.[110] On his reading, the goddess's surviving speech was an indictment of the defendants, who had not only committed murder but challenged a divinely sanctioned pattern in the process. As Garvie notes, however, "a trial of the Danaids raises its own particular problems."[111] For one thing, blood relatives of the slain would make more suitable prosecutors than Aphrodite.[112] Absent their father, Aegyptus, the surviving brother Lynceus could also have assumed the role.[113] Moreover, if fragment 44 records Aphrodite's contribution to a trial, its emphasis on ἔρως would be at odds with the facts of the case. Throughout *Suppliant Women* the Danaids have portrayed the Aegyptids as hubristic, with the Egyptian herald's threats and demeanor only strengthening the claim. So it is difficult to map their fraught relations onto the harmonious union between sky and earth envisioned by Aphrodite. On the contrary, Aeschylus may even have structured the end of the second and the start of the third play to intimate that the parties were driven by hatred instead of *eros*: the Aegyptids' plan to deflower their resistant brides evokes an equally violent response.[114]

We should therefore consider the possibility that *Danaids* contained no trial at all. As noted above, Athenaeus says nothing about the context in which Aphrodite delivers her famous speech.[115] And Pausanias, writing some six centuries after Aeschylus, derived his version of events "not so much from literary sources as from the explanations of his guides as he visited the curiosities and tourist-sites of Argos."[116] His primary purpose was to describe for others the topography and monuments he had seen. And so he attributes the existence of a cult to Aphrodite in her aspects of Πειθώ (Persuasion) and Νικηφόρος (Victory-Bringer) to the legal help the goddess allegedly gave Hypermestra. He likewise links the local toponym for the cultic area (Κριτήριον) with the claim that the Argives sat there in judgment (κρίσις) of the daughter's case.[117] It is thus entirely possible that the trial of Hypermestra is a local invention dating to well after the time of Aeschylus.

Yet even without a trial *Danaids* must have resolved the murder of the Aegyptids in one way or another. While Hypermestra and Lynceus apparently proceed to found a new dynasty at Argos,[118] the remaining sisters must also be dealt with. For one thing, the title by which the play was widely known bears their name. Moreover, as R. P. Winnington-Ingram reasons, "If Aeschylus could not, at *Eumenides* 778, leave a chorus of angry Furies 'in the air,' no more could he leave in the air a chorus of Danaids, bloodguilty as well as aggrieved. In point of dramatic structure, they must have had an *exodus*: whither and to what fate?"[119] In several ancient accounts, the Danaids' story culminates in their eternal punishment in the underworld, where they ceaselessly fetch water in leaky vessels.[120] Yet these sources are comparatively late, with none preceding Aeschylus. Moreover, while the text of *Suppliant Women* contains numerous allusions to the impending murders, nowhere does it hint at the daughters' watery labors.[121] Finally, all surviving accounts of the Danaids' punishment agree that it takes place in Tartarus after their deaths; but thus far no one has offered a convincing scenario for their descent from this world to the next. As Garvie drily remarks, "It would indeed be awkward to have the chorus executed in the middle or at the end of the play."[122]

How then did the trilogy conclude, if not with the Danaids' punishment? According to Kurt von Fritz, following the murder of the Aegyptids "only two possible outcomes remain: either the complete ruin of the Danaids . . . or the recreation of the divine order through expiation."[123] And there is in fact an alternative tradition in the ancient sources tracing a second path: the Danaids are purified and subsequently remarry. According to Pseudo-Apollodorus, "Athena and Hermes cleansed [the Danaids] at Zeus's command. Danaus later settled Hypermestra on Lynceus, and gave his other daughters in marriage to the winners of an athletic contest" (καὶ αὐτὰς ἐκάθηραν Ἀθηνά τε καὶ Ἑρμῆς Διὸς κελεύσαντος.

Δαναὸς δὲ ὕστερον Ὑπερμνήστραν Λυγκεῖ συνῴκισε, τὰς δὲ λοιπὰς θυγατέρας εἰς γυμνικὸν ἀγῶνα τοῖς νικῶσι ἔδωκεν, 2.22). While the *Library* dates to the first or second century CE, mention of the athletic contest also appears in one of Aeschylus's contemporaries, Pindar. In *Pythian* 9, dated to 478 or 474 BCE, the lyric poet depicts Danaus as arranging for the marriages of his remaining forty-eight daughters[124] by lining them up at the edge of the stadium and awarding them to the swiftest runners.[125] That the ode does not explicitly mention the Danaids' purification likely arises from the conventions of epinician poetry, and from the fact that what Pindar wished to emphasize was the race.[126] He was after all writing the poem to celebrate the swiftness of Telesicrates, victor in a different foot-race.[127] In sum, Sommerstein offers arguably the best way to account for fragment 44 of *Danaids*: "It would be highly fitting if [Aphrodite's speech] were followed up by the marriage of the Danaids other than Hypermestra to new husbands with whom they *could* form a union as true as that of Heaven and Earth."[128]

The idea that Aeschylus's trilogy might have ended with the purification and remarriage of the Danaids gains further support from the text of *Suppliant Women*. At line 1018, the women begin a choral song to accompany the *exeunt*, exhorting one another to glorify the gods of Argos.[129] At lines 1022–23 they address an unnamed set of companions, saying, "Listen carefully to our song, companions" (ὑποδέξασθε δ' ὀπαδοί / μέλος). The identity of these companions has been the subject of significant debate. The noun describing them, ὀπαδοί, normally means "attendants" and elsewhere in tragedy refers to both men and women of various stations.[130] Given that these companions sing parts of the *exodos* in responsion with the Danaids, they are generally taken to be a secondary chorus consisting "either of the Danaids' handmaids . . . or of Danaus' Argive bodyguard, whose protective role makes them an equally suitable singing partner."[131] Most scholars now agree that the evidence favors the Argive men.[132] For one thing, the only certain mention of any maids occurs at lines 977–79.[133] And these women's overall role in the play is so scanty and problematic that the lines themselves may be part of a larger interpolation.[134] For another, Danaus refers to his Argive escort with the very same word used by the Danaids: at line 985 he says that "the Argives assigned these spear-carrying men to me as ὀπαδοί."

Even stronger reasons for assigning the secondary chorus to the Argives come from considerations of stagecraft. Dramatic economy makes it likely that these same men have heretofore served several functions in the play. They accompany Pelasgus when he first comes to investigate the newcomers; they escort Danaus into town to attend the assembly; and they reappear with Pelasgus to thwart the Egyptian herald.[135] Moreover, as we saw above, the assembly that granted the Danaids metoikia voted for the measure unanimously and πανδημίαι ("with the whole people taking part," 607). The decree that was passed called on all citizens to protect the newcomers, threatening exile if they failed to do so. By standing with Pelasgus against the Egyptians and then escorting the women into town, the Argive men fulfill in person their promise made earlier in the play.

As *Suppliant Women* nears its end, there are thus two separate choruses, one consisting of the Danaids and the other of Argive men. The latter do more than simply listen to and accept[136] the song of the former.[137] After the women sing the first strophe and antistrophe of the *exodos* (1018–33), the men sing the second (1034–51).[138] The Danaids conclude their section with several wishes (1030–33):

May holy Artemis look upon
our expedition with pity, and may no
forced rite of Aphrodite come: may this contest
end in death.

ἐπίδοι δ' Ἄρτεμις ἁγνὰ
στόλον οἰκτιζομένα, μηδ' ὑπ' ἀνάγκας
τέλος[139] ἔλθοι Κυθερείας.
Στύγιον πέλοι τόδ' ἆθλον.

Conspicuously, the men do not join the women's prayer, but actively work against it. They claim to be mindful of Aphrodite,[140] and of Hera (the goddess of marriage) as well (1034–35). They then acknowledge the power of Desire (Πόθος, 1039), Persuasion (Πειθοῖ, 1040), Harmony (Ἁρμονίας, 1041), and the pathways[141] of Loves[142] (τρίβοι τ' Ἐρώτων, 1042). And they close their antistrophe by predicting that the Danaids, like other women in earlier days, will marry (1050–51).[143]

Friis Johansen and Whittle argue that the Argives intend these last two lines about marriage as "a common type of expression of consolation, extenuation, etc., to the effect that an individual misfortune (or error) is not peculiar to the person(s) addressed."[144] Simply put, the men are telling the women to buck up: the mind of Zeus is inscrutable, there are worse things than marrying one's cousins, and the Danaids have plenty of company in their misery. Yet their reading of lines 1050–51 is too limited. The Argives have just finished praising Aphrodite and her ways in generous terms; they should not then turn and immediately characterize marriage as a thing to be endured. Moreover, while the distribution of parts in the third strophe and antistrophe that follow (1052–61) is extremely uncertain, scholars agree that the two choruses engage in dialogue.[145] As Seaford notes, the pattern of two same-sex choruses exchanging song, with the men capping or correcting the women's claims about marriage, is in essence that of an *epithalamion*. According to him, the entire *exodos* "is influenced by, and would evoke in the minds of the audience, the wedding song."[146] The final ode therefore seems intended (at least in part) as a prelude to marriage. But who is to marry whom?

The fourth strophe and antistrophe are once again spoken by the Danaids alone, and acquire added weight from being the play's last lines. Here the women repeat their opposition to marriage, albeit in more qualified terms than before (1062–73):

May King Zeus take from [us]
a badly manned, hostile
marriage, he who well freed Io from grief,
restraining her with healing hand,
making the violence kind;
and may he distribute
power to women.
I accept the lesser evil
and the glass half-full,
and hope that with my prayers and the
delivering tricks of the god,
Justice may follow justice.

Ζεὺ⟨ς⟩ ἄναξ ἀποστεροί—
η γάμον δυσάνορα
δάϊον, ὅσπερ Ἰὼ
πημονᾶς ἐλύσατ' εὖ
χειρὶ παιωνίαι
κατασχεθών, εὐμενῆ βίαν κτίσας·
καὶ κράτος νέμοι γυναι—
ξίν. τὸ βέλτερον κακοῦ
καὶ τὸ δίμοιρον αἰνῶ
καὶ δίκαι Δίκαν[147] ἕπεσ—
θαι ξὺν εὐχαῖς ἐμαῖς
λυτηρίοις μηχαναῖς θεοῦ πάρα.

The women do not ask Zeus to prevent all marriages, but those that are "badly manned" (δυσάνορα) and "hostile" (δάϊον). By implication, some unions might conceivably involve good men (εὐάνδρος) rather than bad (δυσ-).[148] Indeed, the subsequent course of the trilogy arguably focuses on the replacement of a bad set of spouses with a better. The women's reference to Io points in the same direction, for it "implicitly admits the existence of acceptable forms of γάμος."[149] Zeus's restraint of the maiden in fact proved the means of her release. His touch brought healing (χειρὶ παιωνίαι), not harm; friendly was his force (εὐμενῆ βίαν). And the participle κτίσας intimates that their union is linked to the foundation of something lasting.

The Danaids' prayer at the start of the final antistrophe asks that Zeus "distribute power to women" (κράτος νέμοι γυναι- / ξίν, 1068–69). Friis Johansen and Whittle note that these words echo and invert the last words of the departing Egyptian herald, "May victory and power belong to the men" (εἴη δὲ νίκη καὶ κράτος τοῖς ἄρσεσιν, 951). On their reading, the prayer expresses the hope that the "female" side—the women and their Argive protectors—will be victorious in the coming military confrontation. Yet the lines of the immediately preceding strophe speak of marriage (γάμον, 1063), not war. And the oxymorons contained in their reference to Io suggest the women might like to reverse her tale as well. In their subsequent dealings with the Aegyptids, the Danaids take on an active, masculine role. Moreover, they do not make violence kindly (εὐμενῆ βίαν κτίσας), but rather turn (feigned) kindness into violence. Though they embrace their cousin-husbands, their right hands hold not healing (χειρὶ παιωνίαι) but daggers. The last line of the play hints at the lengths to which the women will go in this regard. The noun μηχαναῖς ("delivering tricks of the god," λυτηρίοις / μηχαναῖς θεοῦ πάρα) recalls the μηχανὴ καλή ("beautiful device," 459) of their loosened girdles, with which they earlier threatened violence. And the adjective modifying it, λυτηρίοις ("delivering"), recalls the brutal methods used by the hero Apis to rid Argos of its snakes long ago (ἄκη τομαῖα καὶ λυτήρια / πράξας, 268–69). The Danaids' desire for victory extends from battlefield to boudoir.

The compressed and powerful language of choral odes lends them an applicability stretching beyond the immediate dramatic context. This is particularly true of the present passage, where the Danaids' wish that Zeus κράτος νέμοι γυναι- / ξίν involves more than their dealings with the Aegyptids. The lack of any direct articles or demonstratives in their wish implies that they want more than the limited ability to choose from among a specific set of prospective husbands. What they are after is power itself: κράτος.[150] Thus even if, as I have argued, the Danaids kill their Aegyptid husbands and remarry their Argive sponsors, the trilogy's ending remains unsettling.[151] As von Fritz remarks, "The fact that the Danaids' freedom to choose is the cause and basis of the entire plot undoubtedly makes them partially masculine, or at least raises them above the Female, so far as contemporaries understood it."[152] In essence, the Danaids' rejection of Greek gender norms and expectations, and their ready resort to violence, gives their desires a revolutionary cast.

Tragic Sisters

Aeschylus's Danaids were doubtless unsettling to the Athenian spectators. They were of course not alone in this; Greek tragedy as a genre recurs time and again to the disruptive effects women could have on the polis.[153] Yet the Danaids have especially close ties to the protagonists of Sophocles's *Antigone* and Euripides's *Medea*. Both of these later women are also marked by an independence from their nominal *kyrioi* and an unwillingness to accept the usual sort of marriage. Moreover, their unruly nature is linked to their sexuality and to their anomalous status within the polis. The trouble ultimately stems from the fact that all these women are, in one way or another, strangers in the poleis they inhabit.

In Sophocles's *Antigone,* produced around 441,[154] the protagonist is marked as an outsider in important ways. Despite the fact that she was born and bred in Thebes, her civic status is deceptively complex.[155] Her father was originally thought to have come from Corinth, which would have led the townspeople to consider her at first the product of a citizen-foreigner marriage. And while the subsequent revelations about Oedipus's identity established him as a Boeotian, they simultaneously undercut the legitimacy of his marriage to his mother, Jocasta. Antigone is therefore anything but the ordinary offspring of a legitimate union between two Thebans. The irregularity of her standing is emphasized by her rejection of the city's laws (νόμοι) broadly speaking and of the *kyrios* they assign her.[156] For the deaths of her brothers Eteocles and Polyneices have paradoxically established her foe Creon as her legal guardian.[157] The same is of course true for Ismene, but here (as in so many ways) the two sisters differ.[158] Whereas Ismene accepts their uncle's authority, Antigone mockingly calls her his ward (κηδεμών)[159] and spends the bulk of the play defying him.[160] Her unusual parentage, her disaffection with the city, and her assertion of independence from her citizen *kyrios* all reveal Antigone as a veritable outsider rather than a loyal daughter of Thebes.

One of the clearest signs of Antigone's foreign status is that the play thrice refers to her with metic terminology.[161] For instance, when she is led away to the cave that will become her tomb, she laments her wretchedness thus (850–52):

Ah, wretched me, [neither a mortal] among mortals
nor a corpse among corpses,
[I am] a metic, [belonging to] neither the living nor the dead.

ἰὼ δύστανος, βροτοῖς
οὔτε νεκρὸς νεκροῖσιν
μέτοικος, οὐ ζῶσιν, οὐ θανοῦσιν.

Shortly thereafter she again terms herself a metic when bewailing the incestuous couplings of her parents (866–68):

From such parents I, wretched, was born.
Toward whom I now go,
accursed, unwed, a metic.

οἵων ἐγώ ποθ' ἁ ταλαίφρων ἔφυν·
πρὸς οὓς ἀραῖος ἄγαμος ἅδ'
ἐγὼ μέτοικος ἔρχομαι.

And roughly twenty lines later, Creon impatiently urges his men to speed up Antigone's entombment so that she "will be deprived of her metoikia above ground" (μετοικίας δ' οὖν τῆς ἄνω στερήσεται, 890).

Most scholars have noted these metic references in passing,[162] or interpreted them loosely. According to Griffith, at the time of the *kommos* Antigone is a metic insofar as she occupies a liminal status, neither living nor dead.[163] Sentenced to death by Creon, she is simply marking time en route. Another common explanation is that Sophocles intended the metic references to evoke loneliness and grief.[164] Yet there is more to them than pathos. For one thing, even as she speaks, Antigone is being led away from the city toward a cavern in a desolate border region devoid of people.[165] Creon's purpose is to insulate Thebes from any potential pollution by having her die of starvation and exposure beyond the city limits.

Significantly, Antigone's depictions as a metic directly precede her marriage. Numerous scholars have remarked that her procession to her tomb is a ghastly conflation of wedding and funeral ritual.[166] She is a woman with simultaneously no and too many husbands. At line 816 she says she goes to wed Acheron (Ἀχέροντι νυμφεύσω). At line 867 she says her fate is to be unmarried (ἄγαμος). And the messenger's description of

Haemon's dying embrace of her corpse (1234–39) is replete with sexual imagery: "the details—a lover's embrace, heavy breathing, the gush of liquid, drops of blood, pale white skin—suggest both the seminal emission of male orgasm and the defloration of a virgin on her wedding night."[167]

In fashioning his Antigone, Sophocles may have been influenced by his predecessor Aeschylus. As in the case of the Danaids, the playwright links Antigone's foreignness and her sexuality; the combination of the two has the ability to destabilize the polis. In marrying either no one or Death, she violates the norm holding that citizen women should wed, and should wed citizen men. Even her planned union with the Theban citizen Haemon cuts against the civic grain. Marriage in classical Greece was as a rule virilocal, with the wife leaving her own natal family to join her husband's. But *Antigone* inverts this movement, making Haemon the mobile element who rejects his family to join a bride clinging excessively to hers.[168] It is noteworthy that the son rejects his father's guidance about marriage.[169] Spurning Antigone as a potential match for Haemon, Creon baldly tells Ismene that "there are other fields [for him] to plow" (ἀρώσιμοι γὰρ χἀτέρων εἰσὶν γύαι, 569). This troublesome outsider should be replaced with a properly submissive Theban wife. Indeed, within the context of male civic ideology, legitimate wives are like land:[170] they are essentially identical parcels, with one tilled acre resembling another. Their primary purpose is to bring forth new life. And, like tracts of earth itself, they can be measured in standard units that simultaneously function as reservoirs of wealth.[171]

Creon's view of marriage was likely shared by many of the spectators attending *Antigone*. His fecund phrase recalls the traditional Athenian wedding formula: "I give you this woman for the plowing of legitimate children" (ταύτην γνησίων παιδῶν ἐπ' ἀρότῳ σοι δίδωμι).[172] In one sense the play vindicates the viewpoint of the watching *kyrioi*. For them, marriage was above all a means of perpetuating *oikoi* and increasing their assets; few things were more disruptive in this regard than a willful son's *eros*-driven marriage to an independent, outspoken woman who might defy the city's laws.[173] Female subjectivity posed significant problems for male citizens both on-stage and off. And Antigone's possession of it in abundance is organically related to her depiction as a *metoikos* about to marry.

Euripides's *Medea*, produced in 431, stars a woman who is not only an outsider, but a barbarian at that. Although the text never explicitly calls Medea a *metoikos*, that is what she is: a free, non-citizen resident.[174]

Leaving her home to marry,[175] Medea acquired in Jason a Greek *kyrios* who attempts to make crucial decisions affecting their *oikos* without regard to her desires.[176] The play's thematic focus is on one of the most significant choices facing families and individuals alike: whom to wed, and on what grounds. Jason's decision to abandon Medea and Creon's choice of him as husband for his daughter clearly drive the plot. But the drama examines past marital choices as well. The play's concern with marriage even extends to the future, with Aegeus and the chorus wondering what sort of spouses fate has in store for them.[177] *Medea* is obsessed with what its protagonist terms the ἀγὼν μέγιστος (235), the acquisition of a spouse.[178]

Medea emphatically rejects the gender role assigned her by Greek society. As Helene Foley notes, "[she] is far from the passive victim of marriage and masculine brutality that she claims to be. . . . She did not in fact need the dowry she complains of to the chorus. . . . She chose her own husband and has won him by her ruthless deeds. Indeed, she often seems to envision herself, contrary to Greek practice, as an equal or even the dominant partner in the marriage."[179] Once, spurred on by *eros*, she defied her father and destroyed her natal *oikos*; in the course of the play she visits the same treatment on her husband and her marital *oikos*.[180]

As a *kyrios* Jason is cool, calculating, and eminently rational. He denies (530) that passion affected his original selection of Medea; it was rather she whom love compelled. For him, tactical help in acquiring fleecy wealth was more alluring. He stresses that his impending marriage to Creon's daughter is rooted in wisdom (σοφία), moderation (σωφροσύνη), and affection (φιλία), a deep and abiding concern for Medea and their children.[181] Once again, his primary thoughts are of political alliance and financial advantage.[182] While Jason's claims are transparently self-serving, they are not just that. To see him solely as reprehensible does not do justice to the play or the society that produced it. Jason does not reject marriage, but instead "insists that he uses it only deliberately, for practical ends."[183] In this, he offers a viewpoint readily familiar to the citizen audience, for whom good marriages were primarily matters of children, household wealth, and political alliance, with affection as a by-product.

Medea arguably depicts the wisdom of Jason's unsentimental approach to marriage. Its characters repeatedly employ the language of profit and loss, calculation and measurement. Forms of ὀνίημι, meaning "to profit, benefit, help, assist," occur five times in the text, while forms of λύω in the sense of "to profit, gain," appear thrice.[184] The famous *agon* scene between Medea and Jason (446–626) could profitably be described as two radically divergent cost-benefit analyses of the same marriage. And in the course of the play Medea ultimately comes around to Jason's way of thinking.[185] At one level this is evident in her murder of Creon's daughter. Deborah Boedeker has argued that this act is a figurative suicide, Medea's eradication of her former starry-eyed self.[186] At another level the change in the heroine also appears in her relationship with Aegeus. When the king passes through on his way to Delphi, she senses a powerful ally and makes him an offer he cannot refuse: progeny in exchange for protection.[187] Although *Medea* is enigmatic about the future, according to one tradition the pair eventually marry, and several textual hints point in this direction.[188] By the end of the play Medea has thus adopted and exploited Jason's view. In the short term marriage is a tactical alliance based on need, while in the longer term it entails providing a man with children and prosperity.

Medea is the most vivid example of the dangers posed by the sexual mores of foreign women. What would the Athenian audience have made of her character? At one level the play was a dramatic demonstration of the disruptive force of *eros*, of what can happen when a citizen marries an exotic outsider accustomed to independence. Many of the spectators undoubtedly agreed with Jason's claim at lines 1339–41:

No Greek woman would ever
have dared this, those whom I passed over
to marry you, a hostile and destructive in-law.

οὐκ ἔστιν ἥτις τοῦτ᾽ ἂν Ἑλληνὶς γυνὴ
ἔτλη ποθ᾽, ὧν γε πρόσθεν ἠξίουν ἐγὼ
γῆμαι σέ, κῆδος ἐχθρὸν ὀλεθριόν τ᾽ ἐμοί.

Medea's airborne departure from Corinth brought the point home in spectacular fashion. Independent, sexually aggressive, foreign women are headed toward Athens, so choose your spouse wisely.[189]

Conclusion

At the time of *Suppliant Women*'s performance in the second half of the 460s, the dimensions of the problems posed by intermarriages with metics were becoming clearer. In the archaic period, marriages between Athenians and foreigners likely occurred mainly at the elite level, and for dynastic considerations. By the end of the sixth century, however, the matrimonial politics of the great clans had begun to fall into disrepute, and with the rise of immigration to Athens, different sorts of marriages with foreigners became more prevalent under the Cleisthenic democracy.[190] As the metic share of the population swelled in the aftermath of the Persian Wars, so too did the number of mixed-status marriages. Stewart, relying on (necessarily tentative) population estimates and the relevant age tables, reckons that "in the 450s, between 350 and 1000 metic *parthenoi* would be reaching marriageable age each year."[191] While these numbers should naturally be treated with great caution, they do provide a rough sense of the scale of the problem. As Rhodes notes, "The Pentecontaetia was the time when Athens' metic population grew most rapidly, and . . . mixed marriages were becoming more frequent."[192]

What made mixed-status marriages so threatening was that, unlike Athenian *astai*, metic women existed in a realm largely beyond the control of citizen *kyrioi*, who were concerned with perpetuating and enhancing their *oikoi*. Put differently, in the imaginary of the Athenian citizen, metic women had a greater possibility of developing an independent subjectivity of their own.[193] And the uses to which they might put their moral agency were frightening. As Stewart notes of the Amazons, "far from the demure virginity prescribed by law and custom, their sexual life is a continual series of flagrantly public one-night stands. In this way they represent not only the threat that every adolescent girl poses to her father's authority and to the stability of the family, but the lure of forbidden fruit as well."[194]

The same statement applies in some ways to Aeschylus's Danaids. As we have seen, they demand to pick their own mates, threaten to remove their garments before strangers, and, under the guise of compliance, kill their cousin-husbands after a single night, even as the men foolishly think they have gained the upper hand. Given all this, the Danaids are intrinsically problematic partners. Their multiple marriages, first to the Aegyptids and later the Argives, are accompanied by destruction for Pelasgus and suffering for the polis and its citizens. The Κύπριος χαρακτὴρ of the Danaids abides.

4

Sons of Earth

Suppliant Women appropriates the complex web of relationships obtaining among natives, newcomers, and the land in historical Athens. Pelasgus's claim to be sprung from Palaichthon ("Ancient Earth") should be read in light of a fifth-century ideological staple, the notion of citizen autochthony.[1] For Athenians, Attica was more than their country: it was also their parent.[2] In the play, Pelasgus's accounts of his ancestry and his land are intertwined.[3] The king also joins together the past of Argos and its present. By recounting the legend of the hero Apis, he tries to demonstrate the circularity of the city's history.[4] His hieromantic predecessor saved Argos from pollution and death by driving out a hostile *synoikia* of snakes. For his part, Pelasgus tries to save the land from a similar threat by offering metoikia to the Danaids. While Apis succeeded, Pelasgus fails, and dies in the attempt.

In *Suppliant Women,* the citizens of Argos are like their leader: they are all depicted as autochthonous γαμόροι. In this regard the Argives resemble real-life Athenians. During the archaic period, the city began to measure and mark off its territory. Solon's census legislation subsequently created an enduring link between citizen and soil. This in turn provided the ideological basis for the ban on *enktesis* by metics.[5] Deprived of the opportunity to own land and houses, non-citizens were compelled to earn their living in different ways, to store their assets in different forms, and to live in different places and manners. The development of twin stereotypes, the agrarian citizen farmer and the urban metic artisan, codified the antithesis between citizens and metics.

Suppliant Women grounds these issues by considering in detail where in Argos the Danaids will live. Although some scholars have argued that the housing motif is meant as preparation for the women's eventual murder of their cousins, it is better understood as another means of underlining their metic status. Although Pelasgus offers the newcomers a variety of housing options, they are not given the chance to own dwellings. The Argive leader instead states that he and his fellow citizens will serve as their citizen sponsors (*prostatai*) and arrange matters for them. The particulars of the Danaids' lodging thus reflect their juridical status and provide ample scope for erotic liaisons that may not be conducive to the well-being of Argos.

Pelasgus and Apis

The start of *Suppliant Women* introduces the Danaids and the play's main themes simultaneously. The subsequent entrance of Pelasgus and his men via the opposite *eisodos* at line 234 is of equal moment. Danaus has finished offering advice to his daughters and likely steps to the side, perhaps even concealing himself behind the altar at which they have taken refuge.[6] We have already discussed in detail Pelasgus's reaction to the women's strange appearance. But their behavior is also highly unusual. At lines 238–40 he comments on the manner of their arrival:

How you fearlessly dared to come to the country
without heralds or *proxenoi* or leaders—
this is astonishing.

ὅπως δὲ χώραν οὔτε κηρύκων ὕπο
ἀπρόξενοί τε νόσφιν ἡγητῶν μολεῖν
ἔτλητ' ἀτρέστως, τοῦτο θαυμαστὸν πέλει.

Their encounter is a tense one. Seas separate many Greek poleis from one another, and even where two or more lands adjoin, the border areas are often rough, contested terrain that forms the backdrop for military clashes. It is therefore no surprise that Pelasgus responds to encroachment on Argos's territory with armed men.[7] While Taplin has argued that his entourage is meant to protect the suppliants, we must remember that unlike the audience, Pelasgus has not had the benefit of attending the play's *proagon*: he does not yet know who the intruders are or why they have come.[8] His response is that of a prudent leader responding to reports of a strange ship offshore and possible disembarkations. Adding to his consternation is the fact that the women have eschewed the ordinary means of peaceful boundary-crossing. Dispensing with heralds (κήρυκες) and lacking local representatives (πρόξενοι), the Danaids have demonstrated both unpredictability and a potentially dangerous character. In this regard they prefigure another incursion of foreigners later in the play. Starting with line 825, more Egyptians again arrive by ship, enter via the same *eisodos* the Danaids used, and proceed to the same location. Like their female quarry, the pursuing herald and his men also appear without permission or *proxenoi*.[9] And Pelasgus responds to their boundary violation in like manner. But while the Danaids threaten to kill themselves to coerce Pelasgus, the Egyptian men threaten to return in force and kill Argives. The king's initial confrontation with the Danaids thus emphasizes the fraught nature of all encounters between newcomers and natives: the potential for violence is seldom absent.

Pelasgus and his men are not the only ones who are wary. Heeding for the moment their father's elocutionary advice, the women keep their remarks short and to the point.[10] At line 246 they concede that Pelasgus is right about their un-Greek dress: "You have spoken an unlying word about our attire" (εἴρηκας ἀμφὶ κόσμον ἀψευδῆ λόγον). Their next words show how bewildering the encounter is to them as well. Pelasgus had guessed at the women's status based on the suppliant branches they carried in their hands and deposited at the altar. But what the Argive carries in his baffles them. At lines 247–48 they question Pelasgus about his identity, asking, "In speaking to you do I address / a private citizen, or a guard with a holy staff, or a leader of the city?" (ἐγὼ δὲ πρὸς σὲ πότερον ὡς ἔτην λέγω, / ἢ τηρὸν ἱερόρραβδον, ἢ πόλεως ἀγόν;). Like their κλάδοι, his staff (ἱερόρραβδον, 247) has a sacral character that in part transcends cultural difference. Yet it also has a political dimension: it symbolizes legitimate authority and is a practical means of applying force.[11] The Danaids want to know in what capacity (and to what ends) Pelasgus wields this implement.[12] Is he an ἔτης, a private citizen?[13] Is he a subordinate who bears the staff for a religious superior?[14] Or is he a, or even the, leader of the political community? Absent further information, the Danaids do not understand Pelasgus's status and are hesitant to say more.

Pelasgus's response to this brief question is expansive. He first recounts his genealogy and position (250–53):

For I am Pelasgus, son of the earth-born Palaichthon,
ruler of this land here, and the Pelasgian people,

appropriately[15] taking their name from me, their king,
reap the harvest of this soil.

τοῦ γηγενοῦς γάρ εἰμ' ἐγὼ Παλαίχθονος
ἶνις Πελασγός, τῆσδε γῆς ἀρχηγέτης.
ἐμοῦ δ' ἄνακτος εὐλόγως ἐπώνυμον
γένος Πελασγῶν τήνδε καρποῦται χθόνα.

Pelasgus's identification of himself as a king (ἄνακτος) of noble blood forms only part of his response. The multiple occurrences of the nouns γῆ and χθών (both alone and in compounds) suggest that who and what he is are tied to the land. In addition, the demonstratives with which these nouns are paired (τῆσδε γῆς, τήνδε . . . χθόνα) are deictics showing that it is his relationship with one particular land that matters: Argos.[16]

The eponymous name of the king's followers was a resonant one for Aeschylus's audience. According to Herodotus (1.56–58), the Pelasgians were the indigenous inhabitants of what eventually became "Hellas" in the aftermath of the Dorian invasion. A number of them reputedly survived the onslaught to establish a *modus vivendi* with the newcomers. Although apparently not Greek-speakers at first, in time the Pelasgians adopted the invaders' tongue. The frequent application of the epithet "Pelasgian" to Argos in particular suggests that the locale was thought to have a special relationship with the *Urvolk* of Greece.[17] Edith Hall has argued that Aeschylus's portrait of Pelasgian Argos reflects this process of cultural mixing: "while in *Suppliant Women* [he] is nodding to the ethnographers' theory about the original Pelasgian population of Argos, *his* Pelasgians are of course simultaneously envisaged as 'Hellenes' . . . and the play depends to a great extent on the contrast between their truly Greek language, customs, and institutions, and those of the barbarous Egyptians."[18] Pelasgus's revelation of his name is thus an assertion that he and his people have a special claim to the land they inhabit, and is made to a new set of immigrants.

The king is not just an indigenous Argive; his self-description styles him a son of the soil. At lines 250–51 he defines himself as an ἶνις of τοῦ γηγενοῦς . . . Παλαίχθονος. The adjective here (γηγενοῦς) is a compound derived from γῆ and γενής, with the primary meaning of "earthborn"—that is, sprung from the ground.[19] The proper noun (Παλαίχθονος) makes the connection even more strongly; his sire Παλαίχθων is literally "Ancient Earth" itself.[20] Despite this surface simplicity, Pelasgus's genealogy is surprisingly complicated.[21] The Palaichthon/Pelasgus duo resemble another pair, the legendary Athenian rulers Erechtheus and

Erichthonius.[22] In each case, autochthonous father and son so closely resemble each other as to be almost indistinguishable. The result is a kind of confusion "in which fathers are the same age as their sons and all the generations are entangled, [and] no eponymous hero has a face that is his own."[23]

Although proud of his ancestors, Pelasgus offers no details about his conception.[24] By comparison, we know far more about the begetting and birth of other autochthonous Greeks. For instance, the famous Sown Men (Spartoi) of Thebes were created from the teeth of a slain serpent that were subsequently planted in the soil. And the Athenian Erichthonius was said to be the product of Hephaestus's semen, which was caught on a tuft of wool and flung to the ground. Pelasgus's silence about how he came to be has an important implication: he apparently has no mother worth mentioning.[25] Nicole Loraux has noted the general tendency of the concept of autochthony to suppress mothers. In the Demosthenic *Epitaphios* (60), for instance, "the land of the fathers takes the place of the mother, to the extent of supplanting her as the signifier: instead of the binominal *meter kai patris*, the couple *pater/patris* will take on the function of a parental couple from this point onward, but it is a parental couple that is wholly masculine."[26] In similar fashion, *Suppliant Women* casts Ancient Land as Pelasgus's *father* while remaining mum about his mother.[27]

Although the play says naught of Pelasgus's begetting, it is more informative about a different miraculous conception. At numerous points the chorus refer to their descent from Epaphus, the son of Io, who was formed by Zeus's gentle touch. Like Pelasgus, he has a mixed ancestry including non-humans: while the Argive ruler was born from the ground, Epaphus descended from a heifer.[28] The Danaids' claim to be Argives ultimately rests on this bovine. What Παλαίχθων is for Pelasgus and his fellow citizens, Io is for the Danaids. Pelasgus's initial statement of his identity implicitly establishes Argos as a place with little room for or need of women. By contrast, the newcomers do not see the land as a preeminently masculine domain. They instead associate it with strong females, especially the goddess Hera and her priestess Io.[29] *Suppliant Women* is by one measure a tale of two competing genealogies, one patrilineal and one matrilineal.[30]

Pelasgus's claim to be autochthonous has two interwoven yet independent strands: (1) he is indigenous to the land; and (2) he is sprung from it. In his study of autochthony as an ideology at Athens, Vincent Rosivach has argued that these two concepts were originally distinct.

According to him, their fusion in the early fifth century formed part of a conscious attempt to buttress the young democracy.[31] In the chaotic environment surrounding the reforms of Ephialtes, the promotion of autochthony was one means of keeping citizens from dwelling on their differences with one another. By emphasizing what Athenians had in common, autochthony fostered unity at home while transposing difference abroad.[32] Pelasgus's on-stage assertion of Argive autochthony may accordingly have had a political resonance for the audience watching *Suppliant Women* in the later 460s. For one thing, it hinted that his regal background was compatible with a commitment to democracy. In this regard Pelasgus resembled the real-life leaders of the Athenian *demos* in the first half of the fifth century, who overwhelmingly stemmed from aristocratic Eupatrid families. Moreover, the fact that Pelasgus's eponymous people share his name suggests that they also share his clan. Palaichthon thereby becomes a noble Pelasgus can safely boast about, because he is by extension the common ancestor of all Argives.

Pelasgus's assertion of his ancestry to the Danaids contrasts with the anonymity he later embraces when confronting the Egyptian herald (938–49).[33] Yet the two scenes are of a piece. In the former instance he stresses his kinship with the Argive people (γένος, 253); in the latter (942–43), the unity they all share. Loraux has noted the centrality of homogeneity to the Athenians' ideology of autochthony. Crucial to the myth was the belief that "the *polis*, an indivisible unity, . . . [owed] its authority to the effacement of its *andres*, valiant citizen-soldiers but identical and interchangeable—the Athenian version of *homoioi*, men of equal standing."[34] In *Suppliant Women* the myth of autochthony likewise functions as a civic leveling mechanism. In Pelasgus's encounter with the Danaids it is ennobling, making ordinary Argives kin to and peers of their leader. Yet in his encounter with the Egyptian pursuers, autochthony democratizes, turning Pelasgus into a nameless everyman standing shoulder to shoulder with his equals among the spear-carrying rank and file.

Autochthony lent a valuable impetus to defending one's country.[35] In confronting first the Danaids and then the Egyptians, the Pelasgians protect not just their soil but also their sire. Theirs is a daunting task, given the geographical extent of Argos in the play. At lines 254–59 Pelasgus traces the perimeter of the area to be guarded:

I rule all the land through which flows holy
Strymon, that toward the west.

And I border the land of the Parrhaebians, and the places
this side of Pindus near the Paeonians,
and the Dodonian mountains. The boundary
of the moist sea terminates [my realm]. All
on this side of it I rule.

καὶ πᾶσαν αἶαν, ἧς δι᾽ ἁγνὸς ἔρχεται
Στρυμών, τὸ πρὸς δύνοντος ἡλίου κρατῶ·
ὁρίζομαι δὲ τήν τε Περραιβῶν χθόνα
Πίνδου τε τἀπέκεινα, Παιόνων πέλας,
ὄρη τε Δωδωναῖα· συντέμνει δ᾽ ὅρος
ὑγρᾶς θαλάσσης· τῶνδε τἀπὶ τάδε κρατῶ.

Pelasgus's repeated use of the verb κρατῶ (255, 259) in an emphatic line-position emphasizes his authority. Yet as we saw earlier, the Argive rules not so much in his own right but as a representative of others.[36] Following Friis Johansen and Whittle, Sandin has argued for the transposition of the nouns Παιόνων and Περραιβῶν. The effect is to turn lines 255–58 into a description of "the northern border of [Pelasgus's] kingdom."[37] Stretching from Thrace in the east to Epirus in the west, this boundary separates the Pelasgians from their (barbarous) neighbors. On the south, Argos extends from the Aegean Sea to the Ionian. The area over which Pelasgus presides thus includes "all of the Greek mainland."[38]

The dramatic motivation for Pelasgus's geographical excursus is not immediately apparent.[39] Similar topographical catalogues occur in a number of other plays by Aeschylus. *Persians* 864–906 includes a list of Greek cities once ruled by Xerxes; *Agamemnon* 289–316 traces the route traveled by the fire beacon from Troy across the Aegean to Mycenae; and *Eumenides* (292–97, 397–402) contains a number of geographical allusions.[40] The frequency and density of these references suggest that Aeschylus may have been influenced by Hecataeus's *Periegesis*,[41] and that his audience found them of interest.[42]

After tracing the extent of his realm, Pelasgus offers a brief history of the region to which the Danaids have come—namely, the Argolid (260–70):

And of the Apian [i.e. Peloponnesian[43]] land, this plain
has long taken its name from a mortal physician.
Having come from the headland opposite Naupactus,
Apis, a physician-seer and child of Apollo, cleansed
this land from man-destroying monsters,
a hostile infestation of serpents,
which the earth sent forth, defiled by

pollutions of ancient bloodshed.
Having blamelessly saved the Argive land with cutting remedies,
he then found recompense in our prayers.

αὐτῆς δὲ χώρας Ἀπίας πέδον τόδε
πάλαι κέκληται φωτὸς ἰατροῦ χάριν·
Ἆπις γὰρ ἐλθὼν ἐκ πέρας Ναυπακτίας
ἰατρόμαντις παῖς Ἀπόλλωνος χθόνα
τήνδ' ἐκκαθαίρει κνωδάλων βροτοφθόρων,
τὰ δὴ[44] παλαιῶν αἱμάτων μιάσμασιν
χρανθεῖς' ἀνῆκε γαῖα †μηνεῖται ἄκη†,
δρακονθόμιλον δυσμενῆ ξυνοικίαν.
τούτων ἄκη τομαῖα καὶ λυτήρια
πράξας ⟨ἀ⟩μέμπτως Ἆπις Ἀργείαι χθονί
μνήμην τοτ' ἀντίμισθον ηὗρετ' ἐν λιταῖς.

As with the geography of Argos, the rationale for this bit of local history is not immediately apparent. Sandin describes the excursus as "somewhat uncalled for, and moreover confusing."[45] Yet the adjective Ἀπίας does provide a link with what precedes. In their earlier prayers to the local divinities, the Danaids twice used this same word to describe the land to which they had come (Ἀπίαν βοῦνιν, 117, 128). In so doing they hoped to link Argos with the Egyptian god-king Apis, who was (according to some) identical with their ancestor Epaphus.[46] Calling Argos an "Apian" land was another method of affirming their ancestral ties with the area. Yet the Apis cited by Pelasgus is a separate figure entirely. He is no foreign bull god born from Zeus, but a son of Apollo. He hails from the north shore of the Corinthian Gulf, not Egypt. And he is a physician-seer rather than a divine ruler.[47] Pelasgus's mention of Apis underlines once again the depths of the mutual misunderstanding between Danaids and Argives. Even when the two groups employ the same words, they mean very different things.[48]

There is a deeper narrative purpose to Pelasgus's aetiology. Earlier in his self-presentation, the ruler dwelt on his link to the Pelasgians; Apis is another eponymous hero. The two men also share a common dilemma: the need to confront enemies who threaten their land with pollution. Apis's opponents are described as "mortal-destroying monsters" (κνωδάλων βροτοφθόρων, 264) and "a hostile infestation of snakes" (δρακονθόμιλον δυσμενῆ ξυνοικίαν, 267) defiling Argos. Apis responds by cleansing the land (ἐκκαθαίρει) with bloodletting. There are numerous verbal echoes between his situation and that of Pelasgus. While the serpents are described as a δρακονθόμιλος (267), the Danaids are an ἀνελληνόστολος ὅμιλος (234).[49] Both Apis and Pelasgus search for ἄκη ("remedies") to their respective crises (268, 367, 451).[50] Like the serpents, the women are a source of possible μίασμα (366, 473).[51] In the rest of the trilogy, the women kill their cousins and must subsequently be purified. To sum up, while Apis defended Argos from one set of marauders, Pelasgus must now confront another. His predecessor set the standard for success against which he will be measured.[52]

At the same time, there are also significant differences between Apis and Pelasgus. To begin with, the two men adopt different methods of dealing with the intruders. To rid Argos of the snakes, Apis employed "cures" that were "cutting edge" (ἄκη τομαῖα καὶ λυτήρια, 268). Sandin notes that elsewhere in Aeschylus, "related expressions are found referring both to the cutting of herbs and, metaphorically, to 'violent remedies', i.e. killing, probably hinting at surgery."[53] By contrast, Pelasgus's approach with the Danaids is milder. His solution is political rather than medical—namely, offering the women residence in the land under a specific set of conditions. He does not ban their συνοικία, but welcomes their μετοικία and seeks to dissipate their potential hostility toward the city. Following their acceptance by the assembly, the women offer the city a benediction (625–709) that begins thus: "Come, let us pray for good things for the Argives, in return for good things" (ἄγε δή, λέξωμεν ἐπ' Ἀργείοις / εὐχὰς ἀγαθάς, ἀγαθῶν ποινάς, 625–26). Yet Pelasgus is not averse to using force when necessary. As we noted above, the Egyptian herald arrives at Argos unapologetic about his lack of *proxenoi*. Pelasgus then rebukes him and says that he may take the women away, but only under certain conditions: "with kindly intent you may lead these women away, / if they are willing and if pious words persuade them" (ταύτας δ' ἑκούσας μὲν κατ' εὔνοιαν φρενῶν / ἄγοις ἄν, εἴπερ εὐσεβὴς πίθοι λόγος, 940–41). However brief their stay, the Egyptians must comport themselves with εὔνοια and εὐσέβεια; things in Argos are done with reasoned argument and mutual consent. When the herald refuses these terms, Pelasgus drives him from the land and offers insults to his departing back.

A second difference between Apis and Pelasgus lies in the degree of responsibility they assume for dealing with their respective crises. Son of a god, endowed with mantic knowledge and a physician's skills, Apis eliminates the snakes all by himself and subsequently receives hero-worship from the grateful Argives.[54] By contrast, input from the entire Argive community is necessary to solve the problem posed by the Danaids. As Pelasgus puts it, "If the whole city is polluted, let the people together work out cures" (τὸ κοινὸν δ' εἰ μιαίνεται πόλις, / ξυνῆι μελέσθω λαὸς ἐκπονεῖν ἄκη, 366–67). The threat is communal, and so the response must be as well. Pelasgus is no demigod, but a single (albeit valiant) member of his community.

Arguably the greatest difference between the two *eponymoi* is that while Apis accomplishes his task, Pelasgus fails at his. Although offering the Danaids metoikia saves Argos in the short run, in the long run it contributes to the city's destruction. To begin with, accepting the newcomers brings war with the Egyptians. At lines 934–37 the herald threatens:

Ares will decide these matters, and not with
witnesses. Nor will the quarrel end with a fine;
but first many men will fall
kicking away their lives.

οὔτοι δικάζει ταῦτα μαρτύρων ὕπο
Ἄρης· τὸ νεῖκος δ' οὐκ ἐν ἀργύρου λαβῆι
ἔλυσεν· ἀλλὰ πολλὰ γίγνεται πάρος
πεσήματ' ἀνδρῶν κἀπολακτισμοὶ βίου.

Visually, *Suppliant Women* resembles other suppliant tragedies, recording war's approach to a polis. The dramatic action culminates in two groups of hostile men facing each other across the level ground of the orchestra. Eventually the Egyptians turn and retreat while Pelasgus hurls invective.[55] The movements of the men resemble a figurative hoplite skirmish marked by a τροπή and subsequent erection of a τροπαῖον.[56] In some senses Aeschylus's *Suppliant Women* is, no less than his *Seven against Thebes*, a "drama full of Ares" (δρᾶμα . . . Ἄρεως μεστόν).[57] And the subsequent plays of the trilogy record the less happy consequences of armed combat.

The source of the conflict between Egyptians and Argives is the taproot of the epic tradition: the wounded τιμή resulting from the seizure of another man's woman. We famously owe the *Iliad* to two such instances: Paris's theft of Menelaus's wife, Helen, and Agamemnon's taking of Achilles's concubine, Briseis. Moreover, Herodotus derives the long-standing historical grievances between Greeks and Persians from generations of tit-for-tat woman-stealing. The historian identifies the removal of Io from Greece as the initial cause. According to his Persian sources, Phoenician sailors arrived in Argos to sell their wares, and departed with Inachus's daughter.[58] The abductions of Europa, Medea, and Helen follow as payback in short order. On this interpretation, the Danaids simply constitute one more link in the chain.

But the idea that claims to the Danaids might spark a war was based on more than epic precedent. The Athenian spectators had seen a similar process play out with regard to a real-life suppliant several years prior to *Suppliant Women*'s performance. In 471/70 the Athenian leader Themistocles was ostracized from Athens and took up residence in Argos. Shortly thereafter, the Spartan general Pausanias, accused of Medizing, was barricaded and starved to death in the temple of Athena of the Bronze House at Sparta. In the course of their investigation the Spartans turned up material implicating Themistocles as well, and requested that the Athenians join them in pursuing him. The Athenians agreed and "sen[t] with the Spartans, who were ready, men with the instruction to seize Themistocles wherever they came upon him."[59] Anthony Podlecki has traced in detail the similarities between this episode and the plot of *Suppliant Women*. He concludes that "it is remarkable that within a very few years of this sequence of events the Argive *demos* should be brought to the center of dramatic attention at Athens for its willingness to give protection to a band of suppliants, even at the expense of war. . . . It seems a plausible inference that Aeschylus, by throwing into high relief the Argive people's heroic reception of the Danaids, was reminding the Athenians of Argos' good services to Themistocles some years before."[60] The two situations are indeed similar in several ways. The commitment to shelter suppliants is treated by both Thucydides and Aeschylus as a likely *casus belli*. Moreover, the instructions given to the Athenians trailing Themistocles bring to mind the language of the Argive decree protecting the Danaids, since the infinitive ἄγειν is contained in both.

These initial similarities fade in light of the greater differences between the two situations, however. To begin with, the history of Argos provides the bedrock for Podlecki's interpretation. Yet in the forty years since his work appeared, scholarly advances have repeatedly shown the Athenocentric nature of tragedy as a genre. Non-Athenian locales are primarily depicted not in their own colors, but as reflections and refractions of contemporary Athens. Moreover, real-life Argos avoided the dilemma tragic Argos could not: Themistocles opted for flight rather than fight. He headed first to Corcyra and later turned to an enemy, King Admetus of the Molossians. He there took shelter for a season, eventually escaping by ship. But the threats of the pursuing Spartans and Athenians proved too much for each successive host. In Aeschylus's play, by contrast, the Danaids stay put, and the Argives suffer for their convictions.

Above all, the particulars of Themistocles's flight differ from those of the Danaids'. The former is pursued on political grounds, implicated though not yet convicted or condemned. By contrast, the Danaids flee to avoid marriage, and stress that they have committed no legal offense. The diverse directions in which the two parties flee are significant. At the time of *Suppliant Women*'s performance, Egypt was under the sway of Persia. Couched in the many antitheses structuring Greek thought of the period, the Danaids' move to Argos thus constitutes a rejection of the decadent, effeminate barbarism of the monarchical "Orient."[61] Yet Themistocles's final destination is nothing less than the court of the Great King himself. He is even said to have made part of the journey disguised as a woman.[62] Upon arriving, he spent the first year adapting himself to Persian ways, "and in that time he learned as much as he could of the Persian language and the customs of the land."[63] The extent of his Medizing was electrifying. When the time came to meet Artaxerxes, Themistocles "was led before the king, performed *proskynesis,* and stood in silence" (εἰσήχθη πρὸς βασιλέα καὶ προσκυνήσας ἔστη σιωπῇ).[64] For the Greeks, this ritual abasement was the ultimate symbol of Persian subservience, the individual equivalent of providing earth and water to the Great King. For many of the play's spectators, who had themselves fought against Xerxes and his successor, Themistocles's embrace of eastern despotism would have been difficult to reconcile with the Danaids' *prima facie* rejection of it.[65] Podlecki is nevertheless right about one important fact: the incorporation of outsiders could indeed create substantial foreign policy risks.

The Danaids and Danger

The choral ode sung by the Danaids at lines 625–709 highlights the danger they pose to Argos. At lines 634–36 in the first strophe, they show an acute awareness of what may well come to pass:

May warlike Ares, insatiable of shouting,
never set this Pelasgian land aflame,
harvesting humans in other furrows.

μήποτε πυρίφατον τάν⟨δε⟩ Πελασγίαν
τὸν ἄκορον βοᾶς κτίσαι μάχλον Ἄρη,
τὸν ἀρότοις θερίζοντα βροτοὺς ἐν ἄλλοις . . .

In the second strophe, however, at lines 659–62, the women again pray that the city may be spared, but this time from a different threat:

May plague of men[66]
never empty out this city,
nor strife bloody the land's plain
with internecine dead.

μήποτε λοιμὸς ἀνδρῶν
τάνδε πόλιν κενώσαι·
μηδ' ἐπιχωρίοις ⟨ ⟩
πτώμασιν αἱματίσαι πέδον γᾶς.

The repetition of μήποτε at line 658 and the identical position of the wish within the strophe show that the second wish is parallel to the first: to avoid war. Yet the lack of an explicit subject for the optative αἱματίσαι has led to a number of conjectures to fill out the missing iamb at line 660. The most successful to date are a pair of words meaning "strife," Bamberger's στάσις and Heath's ἔρις.[67] What the women apparently fear is some sort of contention that will lead to bloodshed related to "internecine struggles" (ἐπιχωρίοις . . . πτώμασιν). Friis Johansen and Whittle have claimed that this dative phrase refers to "the loss of Argive lives brought about by a military invasion of the country,"[68] with the adjective ἐπιχωρίοις denoting where the men will fall. Yet the phrase applies equally well to struggles between natives of the same country. After all, *stasis* is often used to describe the bloody political conflicts between citizens in ancient Greek poleis. According to Thucydides, the tendency toward it was so pronounced that in the course of the Peloponnesian War "the whole Greek world, so to speak, was disturbed."[69]

At the start of the third strophe, the women combine both wishes, praying that Argos may be spared both war and *stasis*. At lines 678–82 they say:

May no man-wearying ruin come upon
this city and ravage it, arming
danceless, songless, tear-begetting Ares
and violence among demesmen.

μηδέ τις ἀνδροκμὴς
λοιγὸς ἐπελθέτω
τάνδε πόλιν δαΐζων,
ἄχορον ἀκίθαριν δακρυογόνον Ἄρη
βίαν[70] τ' ἔ⟨ν⟩δημον ἐξοπλίζων.

In the second participial clause, the twin dangers of war and civil strife are brought under a single umbrella, serving as direct objects of the participle ἐξοπλίζων. The combination is understandable, given that the two are in some sense different facets of the same problem: the violence that may result from introducing strangers into a city.[71]

Pelasgus's recurring fears throughout *Suppliant Women* about what the Argives will say are related to the threats the Danaids pose. We discussed earlier his refusal to grant the women's plea for sanctuary without the consent of the *demos* (398–400) and his request that Danaus move his daughters' suppliant branches to a more visible location (480–85).[72] In his sensitivity to public opinion, Pelasgus bears a striking resemblance to an Athenian magistrate conscious of the fact that his *euthuna* will come.[73] Indeed, military defeats and significant casualties were a reliable way to produce political strife in classical Athens.[74] In addition, we find popular reproach for unsuccessful leaders scattered throughout other Aeschylean plays. In the first stasimon of *Agamemnon,* the chorus note the civic unrest arising from the Argive losses at Troy. As the ashes of dead warriors arrive home in urns, the families mutter about the waste, all "for the sake of another's woman" (ἀλλοτρίας διαὶ γυναικός, 448). They direct their anger at the expedition's leaders, the Atreidae: "the citizens' voices are heavy with rage, and stretch out their curses" (βαρεῖα δ' ἀστῶν φάτις ξὺν κότωι, / δημοκρά⟨ν⟩του δ' ἀρᾶς τίνει χρέος, 456–57).[75]

In the *Oresteia,* threats of war and *stasis* combine to produce a third sort of danger: coup d'état. In *Agamemnon* and *Libation Bearers,* Aegisthus seizes power and then wields it tyrannically. And as we saw earlier, in the Danaid trilogy the newcomers constitute a kind of fifth column that subsequently takes control of their host city.[76] Read in this way, *Suppliant Women*'s award of metoikia is but the opening act of a drama featuring war, civic turmoil, and the rise of a crafty outsider to power.[77] Pelasgus's worst fear ultimately seems to have been realized. Unlike Apis, who was venerated for his ability to save Argos, Pelasgus contributes to his city's downfall. His sole consolation may be to die before hearing his eponymous people say "ἐπήλυδας τιμῶν ἀπώλεσας πόλιν."

Argives and Athenians: Common Ground

Just who were the Argives whose judgment Pelasgus feared? A representative sample were visible on stage as his silent retainers.[78] These citizens perform a variety of functions. They first attend their leader and then escort Danaus to the meeting of the assembly; they later reinforce Pelasgus when he rebuffs the Egyptians, and finally they lead the newcomers toward the *asty* in the play's *exeunt*. Arguably their most important task occurs off-stage, when they join their peers in assembly and vote to bestow metic status on the Danaids.[79] We analyzed above both the proceedings of the assembly and the terms of the metoikia it grants. One particular section of the measure separated people into two categories: native inhabitants (ἔνοικοι) and foreigners (ἐπήλυδες). The people's decree holds that no one from either group may forcibly remove the Danaids. It then adds a further enforcement clause (612–14):

And if [someone] does use force,
whoever of the landholders here does not help
will lose his rights and be sentenced to exile by the people.

. . . ἐὰν δὲ προστιθῆι τὸ καρτερόν,
τὸν μὴ βοηθήσαντα τῶνδε γαμόρων
ἄτιμον εἶναι ξὺν φυγῆι δημηλάτωι.[80]

We saw earlier that as Pelasgians, the Argives share their leader's name and his autochthony. The noun used here to delineate them, γαμόροι, likewise foregrounds their relationship with the earth. It is the Doric version of a compound formed from γῆ and μείρομαι ("receive as one's portion, obtain one's share of").[81] Citizens are paraphrased as those having a share in the land of Argos. The demonstrative adjective τῶνδε paired with them suggests that all those attending the assembly meet this definition.

Elsewhere in Greek literature, the Attic version of the noun (γημόροι) admits of a number of meanings. For instance, Herodotus uses it to denote the wealthy in Syracuse (7.155). In *AthPol* it denotes those of intermediate status, neither nobles (εὐπατρίδαι) nor common artisans (δημιουργοί).[82] To determine the sense of the word here in *Suppliant Women*,[83] we need to return to the connotations of autochthony. For the play's Argives, the land was not just a commodity to be owned. The citizens are descended from it, and work it for a season.[84] And they presumably return to it via death and burial.[85]

One measure of the Argives' commitment to the Danaids is the punishment they impose on themselves if they fail to protect the new metics (614): "to lose citizen rights and be driven into exile by the people" (ἄτιμον εἶναι ξὺν φυγῆ' δημηλάτωι).[86] The phrase φυγῆ' δημηλάτωι stands in contrast to the Danaids' self-description in the prologue, where they say (5–8):

. . . we flee
but have not been driven into exile for any sort of blood offense
by a vote of the city;
[we] rather have chosen to flee men.

. . . φεύγομεν,
οὔτιν᾿ ἐφ᾿ αἵματι δημηλασίαν
ψήφωι πόλεως γνωσθεῖσαι,
ἀλλ᾿ αὐτογενῆ φυξανορίαν.

The noun in the assembly's decree, φυγῇ, echoes the Danaids' verb φεύγομεν, and its adjective δημηλάτωι picks up on their noun δημηλασίαν. On the surface, the two situations might appear commensurate: the Danaids have fled from Egypt and are homeless, while any Argive who fails to protect the newcomers will himself be made homeless. The measure thus fits punishment to crime: citizens who fail to protect metics will be forced to become metics themselves. Yet the differences between the two situations outweigh the similarities. The Danaids' exile is, from a legal perspective, voluntary. If the suitors had had their way, the women would still be ensconced in Egypt. By contrast, any Argives who fail to act will be driven out by their fellow citizens. In addition, the Danaids have fled to a land they claim by ancestry. Yet any Argives to suffer *atimia* will lose the only home they have ever known. For autochthonous citizens, this is tantamount to being disowned and orphaned.[87]

The citizenship of Aeschylus's Athenian spectators was similarly grounded. When Cleisthenes instituted the democracy in 508/7,[88] he did not do away with important underlying aspects of the previous constitution. On the contrary, he maintained the ideological connection established by his predecessor Solon between Athenian citizenship and Attic soil. Among his reforms in the early sixth century, the great poet-lawgiver instituted a census classifying citizens for the purpose of regulating access to political office.[89] The fullest description of his schema comes from *AthPol*, composed some two and a half centuries later.[90] According to the author, Solon "separated [them] into four classes with respect to their worth, as had been done previously, into *pentecosiomedimnoi* and *hippeis* and *zeugitae* and *thetes*" (τιμήματι διεῖλεν εἰς τέτταρα τέλη, καθάπερ διῄρητο καὶ πρότερον, εἰς πεντακοσιομέδιμνον καὶ ἱππέα καὶ ζευγίτην καὶ θῆτα, 7.3). Shortly afterward *AthPol* describes the basis for these four categories: "to the *pentecosiomedimnoi* belongs whoever produces from his own [land] five hundred measures, counting both dry and wet; to the *hippeis* belongs whoever produces 300 measures, or as some say, whoever is able to maintain a horse; . . . to the *zeugitae* those producing 200 measures of both sorts; and the rest are *thetes*" (ἔδει δὲ τελεῖν πεντακοσιομέδιμνον μὲν ὃς ἂν ἐκ τῆς οἰκείας ποιῇ πεντακόσια μέτρα τὰ συνάμφω ξηρὰ καὶ ὑγρά, ἱππάδα δὲ τοὺς τριακόσια ποιοῦντας, ὡς δ' ἔνιοί φασι τοὺς ἱπποτροφεῖν δυναμένους . . . ζευγίσιον δὲ τελεῖν τοὺς διακόσια τὰ συνάμφω ποιοῦντας·τοὺς δ' ἄλλους θητικόν, 7.4). One of the most noteworthy features of Solon's scale is its agricultural basis: citizens are categorized according to their ability to produce crops from their own land.[91] *Pentecosiomedimnoi* produce the most; *hippeis* the next most; *zeugitae* the third most; and *thetes* produce annual harvests falling below 200 measures.

Solon's poetry shows that the lawgiver was aware that wealth in the archaic period could derive from a number of sources, including non-agricultural livelihoods such as trade and manufacturing.[92] Nevertheless, there is no evidence that his census categories were ever understood in antiquity as general rubrics for abstract levels of wealth.[93] Moreover, it is extremely unlikely that his census classifications established precise brackets for annual income deriving exclusively from agriculture. For one thing, Solon apparently allowed farmers to combine varying amounts of different produce to reach the specified threshold of commodity measures. For another, market prices were not the same for "dry" and "wet" crops. Even within these subsets, wheat regularly fetched more than barley, and wine than oil.[94] A third difficulty is that Solon neglected other important crops (e.g. grapes, olives, nuts, and figs) and completely ignored livestock (cows, goats, sheep, and pigs).[95] A final, overarching complication lies in the rudimentary nature of ancient Greek accounting practices. According to G. E. M. de Ste. Croix, the Athenians did not even draw the most basic distinction between capital and income.[96]

Solon's census clearly did not classify Athenian citizens on the basis of their annual income. What then did it seek to measure? We recur to the fact that it was explicitly calibrated according to agricultural output. Now, a number of factors naturally affected crop yield at Athens, including each man's farming skill, equipment, choice of crops, and seed or vine stock. Microclimate, weather, soil fertility, and the availability of labor (whether familial, hired, or slave) were important considerations as well.[97] But the extent of a man's landholdings must have played a crucial role. The roughest of calculations suggests that it took a considerable acreage to achieve even zeugite status. According to Alfred French, for instance, whose assumptions are tentative but plausible, there was "a theoretical upper and lower limit of say 65 and 10 acres for a Zeugites farm producing the minimum assessment [of 200 measures]: there is however no way of striking an average, because we have no idea of the statistical distribution of the farms between the two limits. The average may be nearer the higher than the lower, if we make the reasonable assumption that many of Attica's farms were run on a near-subsistence basis."[98] *Ceteris paribus*, the range of acres required to reach the level of the *hippeis* or *pentecosiomedimnoi* will ordinarily have been higher still. Thus on French's estimates the members of the top three Solonian categories were significant landholders.

Rosivach has arrived at a similar conclusion via a different route. Basing his analysis on per capita food consumption per annum, he maintains that the top three census tiers comprised farmers who had enough land to feed others in addition to their own families.[99] It is thus plausible that Solon's categories were a way of measuring roughly how much land individual Athenians owned. This hypothesis receives additional support from a suggestion made by de Ste. Croix. He reminds us that one (and perhaps the) main purpose of the Solonian census was to determine who was eligible to serve as archon. One important consideration was to provide the city with recourse in the event of embezzlement by its chief magistrates. The lawgiver thus sought to ensure that all those holding high office had a visible form of collateral that could be seized by the city if necessary.[100] His categories essentially linked political privileges to the amount of land men possessed. Put differently, they functioned as a crude measure of land ownership: the more land one owned, the higher one's standing as a citizen.[101]

It is not just Solon's reliance on crop yields that points to the agricultural roots of his census system. So do the names assigned to his categories. The *pentecosiomedimnoi* are literally the "500 bushel men." *AthPol* paraphrases the *hippeis* as those "able to maintain a horse" (7.4). The infinitive used, ἱπποτροφεῖν, seems on its face to mean "to breed or keep horses," and hints at access to pasturage.[102] Yet Whitehead has argued that other compounds prefixing forms of τροφέω with animals such as oxen describe not the raising of the animals, but the ability to yoke them and put them to work. For him, a more appropriate meaning of ζευγίτης would be something like "teamster."[103] And he and others have now embraced a thoroughly revisionist view.[104] According to them, the fundamental basis for Solon's census was not agriculture but warfare. On their understanding, its different categories reflect the different roles played by citizens in the Athenian military. The *hippeis* were the cavalrymen,[105] the *zeugitae* the hoplites,[106] and the *thetes* the sailors and light-armed troops (and in some instances the ship-board marines). This approach has considerable *a priori* appeal, given the explicit links between military service and political standing in other ancient cultures.[107] Yet it is also complicated by a number of factors. First of all, it is not clear when the Athenians began to field a cavalry force. Although some have argued for its existence in the archaic period, others are more skeptical and place its beginnings in the classical era.[108] Moreover, Athens did not begin to develop its substantial navy until approximately the 490s, when Themistocles proposed devoting the revenue from the Laureion mines to building triremes.[109] De Ste. Croix and Raaflaub have accordingly advanced an even more radical thesis: that these census categories were in essence a fifth-century creation that was retrojected into the archaic past and ascribed to Solon.[110]

There are thus two distinct alternatives: Solon's census had either an agricultural or a military basis. The available evidence does not permit a definitive choice between the two. The dichotomy may, however, be more apparent than real. Victor Hanson has noted that in archaic Greece, agricultural activity and military development went hand-in-hand. On his view, the prehistory of democratic Athens is to a substantial extent the story of the development of a new class of "middle" citizens who used innovative farming techniques to wring increased crop yields from previously marginal lands. And these small farmers, the *mesoi*, in turn formed the core of the emerging hoplite phalanx in eighth- and seventh-century Attica.[111] We are thus on solid ground if we conclude that Solon's census reveals the extent to which the military and agriculture were intertwined, like the vine around the elm. Hanson summarizes thus: "small plots, not large herds or rich estates; infantry, not horsemen or skirmishers[;] agricultural competence, not birth, become the backbone of the Athenian polis."[112]

At first glance, the existence of a Solonian category for thetes presents a formidable obstacle to the idea that Athenians understood themselves as a group of autochthonous citizen γαμόροι.[113] While some thetes were doubtless landowners, others clearly were not. Elsewhere in his poetry, Solon writes of his attempts to help groups at the social margins. For instance, the *hektemoroi* ("sixth-parters") were apparently sharecroppers with smaller *moroi* ("portions") than their fellow citizens.[114] And the *pelatai* may have been transients drawing their name from the verb πελάζω ("approach, draw near").[115] While Solon responded to the plight of both groups, he boasts that he did so without redistributing land, despite considerable pressure to the contrary. It thus seems indisputable that a significant number of Athenians lacked private lands of their own, both before and after 594/93.

Nevertheless, the ideological link between citizenship and the soil remained powerful at Athens. It is not clear when, or to what extent, the notion of alienable property became applicable to Attic land. By the time of Aristotle, owning a thing meant having the right to transfer or sell it as one saw fit.[116] Yet Alison Burford has suggested that at first all land was held communally, and that distinct patterns of usage and types of ownership emerged gradually. On her view, the first landholders were primarily not individuals, but groups such as phratries, tribes, religious bodies, and clans, all of whose lands were inalienable.[117] As time went on, however, individuals began to acquire land in their own right, and to dispose of it more freely.[118] Solon's census apparently stemmed from an era in which some lands were owned corporately and others individually. Even following the reforms of Cleisthenes in 508/7, a significant portion of Attica was owned by associations. According to Philip Manville, down to the classical period at least 10 percent of agricultural land was corporately owned.[119] Thus even the poorest fifth-century Athenians without land of their own could still consider themselves property owners through their membership in kinship groups and the Cleisthenic administrative divisions of *phylai*, *trittyes*, and demes. Moreover, when sitting together in law courts and assemblies, they possessed the power to appropriate the possessions of others. A common punishment levied against those convicted of serious offenses was the confiscation and auction of their assets, including land, with the proceeds going to the *demos*.[120] The existence of a set of individually landless thetes was therefore not, strictly speaking, incompatible with the rise of an agrarian civic ideology. On the contrary, Athenians' willingness to embrace a mythic identity rooted in agriculture and autochthony may have been enhanced by the urbanizing, increasingly cosmopolitan fabric of their fifth-century world.

The Solonian census distinctions performed a number of important political functions, including determining eligibility for the archonship and (perhaps) regulating membership in the liturgical class.[121] *AthPol*'s mention (26.2) that *zeugitae* became eligible for the archonship in 458/57 suggests that Solonian distinctions were still observed at that time. Yet the maintenance of these divisions ultimately depended on Athenians' ability to distinguish who belonged to which group. Although hard evidence is lacking, some scholars believe that in the years following

Cleisthenes, the deme registers (*lexiarchika grammateia*) listed not just citizens' names but their census classifications as well.[122] Much of the recent scholarship on ancient literacy has, however, cautioned against ascribing too much bureaucratic efficiency to ancient Athens.[123] It is, for instance, unclear whether the Athenians maintained a centralized standing register for something as important as the men susceptible to call-up for hoplite duty.[124] It is thus possible that the city depended on its citizens to declare their own census status—for example, when they stood for various magistracies.[125] Indeed, one passage from *AthPol* has long been understood as an instance of such self-advertisement. At 7.4, [Aristotle] claims that Anthemion dedicated an equestrian statue of Diphilus on the Athenian Acropolis to mark his rise from thete to *hippes*.[126] Keesling, however, has indicated some of the difficulties of this position.[127] There is in sum little evidence that the city kept official track of the census categories of its citizens. Presumably much of the control it did exert in this regard was oral and social, mediated through, for example, the testimony of witnesses in various deme and polis-wide bodies.[128]

Although unmistakable signs of class standing were largely lacking in ancient Athens, signs of indebtedness were not. Inscribed stone markers, *horoi*, were ubiquitous throughout Attica. Some of these inscriptions established land boundaries of various sorts: for example, those separating polis from polis, sacred space from secular, and public land from private.[129] But *horoi* could also delineate the landholdings of individual citizens and were frequently used to denote legal encumbrance.[130] One of Solon's proudest claims was that he had freed the Attic land (Γῆ) from her burdens by removing a number of these *horoi*.[131] Although dispute persists about what exactly he did, and what it meant, many scholars link his action to the abolition of borrowing on the security of one's own person.[132] In short, by taking up the markers Solon is said to have done away with debt bondage, freeing citizens and soil simultaneously.[133] This *seisachtheia* ("shaking off of burdens") was accompanied by the repatriation to Attica of Athenians who had been enslaved and sold abroad.[134] By bringing Athenians back home, Solon reunited them with their mother, who for her part was freed from a number of burdens.[135] The lawgiver adds that many returnees had lost their power of native speech: "they no longer spoke the Attic tongue, as often happens with wanderers" (γλῶσσαν οὐκέτ' Ἀττικὴν / ἱέντας, ὡς δὲ πολλαχῆι πλανωμένους, fr. 36.11–12).[136]

In his surviving poems Solon defends the way he discharged his duties as lawgiver. Responding to criticism, he uses a bold simile to stress that he sided with neither rich nor poor: "I stood between these [two groups] just like a *horos* on the frontier" (ἐγω δὲ τούτων ὥσπερ ἐν μεταιχμίῳ / ὅρος κατέστην).[137] Solon did not simply uproot existing *horoi*: he established himself as a *horos*. As we saw earlier, boundaries are also important to *Suppliant Women*,[138] but in the play external rather than internal divisions are paramount. Pelasgus emphasizes the borders separating Argos from other lands, not those separating citizen from citizen. Indeed, the Argives are in important measure interchangeable and indistinguishable. Consider the assembly granting metic status to the Danaids, for instance. According to Danaus, those attending the assembly are all of one mind: they vote the same way (οὐ διχορρόπως, 605) with the same gesture (χερσὶ δεξιωνύμοις, 607). And in the play Pelasgus uses a striking verb to describe his role. At lines 256–58 he says:

I mark off as mine the land of the Perhaeboi
and the areas this side of Pindus near the Paionoi
and the mountains of Dodona.

ὁρίζομαι δὲ τήν τε Περραιβῶν χθόνα
Πίνδου τε τἀπέκεινα Παιόνων πέλας
ὄρη τε Δωδωναῖα.

Like Solon, the Argive leader might be said to function as a *horos*. But whereas the Athenian faced inward, separating factions within his own city, Pelasgus faces outward. He embodies the united Pelasgian community, differentiating home from abroad and Argives from *barbaroi*.

Pelasgus's description of himself as τῆσδε γῆς ἀρχηγέτης (251) elsewhere in the same passage is similarly revealing. The nominative noun's iambs make it useful as a synonym for "leader, chief" in tragedy.[139] But Pelasgus's eponymous status lends the phrase another dimension as well. The primary meaning LSJ assign ἀρχηγέτης is "*first leader, author,* esp. *founder* of a city or family."[140] As we saw earlier, Apis drove out the snakes inhabiting the Argive plain. This act of clearing the land of monsters was a necessary prerequisite for putting it to civilized agricultural use.[141] As Apis's successor, Pelasgus is akin to other founders of poleis and colonies who established and distributed plots of land (*kleroi*) to members of the community. Given *Suppliant Women*'s emphasis on the autochthony, unity, and homogeneity of the Pelasgians, they might all be imagined as having equal shares in the land of Argos as well. At Sparta, for instance, the myth of equality among the Spartiate *homoioi* was rooted in their *kleroi*. Originally equal, indivisible, and inalienable, these 6,000 plots of land remained so (at least in theory) throughout much of the classical period. In some of the Greek colonies founded during the archaic period, equality of *kleroi* among colonists was likewise the ideal and sometimes the rule.[142] And Plato's *Laws* (737c2–6) offers a subsequent vision of a city planned to maximize civic unity: its 5,040 citizens, tellingly termed γεωμόροι, share the community's land and dwellings as equally as possible. In calling him an ἀρχηγέτης, *Suppliant Women* may suggest that Pelasgus ensures Argos's citizens equal access to their common parent, the earth.[143]

Aeschylus's portrait of the Argives as autochthonous landholders resonated with his Athenian spectators, many of whom still lived in rural Attica. According to Thucydides (2.16.1), a substantial number of Athenians remained in their ancestral country homes down to the outbreak of the Peloponnesian War in 431;[144] when they were forced to move into the *asty*, their distress was acute. Six years later, in 425, Aristophanes's *Acharnians* depicted the farmer Dicaeopolis as the Athenian everyman par excellence, whose deepest longing was to celebrate the rural Dionysia on his own lands in peace.[145] Following another decade of warfare, the Spartans adopted the advice of the traitor Alcibiades and occupied Decelea continuously. According to Thucydides this harmed the Athenians greatly, "depriving them of their entire countryside" (τῆς τε γὰρ χώρας ἁπάσης ἐστέρηντο, 7.27.5). And after the city capitulated to the Spartans, Phormisius gave voice to what many of his compatriots had doubtless felt for years: that the woes of Athens resulted from paying too much heed to its landless riffraff. He therefore urged the recall of the oligarchs from Eleusis and proposed restricting citizenship to landowners. On Martin Ostwald's reckoning, "he will have opposed popular sovereignty, which considered as citizens all Athenians regardless of their source of income. . . . The bill would have excluded from citizenship those of them who derived their livelihood from industry and sea-borne commerce."[146] Although the Athenian assembly rejected his measure, the ideal of an agrarian, land-holding citizenry was clearly an enduring one.

Metics and *Enktesis*

In contrast to citizens, even the wealthiest metics at Athens had a more tenuous connection with the ground they trod. As newcomers, they could claim neither indigeny nor autochthony. The prospect of exile, held in reserve to punish unhelpful Argives in *Suppliant Women*, apparently did not terrify many metics. Times of crisis and war tended to produce an exodus of such folk from Athens.[147] One of the most damning charges leveled against the Athenian citizen Philon at his *dokimasia* for membership on the *boule* around 403–401 is that when Thrasyboulus was struggling to retake the city, Philon took what possessions he could and fled over the border to Oropos. Playing on stereotypes held by the jurors, the accuser claims that Philon acted like a metic rather than a citizen.[148] As he explains (Lys. 31.6), "all those who are citizens by birth, but think that their homeland is wherever they can make a living, these men clearly would abandon the common good of the city to pursue their own private advantage, because they think that their country is not the city but their property" (ὅσοι δὲ φύσει μὲν πολῖταί εἰσι, γνώμῃ δὲ χρῶνται ὡς πᾶσα γῆ πατρὶς αὐτοῖς ἐστιν ἐν ᾗ ἂν τὰ ἐπιτήδεια ἔχωσιν, οὗτοι δῆλοί εἰσιν ὅτι κἂν παρέντες τὸ τῆς πόλεως κοινὸν ἀγαθὸν ἐπὶ τὸ ἑαυτῶν ἴδιον κέρδος ἔλθοιεν διὰ τὸ μὴ τὴν πόλιν ἀλλὰ τὴν οὐσίαν πατρίδα ἑαυτοῖς ἡγεῖσθαι). By placing his own good(s) above the good of the city, Philon demonstrated that he did not really belong to it, nor it to him. On the contrary, he recognizes no homeland but his wealth. He and others like him may be citizens by accident of birth; their belief that home is where the heap is makes them into metics.[149]

Athenians saw in metics' livelihoods confirmation of the idea that for non-citizens all lands were in essence interchangeable. By contrast, ancestral tradition, Solonian census categories, the ideology of autochthony, and the need to eat all provided fifth-century Athenians with incentives to till the Attic soil. Despite the ongoing transformation of the city's economy, many citizens (including some of the wealthiest and most influential) still derived their living from farming. According to Nicholas Jones, "separation, isolation, local community, and the resulting survival of a preurban agrarian social and cultural order are . . . the terms with reference to which we should view the great mass of the population of [fifth-century] Attica."[150] In contrast to these citizens, metics tended to earn their keep in different ways. Some of the earliest evidence for foreign craftsmen comes from pottery, whose makers brought their native styles and workmanship to Athens.[151] In the early sixth century, Solon sought to restrict immigration to those who knew a trade.[152] The Peisistratids subsequently encouraged the flow of skilled labor to Athens to promote their building and cultural agendas.[153] And the abiding demand for Attic ceramics may have produced a further increase in foreign potters and painters during the same period.[154]

Following the Cleisthenic reforms and the Persian Wars, the economic expansion of Piraeus and the rebuilding of the upper city sparked a veritable boom in immigration. By the late fifth century, metics dominated crucial niches of the economy, which was increasingly centered on the *asty*. They practiced trades and crafts; they managed workshops and banks; they played dominant roles in sea-borne commerce.[155] According to Balbina Bäbler, the epigraphic record shows that metics made up as many as 70 to 80 percent of the free people involved in such activities.[156]

The dichotomy between citizen farmers and metic artisans should nevertheless not be exaggerated. To a certain extent the divide between the two groups was an artificial construct reflecting the ideological and rhetorical tendencies of our ancient sources as much as reality. The building accounts of the Erechtheum (*IG* i³ 474–79) provide a healthy caution. These inscriptions, dating from 409/8–406, contain detailed lists of the workmen involved in the construction, the tasks they performed, and the wages they were paid. In addition, they provide invaluable information about the civic status of many of the workmen. Citizens are listed with their demotic, metics with the preposition ἐν plus their deme of residence, and slaves with the name of their master in the genitive. According to Richard Randall's calculations, of the 107 identifiable individuals in these inscriptions, at least 24, or 22 percent, are citizens, while at least 42, or 39 percent, are metics.[157] Moreover, in a number of instances we find citizens, metics, and slaves working side by side, performing roughly equal tasks for equal pay.[158] At least one conclusion is inescapable: a considerable number of citizens during this period earned their living as artisans.

Another important inscription demonstrates the converse, that some metics worked as farmers. *IG* ii² 10 records the benefits conferred upon the metics and slaves who assisted Thrasyboulus and the Athenian democrats during their return from Phyle in 403. Significantly, the document does not identify metics with the usual formula involving their demes of residence, but rather by their livelihoods. Among the eighteen individuals whose occupations survive are a cook, an architect, a muleteer, a builder, a tanner, a day laborer, and a sculptor. But far the greatest proportion of those listed are farmers, γεωργοί.[159] In addition to the five men thus described, there are another three whose occupations involve work with gardens, olives, and nuts respectively.[160] While the size of our sample here is admittedly quite small, at least some fifth-century metics apparently survived by tending the earth.[161]

Occupational facts on the ground notwithstanding, the ideological connection between citizenship and soil was firmly entrenched in Athenian laws about property ownership. By the mid-fifth century at the latest, *enktesis* had been restricted to citizens: in principle only they could own immovable property such as land or houses.[162] These assets constituted the most desirable form of wealth in classical Athens.[163] By contrast, metics were denied this opportunity outright. Although the city could grant exemptions to the rule, it seldom did. Moreover, any exceptions were generally intended as an honorific gesture to the city's staunchest supporters abroad, for whom residence in Attica was an insurance policy rather than an immediate plan.[164] According to Jan Pecirka, the first known grant of *enktesis* to non-citizens occurred a generation after the performance of *Suppliant Women*.[165] Xenophon's fourth-century treatise *Resources* (Πόροι) implies that over time, however, the nature of grants of *enktesis* shifted; they eventually became a practical and valued privilege. The author in fact recommends (2.6) that the city use them as a lure to increase the number of metics (and thus the revenue paid in to Athens). Yet even he does not counsel awarding this benefit indiscriminately. *Enktesis* should be granted only to those metics approved by the assembly; these were likely to be fellow Greeks hailing from other poleis.[166]

There is scant evidence that the city ever acted on his suggestion. From the time of *Suppliant Women* on down to *Poroi*, almost all metics were legally barred from the most concrete way of identifying with the Attic land. Denied the chance to own plots or houses of their own, they were forced to store their assets in portable forms (ἀφανὴς οὐσία): jewelry, loans, foodstuffs, ships, and the like.[167] If they felt an insurmountable urge to own real property, subterfuge was necessary. Even in the more enlightened third century, the Athenian philosopher Epicurus had to use citizen intermediaries to bequeath his celebrated Garden and its effects to his successor Hermarchus, a non-citizen. A number of features of his will are decidedly unusual.[168] For one thing, he names as co-heirs Amynomachus and Timocrates, two Athenians to whom he had no known tie of blood or sentiment. Moreover, they receive at first only limited control over the inheritance. As long as Hermarchus lives, they must consult with him about how to manage Epicurus's bequest. Only after Hermarchus's death will they receive the house (located in the metic-heavy deme of Melite) to dispose of as they please. Martti Leiwo and Pauliina Remes suggest that "by appointing two men to take care of his property [Epicurus] ensured that the heirs, keeping an eye on each other, would respect the conditions of his last will."[169] Put differently, Epicurus apparently thought it safer to rely on the competitive instincts of his fellow citizens than their trustworthiness. By making them co-heirs, and by making them wait to inherit, Epicurus gave each man an incentive to leave the metic Hermarchus in effective control of his property. The famous philosopher was sagacious indeed in seeing to both the philosophical and the material interests of his non-citizen pupils.

The Danaids' Residence at Argos

The ban on metic *enktesis* forms an important backdrop to *Suppliant Women*. Traditionally scholars have been puzzled by the amount of attention the play devotes to where in Argos the Danaids will stay. For instance, Friis Johansen and Whittle say that "Pelasgus dwells in surprising detail on the question of accommodation, and its importance is emphasized by the Danaids' referring the decision to their father (970–72) and by Danaus' further mention of the matter (1009–11)."[170] They conclude that the matter must have a bearing on subsequent events in the trilogy.[171] Similarly Garvie, following Wilamowitz, has suggested that "Aeschylus may be preparing the most suitable conditions for the murder"[172] of the Aegyptids. The idea is not impossible, or even perhaps implausible.[173] Yet to date no one has shown why one housing arrangement would be more conducive to spousal murder than another. One surviving fragment of *Danaids* (fr. 43) describes the morning after the wedding, when young male and female choruses prepare to serenade the apparently sleepy newlyweds: "Let them gladden the bridegrooms with song, together with youths and maidens" (πρευμενεῖς τοὺς νυμφίους / νόμοισι θέντων σὺν κόροις τε καὶ κόραις). But the singers could have attempted this no matter where the bridal couples were lodged. The grooms' affectless response would in any case have remained the same.

The best explanation for Aeschylus's emphasis on the housing issue in *Suppliant Women* is that it underlines the Danaids' status as metics at Argos.[174] We touched earlier on the accommodations offered by Pelasgus (957–63):[175]

And there are many public dwellings,
nor have I built with a stingy hand,

where it is possible for you to inhabit well-built houses
with many others. And if it pleases you better,
it is also possible to inhabit "single-rhythmed" houses.
Of these, choose the best and most agreeable:
you are free to do so.

καὶ δώματ' ἐστὶ πολλὰ μὲν τὰ δήμια,
δεδωμάτωμαι δ' οὐδ' ἐγὼ σμικρᾶι χερί,
ἔνθ' ἐστιν ὑμῖν εὐτύκους ναίειν δόμους
πολλῶν μετ' ἄλλων· εἰ δέ τις μείζων χάρις,
πάρεστιν οἰκεῖν καὶ μονορ⟨ρ⟩ύθμους δόμους.
τούτων τὰ λῶιστα καὶ τὰ θυμηδέστατα,
πάρεστι, λωτίσασθε.

What is most noteworthy is what Pelasgus does not offer the Danaids—namely, a home of their own. Although they are honored guests, there will be no *enktesis* for them and their father.[176] The verbs Pelasgus uses (ναίειν and οἰκεῖν—not, e.g., κτᾶσθαι, κτίζειν, or some form of ἔχειν) denote occupancy rather than possession. In addition, the ownership of the buildings in question is spelled out. Those mentioned first, the δώματ' . . . δήμια, belong not to individuals but to a group or groups. According to LSJ, δήμιος means "belonging to the people or state" and is a synonym for δημόσιος.[177] On this understanding of the adjective, the owner of the buildings is the Argive *demos*. Given the play's emphasis on the Argives as a uniform, undifferentiated group of citizens, this is the likeliest meaning here.[178]

It is, however, worth recalling that in fifth- and fourth-century Athens, there were also numerous smaller groups of citizens that owned and let real property.[179] Based on a survey of the available evidence, Robin Osborne has concluded that in the fifth century "public land was already being leased out on a considerable scale. . . . The Athenians expected to exploit the land on which temples and shrines stood by leasing it out to private individuals, and they had devised a more or less standard system for doing so."[180] Returning to Pelasgus's offer, the presence of the additional adjective πολλά indicates that there are many such δώματ'. This passage might therefore be understood in light of the notion that a significant percentage of Attica was corporately owned and let out at the time of *Suppliant Women*'s production.[181]

Pelasgus's words δεδωμάτωμαι δ' οὐδ' ἐγὼ σμικρᾷ χερί describe a second housing alternative offered the women. The opposition between the two choices is emphasized by the antithetical placement of the particles μέν and δέ. One way in which the options differ is ownership:

Pelasgus's first person singular verb δεδωμάτωμαι suggests that the second set of structures belongs to him.[182] The dative litotes οὐδ' . . . σμικρᾷ χερί suggests additional differences. Rösler has argued that grammatically speaking, the subsequent clause ἔνθ' ἐστιν ὑμῖν εὐτύκους ναίειν δόμους / πολλῶν μετ' ἄλλων should be a further comment on the δόμοι of Pelasgus.[183] On his reading, Pelasgus's assertion of his liberality as a builder could stem from several things. Although the *demos* has many houses, he as its leader may have even more. Perhaps his dwellings are fewer, but larger and more extensive. Or it may be that the emphasis belongs on the words εὐτύκους . . . δόμους. According to Friis Johansen and Whittle, the phrase means "well-suited for habitation"[184] and might imply that Pelasgus's dwellings were particularly well-built or lavishly furnished.[185]

When the women hesitate to commit themselves to one alternative or the other, Pelasgus adds another crucial piece of information (963–65):

> I and all the citizens will be *prostates*
> of what the decree enjoins. Why do you wait
> for men more authoritative than these?

> προστάτης δ' ἐγώ
> ἀστοί τε πάντες, ὧνπερ ἥδε κραίνεται
> ψῆφος. τί τῶνδε κυριωτέρους μένεις;

At Athens every metic was legally required to have an Athenian sponsor, a προστάτης; failure on this score brought considerable danger. Any citizen who wished could bring a public prosecution of *graphe aprostasiou* against a metic, and many apparently did.[186] Defendants who were convicted were sold into slavery.[187] Although the precise functions of the *prostates* remain a subject of scholarly dispute, one of his chief duties was probably to preside over his charge's enrollment in a deme.[188] While citizens' demotics were heritable, metics' were not: a metic's deme was ordinarily his deme of residence. Later in the fifth century, the locution οἰκῶν (or οἰκοῦσα) ἐν + deme name became the standard way of denoting a metic. Gerhard Thür's conjecture that a *prostates* was involved in arranging his metics' lodging is thus attractive.[189] And this is precisely the scenario we find in *Suppliant Women*. Pelasgus and the citizens act jointly as the newcomers' προστάτης, and therefore seek to find them housing as well.

Despite the Argives' prompting, the women still prefer to await the advice of their father before deciding. Somewhere between lines 965 and 979, Pelasgus departs.[190] When Danaus arrives shortly afterward

(980), accompanied by a set of Argive bodyguards (ὀπαδοὺς τούσδε καὶ δορυσσόους, 985), he counsels his daughters thus (1009–11):

> A double dwelling is possible.
> Pelasgus is providing one, the city the other,
> [for us] to inhabit without payment. These things are favorable.

> οἴκησις δὲ καὶ διπλῆ πάρα.
> τὴν μὲν Πελασγός, τὴν δὲ καὶ πόλις διδοῖ,[191]
> οἰκεῖν λάτρων ἄτερθεν. εὐπετῆ τάδε.

Here Danaus lives up to his daughters' billing as thoughtful and shrewd (πρόνοος, 970; τοῦ . . . μῆτις, 971). He urges them to take advantage of both offers, especially since they may live there without λάτρων. The Suda equates this Greek noun with μισθός; LSJ define it as "pay, hire," translating the passage as "without charge or payment."[192] Given that he and his daughters are metics and barred from *enktesis*, the offer of rent-free lodging is opportune.[193]

Suppliant Women's emphasis on the Danaids' housing clearly underscores their status as metics. From this basic point spring a number of important details. The sentence spoken by Pelasgus at lines 960–61, εἰ δέ τις μείζων χάρις, / πάρεστιν οἰκεῖν καὶ μονορ⟨ρ⟩ύθμους δόμους, offers a significant interpretive challenge. It occurs immediately after Pelasgus has mentioned both the δώματ' . . . δήμια and his own δόμοι. The most basic question is whether this new sentence offers yet a third possibility, or whether it instead refers back to one (or both) of the housing alternatives already described. Friis Johansen and Whittle, noting the presence of the superlatives τὰ λῷστα καὶ τὰ θυμηδέστατα immediately following in line 963, argue that the μονορ⟨ρ⟩ύθμους δόμους constitute a separate option altogether.[194] Rösler, by contrast, claims that Pelasgus gives the Danaids only two choices, and that the εἰ δέ τις μείζων χάρις sentence must refer back to the δώματ' . . . δήμια. According to him "the king's proposal thus has the following chiastic structure: the offer to live in δώματ' . . . δήμια—the offer to live in the palace—the explanation of the latter possibility—the explanation of the first possibility."[195] Although certainty is impossible, on balance Rösler's chiasmus is preferable; tragic diction is frequently elastic, and Aeschylus was a playwright, not a grammarian. His superlatives here may function as comparatives. The μονόρ⟨ρ⟩υθμοι δόμοι thus seem a periphrasis of the δώματ' . . . δήμια.

But what exactly are "single-rhythmed houses"? The adjective is a *hapax* that some commentators understand as the opposite of the crowded lodgings (πολλῶν μετ' ἄλλων) proffered by Pelasgus; put differently, the δώματ' . . . δήμια offer the Danaids the chance to live in homes by themselves, *monoi*. Rösler, however, focuses on the second part of the compound, -⟨ρ⟩ύθμος. Citing a passage from Pindar, he argues that the phrase actually means "houses of unitary form."[196] Moreover, he links the description to a new style of architecture pioneered in Piraeus following the Persian Wars.[197] In his study of Hippodamus as a city planner, Alfred Burns has argued that the Milesian "originated the concept of land allocation and city design according to a master-plan prepared . . . with all aspects of community life in mind."[198] In addition, Hippodamus seems to have employed an orthogonal grid system for his streets and *insulae*.[199] This system was well suited to creating "blocks for buildings . . . [exemplifying] certain criteria of absolute equality among residential blocks."[200] Rösler concludes that Aeschylus's μονόρ⟨ρ⟩υθμοι δόμοι correspond to "the concept of a housing development formulated by Hippodamus of Miletus . . . of which a unitary type of citizen house was a constitutive part."[201]

Rösler's theory is attractive, not least because it helps to explain why such dwellings might be attractive to the Danaids. As Aristotle notes, "the arrangement of private dwellings is considered more pleasant and more useful for various affairs, if it is well divided and in accordance with the newer, that is, Hippodameian, fashion."[202] The comparative adjective the philosopher uses, more pleasant (ἡδίων), could serve as a periphrasis for Pelasgus's phrase "if it pleases you better" (εἰ δέ τις μείζων χάρις, / πάρεστιν οἰκεῖν καὶ μονορ⟨ρ⟩ύθμους δόμους). There are, however, a number of complications. For one thing, we have no physical evidence of any such unitary residential compounds within Athens itself.[203] To date only one block of classical houses in the city has been excavated. While each house does feature a courtyard that is more or less centrally located, the houses themselves vary considerably in size and layout. Excavated houses that were not part of this block display still greater variation in their shape, number, and types of rooms.[204] Furthermore, it is difficult to determine how fully Hippodamus's designs were realized in Piraeus. While a number of *horoi* demarcating various sections of the port deme have been found,[205] very few remains of housing have been excavated.[206] It is entirely possible that at the time of *Suppliant Women*'s performance in the later 460s, no "houses of unitary form" yet existed either in Piraeus or elsewhere in the city.[207] Moreover, even if the deme did feature some μονόρ⟨ρ⟩υθμοι δόμοι, these may have been less regular than the adjective implies. The best extant examples of largely identical houses built along a rectilinear city grid plan come from different poleis in somewhat later periods.[208] Prior to that, tract housing may have been far from uniform, particularly if construction stretched over a number of years and was carried out along the lines of the public/private model proposed by Wolfram Hoepfner.[209]

Nevertheless, the potential connection between the μονόρ⟨ρ⟩υθμοι δόμοι and the Danaids' metoikia is worth pursuing. For one thing, the new style of Hippodamian architecture was centered in Piraeus, home to one of the largest concentrations of metics in all Attica. According to Whitehead, of the 366 metics with known demotics from the last quarter of the fifth to the last quarter of the fourth century, 69, or 19 percent, resided in Piraeus; the deme ranks second only to Melite in this regard.[210] For metics arriving by ship, the port was their first contact with Athens and offered numerous opportunities to pursue their economic interests. Moreover, the presence of preexisting metic communities, some organized along ethnic lines, will have made the area even more attractive.[211] Inscriptional evidence and material remains show that by about 430 at the latest, groups of foreigners from abroad were setting up new sanctuaries for their native deities in Piraeus.[212] And the process likely began even earlier. Rösler's μονόρ⟨ρ⟩υθμοι δόμοι would thus have had much to offer such newcomers.

The play's treatment of the Danaids' housing choices reflects the link between their metic status and their erotic potential. To begin with, the advice Danaus offers his daughters about their lodging (1009–11) is couched within a broader framework: the need for the women to preserve their chastity. In the lines immediately preceding (1000–1009), he reminds them of their allure, adding a fervent wish (1008–9): "May we not shame ourselves and delight my enemies" (μηδ' αἶσχος ἡμῖν, ἡδονὴν δ'ἐχθροῖς ἐμοῖς / πράξωμεν). And in the lines just after his remarks about lodging, he is yet more direct. Here he exhorts his daughters thus (1012–13): "Only guard these instructions of your father, / valuing your modesty more than your life" (μόνον φύλαξαι τάσδ' ἐπιστολὰς πατρός, / τὸ σωφρονεῖν τιμῶσα τοῦ βίου πλέον).[213] These are the last words Danaus utters in *Suppliant Women.*

The Danaids promptly seek to reassure their father on this score, responding (1014–17):

With regard to other things may we fare well, by the Olympian gods;
but as for my virginity, take heart, father:
for unless something new is contrived by the gods,
I will not change the previous track of my thoughts.

τἄλλ' εὐτυχοῖμεν πρὸς θεῶν Ὀλυμπίων·
ἐμῆς δ' ὀπώρας οὕνεκ' εὖ θάρσει, πάτερ·

εἰ γάρ τι μὴ θεοῖς βεβούλευται νέον,
ἴχνος τὸ πρόσθεν οὐ διαστρέψω φρενός.

The Danaids insist that they have no intention of changing their previous habits, even as they adapt to a new city and new accommodations. Yet their remarks contain an unsettling undercurrent. The women do not meekly accept the gods' power to control their lives; on the contrary, they seem to want to limit the divine jurisdiction. Friis Johansen and Whittle explain lines 1014–15 thus: "In all other respects (e.g. with regard to the result of the war with the Aegyptiads) the Danaids cannot influence their fate but can only pray to the gods for εὐτυχία (1014); but they do have control over their personal behavior, though this may of course be overridden by divine designs (1015–17)."[214] But their interpretation here underestimates the Danaids' resistance to marriage. Their earlier threat to pollute Argos with suggestive suicide was certainly not the stance of women resigned to whatever fate the gods might send. Instead, it demonstrated forcefully their insistence on controlling their sexuality, even at the cost of offending the ἀγώνιοι θεοί.

Yet the passage simultaneously shows that the Danaids have few illusions about the ability of mortals to defy the divine.[215] The caveat they offer, "unless something new is contrived by the gods" (εἰ γάρ τι μὴ θεοῖς βεβούλευται νέον), is not an offhand possibility, but a regular feature of the world they inhabit. They themselves admitted earlier in the play that the gods are nothing if not unreckonable. At lines 92–95, for instance, they stressed that

The desire of Zeus is not easily traced.
The ways of his wits
stretch thick and shaggy,
impossible to point out and behold.

Διὸς ἵμερος οὐκ εὐθήρατος ἐτύχθη·
δαυλοὶ γὰρ πραπίδων
δάσκιοί τε τείνου—
σιν πόροι, κατιδεῖν ἄφραστοι.[216]

Sandin notes of *Suppliant Women* in general, and of this passage especially, that "the focus is, even more explicitly than in the [comparable] verses from *Agamemnon* [i.e., the "Hymn to Zeus" at 160–83], on the might of Zeus, in particular on his unlimited power to change human fortune."[217] The women earlier noted (100–104) that the gods can accomplish whatever they wish without so much as rising from their seats. And the very words with which they express their steadfast intent at line 1017 (ἴχνος τὸ πρόσθεν οὐ διαστρέψω φρενός) suggest that change is in fact already afoot. For in *Suppliant Women* the word ἴχνος leads unmistakably back to their ancestor Io. At line 538 the Danaids claimed that they were following in her footsteps: "I embarked on the ancient path, the flowery places where [my] mother was watched" (παλαιὸν δ' εἰς ἴχνος μετέσταν, / ματέρος ἀνθονόμους ἐπωπάς). In some senses the Danaids are now reversing their mother's journey: while she left Argos, they return there.[218] However, Io's route was extremely roundabout. As the Danaids note (540–60), she wandered through all of Asia and much of the known world before fetching up in Egypt. In addition, the fate that befell her there was impregnation by Zeus and not celibacy. The Danaids' vocabulary thus calls into question their ability to remain chaste. The audience almost certainly knew that the women's fate would resemble Io's in several ways: they would be lustily observed, pursued down wandering ways, and bedded in the end. Following the Danaids' rejoinder, a supplementary chorus of Argive men supplant Danaus as interlocutors.[219] And their presence confirms his worst fears: as they lead the women toward their new dwellings, they hint at their own interest in the women's charms.

Conclusion

Suppliant Women takes considerable pains to establish the identity and genealogy of Pelasgus. As ruler, he follows in the footsteps of Apis, the legendary physician-seer who drove a band of poisonous snakes out of the Argolid. Like his predecessor, his task is to protect the land from potential enemies who threaten to poison and blight it forever. In short, he must defend the community against violence from those who do not belong to the citizen community. At the same time, he also boasts of his descent from Palaichthon, Ancient Earth itself. He is, in a word, autochthonous. He is also an eponymous hero who has lent his name to the Argives, making them all Pelasgians. The play's citizens are thereby cast as descendants of the land they inhabit. This shared ancestry gives them a homogeneous communal identity, in which they are both interchangeable citizens and close kin.

In this regard, the Argos of *Suppliant Women* bears a strong resemblance to classical Athens. From time immemorial, the Athenians had grounded their citizenship in their possession of Attica.[220] As population pressures increased during the sub-Mycenaean and Iron Ages, they began to demarcate and farm the land with increased vigor. Under Solon the relationship between citizen and soil became a matter of law: his census, rooted in agriculture, made Athenian-ness directly proportional to land ownership. This connection later bore fruit in the myth of citizen autochthony. Originally formulated as a means of increasing political unity among citizens of the democracy, the myth had the added effect of emphasizing the differences between citizens and non-citizens. When immigration surged following the Persian Wars, these differences, both real and imagined, assumed still greater importance.

In *Suppliant Women*, the Argives' special relationship with their land is summed up by the noun used to describe them in the assembly's decree: γαμόροι. As autochthonous, land-sharing citizens, they are the antithesis of Danaus and his daughters. The play's emphasis on the question of where the newcomers are to live underlines their status as metics. Barred from owning real property, they must take citizen sponsors (*prostatai*) who arrange for their housing and lead them into the walled city with *eros* on their mind.

Conclusion

Suppliant Women offers a poetic portrait of a specific time and place. But its treatment of the Danaids' flight from Egypt and the sanctuary they find in Greece is noteworthy not for what it reveals about Bronze Age Argos, but for the light it shines on classical Athens. In staging the myth, Aeschylus drew upon his own community's experiences with immigration. The play's stagecraft emphasizes the newcomers' liminal status. The decree of its citizen assembly (ἡμᾶς μετοικεῖν τῆσδε γῆς ἐλευθέρους, 609) awards them metoikia. And its dramatic particulars explore what the presence of these metics portends for the polis.

The juridical status of metoikia was likely created in the late 470s at Athens. The play thus offers a mythic pedigree for a political innovation. By linking metoikia to the older customs of supplication and guest-friendship, the playwright lent the new institution legitimacy, showing how aristocratic tradition might be accommodated within and adapted to a democratic context. In this aetiological dimension, *Suppliant Women* resembles *Eumenides,* a slightly later Aeschylean work that provided a legendary origin for the Areopagus and its supervision of homicide trials.[1] But the similarities between the two plays go deeper. Both conclude with the introduction of a secondary chorus and a politically significant *exeunt* in which a joint procession of metics and citizens departs the theater.[2]

As in *Suppliant Women,* so too in *Eumenides* the secondary chorus is composed of the citizens who earlier performed a political function. In this instance they are the jurors who helped decide the fate of Orestes.[3] Athena addresses them at lines 1010–12, telling them to lead the Furies to their new home beneath the citadel:

You Acropolis-holding children of Cranaos,
lead these metics. And may the citizens' intention
be good in return for good.

ὑμεῖς δ' ἡγεῖσθε, πολισσοῦχοι
παῖδες Κραναοῦ, ταῖσδε μετοίκοι⟨ς⟩·
εἴη δ' ἀγαθῶν ἀγαθὴ διάνοια πολίταις

The goddesses are here described as metics (μετοίκοις), while the adjective πολισσοῦχοι ("citadel-holding") suggests that their escorts are citizens.[4] The goddesses are also contrasted with the Athenians more broadly via the term πολίταις ("citizens"); its case and line position match those of the μετοίκοις just two lines above. Athena's hope is that concord will mark relations between the two groups in her city.[5] The final tableau of *Eumenides* stresses this civic unity, incorporating several features of an idealized Panathenaic procession.[6] And "the chorus' final strophe and antistrophe are each introduced by a repeated χαίρετε (996, 1014) which is both a *salvete* from these new μέτοικοι to the city that is receiving them and a *valete* from the performers of the *Oresteia* to its audience."[7]

Suppliant Women and *Eumenides* are similar in theme as well as stagecraft. Each play revolves around what to do with a suppliant and presents persuasion (*peitho*) as superior to violence (*bia*).[8] And in each the issue is put before a group of citizens who hear arguments and express their collective opinion by voting.[9] There are admittedly differences between the two works.[10] In *Suppliant Women* the political venue is the Argive assembly; debate and voting take place off-stage; the latter occurs by show of hands (χερσὶ δεξιωνύμοις, 607) and is unanimous (οὐ διχορρόπως, 605). In *Eumenides*, by contrast, the venue is the council of the Areopagus; the process involves ballots that are cast on-stage (ψῆφον αἴρειν καὶ διαγνῶναι δίκην, 709) and results in a split vote (ἴσον γάρ ἐστι τἀρίθμημα τῶν πάλων, 753). But taken together these two plays endorse a crucial element of popular sovereignty: the primacy of persuasion in democratic bodies.[11] Aeschylus's sympathy for the political institutions of his own city is a hallmark of his dramaturgy.

Suppliant Women clearly functioned as a charter myth, creating a historical *aition* for an important contemporary phenomenon. But it also gave the spectators the mental license to think through a pressing issue in an extended way, and at a safe remove. Who should share in the city? And on what terms? As an institution, metoikia was theoretically a voluntary arrangement based on *peitho*. The Danaids had to convince the Argives to accept them, while the Argives in turn had to persuade the Danaids to accept the status they were offered. Metoikia rested on the possibility of mutual benefit, for citizens and newcomers alike.

Despite these significant parallels with *Eumenides*, *Suppliant Women* is nevertheless a more somber play; its final tableau cannot dispel the very real anxieties the Danaids have created in the polis that has taken them in. At one level, this is apparent in the fact that the Argive decision to accept them is not a free and unconstrained choice. Pelasgus and the assembly act in response to threats, with the fear of pollution and divine disfavor sweeping aside reluctance. After they are established at Argos, the newcomers precipitate a civic crisis. Their dress and speech are anomalous, and their differences in thought and manner greater still. They are ignorant of or, worse yet, indifferent to democracy. They use violence and guile to further their own interests at the expense of the community. The women display an un-Greek, headstrong independence and mores that are at once exotic and erotic. Finally, they have no abiding connection to the land that they now inhabit. By stressing all these details—the Danaids' penchant for bold speech (θρασυστομεῖν), their licentiousness (Κύπριος χαρακτήρ), and the fact that they are not autochthonous (γαμόροι)—*Suppliant Women* highlights a broader issue: namely, the formidable difficulties surrounding the incorporation of newcomers into a polis. Non-citizens remained a group apart, with a distinct set of interests and values.

Historically speaking, the Athenians responded by watching metics carefully. Approximately ten years after the performance of *Suppliant Women*, they enacted Pericles's citizenship law as one means of enforcing a separation between metics and citizens. Although the former might be permitted to dwell in the land (μετοικεῖν τῆσδε γῆς), they would never be granted a full share in the city (μετέχειν τῆς πόλεως). And their presence was hedged about with restrictions. Politically, metics were barred from serving on the deliberative bodies (*boule, ekklesia, dikasteria*) governing the democratic city. Socially, the city created disincentives to mixed-status marriages and later banned such unions outright. Economically, metics were denied the chance to acquire land and houses of their own. Taken as a group, these restrictions (and others like them) created a juridical chasm that any number of daily interactions between individual citizens and metics could not bridge.

The Athenians resolutely maintained the legal distinction between citizens and metics for a century and a half. Despite the manpower losses of the Peloponnesian War and the great plague of 430, the city never suspended Pericles's law.[12] Although the vicissitudes of a generation had demonstrated that some allies' devotion could match or exceed that of some citizens, the Athenians responded not by erasing the citizen/metic divide, but by transferring exceptionally deserving groups from one side of the line to the other.[13] Even at its postwar nadir, democratic Athens was unwilling to loosen its criteria for citizenship. As Osborne notes, "the preserved record bears out the view that in the fifth century, prior to the Peloponnesian War, grants [of citizenship] were made very infrequently—a mere five cases are known. There was some increase in the War period, and the need to take in the Plataian refugees and, more particularly, the enforced laxities of the last years of the War confused the situation. But there was an observable reaction when the War ended."[14]

In 402 the Athenians were faced with the task of reestablishing their ancestral constitution. They thus had the chance to reconsider systematically the issue of metoikia. The Thirty Tyrants had recently shown the depths to which citizens could sink, and the campaign of Thrasyboulus, the heights to which metics might rise.[15] Even so, the Athenians did not budge. Given the opportunity to eliminate, or at least recalibrate, the citizen/metic divide, the *ekklesia* voted instead to enact the motions of Aristophon and Nicomenes reaffirming Pericles's restrictive citizenship law of 451/50.[16] As late as the 350s Xenophon was left to plead (*Resources* 2.6), apparently in vain, for loosening the restrictions on metics. But the distinction between citizens and metics was so important to the city's self-understanding that the Athenians preferred ideology to manifest self-interest. As a culture they had apparently internalized an important lesson of *Suppliant Women*: that newcomers could have destabilizing—nay, devastating—effects on a polis. In the late 460s, Aeschylus's spectators had watched a democracy modeled on their own[17] succumb to military defeat, *stasis*, and coup d'état following its decision to admit metics. And the judges had responded by awarding his Danaid trilogy the first prize.

Notes

Introduction

1. On the process see especially Grethlein 2003, 45–108.

2. Murray 1958, 3–4; Garvie (2006, 211–12) offers relevant bibliography.

3. Podlecki 1966, 52–57.

4. Sicherl 1986, 99: "Danaos und seine Töchter glauben, dem Orakel ausweichen zu können, während in Wirklichkeit seine Erfüllung bereits feststeht."

5. Farenga (2006, 352–53) defines this as "the disquieting thought that each citizen self, and the collective citizen body, relies for its apparent autonomy and its harmony on a network of alliances with non-citizen others."

6. Zeitlin 1992.

7. While the approaches of Zeitlin 1992 and Farenga 2006, 346–423, are particularly conducive, each suffers from an important limitation. On Zeitlin, see below and ch. 3. On Farenga, see ch. 1.

8. Zeitlin (1992) argues that one of *Suppliant Women*'s main themes is the acculturation of the Danaids to life at Argos.

9. Zeitlin 1992, 211.

10. The same infinitive μετοικεῖν is likewise used in a technical sense at Aristophanes *Birds* 1319, where the chorus lists the advantages that might lead a man to become a resident foreigner in Pisthetaerus's new city.

11. Vidal-Naquet (1997) starts his study titled "The Place and Status of Foreigners in Athenian Tragedy" with a consideration of metic terminology, yet does not discuss the appearance of the term in Aeschylus's *Suppliant Women*.

12. E.g. Clerc 1893, 225n2. Grethlein (2003, 93n168) offers bibliography but is himself somewhat skeptical (95–96). Wilamowitz (1887, 247, 256–59) and Whitehead (1977, 34–35) constitute the main exceptions in this regard. On their importance for the current study see below.

13. FJW 1980, 2.497. See also Mitchell (2006, 216), who focuses instead on the newcomers' identity as *barbaroi*.

14. Whitehead 1977, 34.

15. The powerful description of birds stripped of their young as μέτοικοι at *Agamemnon* 57 is perhaps influential in this regard.

16. Whitehead 1977, 38: "all three poets introduce the metic in contexts which, to a citizen audience, suggested something unattractive, precarious (except after death!) and pathetic."

17. Pace Zeitlin (1992, 237), who believes that the trilogy depicts the newcomers' transformation from *astoxenoi* to *metoikoi* to "citizen wi[ves] of the Thesmophoria."

18. Meier 1993, 43.

19. Goldhill 1987, 68.

20. Goldhill 1987, 74.

21. Zeitlin 1990 (first published in 1986).

22. E. Hall 1989.

23. Rhodes 1993 (first published in 1981).

24. E.g. Ober 1989.

25. Whitehead 1986.

26. Davies 1977; Patterson 1981; Manville 1990. In this regard they have been followed by Blok 2009.

27. Loraux 1986.

28. Anderson 2003.

29. On boundaries in general see Cole 2004, 78–79. On *horoi* ("boundary markers") see Ober 1995, 106–11.

30. This was visible in e.g. the growth of the Agora. See Anderson 2003, 87–103.

31. Sealey (1983) argues that the distinction between *epitimos* and *atimos* preceded that between citizen and alien.

32. Manville 1990, 183: "Solon's reforms had been most concerned to distinguish free Athenians from slaves."

33. Speaking of archaic Athens, Whitehead (1977, 141) claims that "pockets of foreign residents will have built up, in the retinues of dynastic families or as independent artists and labourers. With no claim to 'naturalisation,' they will simply have merged into the appropriate socio-economic group, their status *de iure* unrecognized." On the reflection of this fact in Aeschylus's *Agamemnon* see Griffith 1995.

34. See ch. 2.

35. Thuc. 1.2. Plutarch (*Solon* 24.4) claims that Solon sought to bring to Athens those who had been permanently exiled from their homelands. Clerc 1893, 318: "aucune autre des cités antiques ne s'est, d'une façon générale, ouverte aux étrangers aussi facilement qu' Athènes, et cela dans toutes les périodes de son histoire."

36. Rosivach 1987.

37. Whitehead 1977, 140: "it is the appearance and rigid maintenance of

the *polites* concept which is one—but only one—of the ideological foundations of the *metoikia*."

38. On the *ethnos* as a basis for studying Athenian history see Cohen 2000.

39. Wilamowitz (1887, 211–12) acknowledges his own debt to others, especially Boeckh, Schenkl, and Mommsen. He avers that "Mommsens Abhandlung über das römische Gastrecht und die römische Clientel lehrt für die hier behandelten Fragen mehr als alle Handbücher der griechischen Alterthümer."

40. Wilamowitz 1887, 247: "der Staat . . . wollte sich durch die Erleichterung des Eintritts und die *unvergleichlich günstige* Rechtsstellung, die er den Einwandernden bot, frisches Blut zuführen. Wir haben es eben mit einem der Mittel zu thun, welche *die überwältigende Grösse* Athens bewirkt haben." (Italics added.)

41. *Les métèques athéniens*. According to Clerc (1893, 5–6), "le plan et les idées principales" of his own work were already formed before he encountered Wilamowitz's views on the topic.

42. Clerc 1893, 2: "l'histoire d'Athènes au cinquième et au quatrième siècles ne s'explique parfaitement que si l'on tient le plus grand compte de l'élément étranger incorporé à la cité."

43. Thus Gauthier 1972, 122. See also Whitehead 1977, 9.

44. Whitehead 1977, 75.

45. Whitehead 1977, 90–92.

46. Whitehead 1977, 80–82.

47. Whitehead 1977, 82–86.

48. Whitehead 1977, 70.

49. On metic access to law courts see Patterson 2001.

50. Whitehead 1977, 18.

51. Whitehead 1977, 1–2.

52. Cohen 2000, 9–10.

53. Cohen 2000, 63.

54. See Whitehead 1977, 60; Blok 2005, 15–17.

55. Cohen 2000, 61.

56. Cohen 2000, 73.

57. Blok 2005, 12. See also R. Osborne 2002, 94: "C[ohen] has no difficulty showing that texts regularly contrast *astoi* and *xenoi*. But that is perfectly compatible with *astos* and *polites* meaning essentially that same thing."

58. Cohen 2000, 129.

59. Blok (2005, 33n131) emphasizes that "although the difference between citizens and metics in social life was indeed not always very striking (as [Cohen] rightfully argues), significant distinctions remained both in the legal and the social-religious sphere."

60. Because of the presumed threat to public welfare, *graphai* could be brought by any Athenian citizen (*ho boulomenos*).

61. Meyer 2009.

62. Numerous scholars have accepted and sought to extend his basic

conclusions, including Bakewell (1997; 1999a); Adak (2003); Niku (2007); and Meyer (2009).

63. E.g. Diamantopoulos 1957.

64. Sommerstein (2008, 278–80) offers the most recent discussion. See also Garvie 2006, ix–xv.

65. If the ἀρ of the papyrus is in fact part of a proper name, Archedemides is the only suitable candidate on the Athenian archon list.

66. Scullion 2002, 87n24.

67. Scullion (2002, 87–90) is dubious; see however Farenga 2006, 351n5.

68. Scullion (2002) rejects the testimony of Plutarch and has revived the argument for an earlier date (i.e. the 470s) on the basis of stylistic criteria and structural considerations. In this he has had few supporters. See Farenga 2006, 351n5.

69. Garvie 2006, x.

70. Sommerstein 2008, 279.

71. Subsequently reissued as Garvie 2006.

72. Griffith 1986, 323.

73. E.g. Griffith (1986, 323), who adds "[FJW] rarely stand back from the scrutiny of individual trees to point out the larger characteristics of the forest unfolding (or enfolding) all around."

74. Sicherl 1986; Zeitlin 1992; Rösler 1993; Sommerstein 1995; Bachvarova 2009.

75. Sandin 2003.

76. Ober (1994, 157) contends that "Athenian political ideology and significant aspects of Athenian social practice were formulated through, maintained by, and revealed in the processes of public speech." See further Heath 2005, 17–18.

77. Patterson (1994, 211) notes that "to the Athenian audience, whether in the theater or the law court, marriage represented the first political bond of the polis and was a potent symbol of the political order."

78. Zeitlin 1992, 234–38.

79. Rosivach 1987, 298n15.

80. Metics themselves apparently persevered because residence at Athens seemed better or more practical than the alternatives. They certainly understood that theirs was a second-class status. For instance, not a single surviving Attic tombstone identifies the deceased as a metic. (Although *IG* i^3 1357 refers to Anaxilas of Naxos as a μετάοικος, it does so in a non-technical way. See Bakewell 1997, 221.) Resident foreigners who died in Athens preferred to associate themselves with their homelands by using their *ethnikon*. As Whitehead (1977, 33) observes, "this is the one stone with which ordinary men were likely to be concerned—the record transmitting them and their status to posterity. . . . Yet every one of [the dead] proclaims himself not as *metoikos* of the city where he had lived and died . . . but as X, son of Y, *of city* Z."

81. Whitehead 1977, 37.

82. Whitehead 1977, 37.

83. Whitehead 1977, 70: "Paradox . . . should cause no surprise in a subject founded upon a patent contradiction: the economic importance of the metics yet their lack of political rights and *enktesis*."

84. While Mitchell (2006, 220) correctly reads the play as representing on one level "the opening up of Athenian attitudes to the non-Greek world, or at least to Egypt," she goes too far in claiming that it "ultimately subverts the Greek-barbarian polarity."

85. Unless otherwise indicated, the Greek text of *Suppliant Women* I refer to is that of West 1990, and all translations are my own.

86. The reading ἡμῖν is that of M.

87. Whitehead 1977, 2: "It is the central paradox of a paradoxical subject that during two centuries of political, social, and economic change in Athens, attitudes toward the metic—and therefore his actual framework of existence—changed extraordinarily little." See further Davies 1977, 121.

88. Forrest (1960) attempts to read *Suppliant Women* in light of the little we know about Argive history. Diamantopoulos (1957) speculates that the play also had a performance in Argos. On democracy at Argos see Robinson 1997.

89. Sparta and its tradition of driving out foreigners (*xenelasia*) are exceptional in this regard.

90. Whitehead 1984, 48–49.

91. Zeitlin 1990, 131. Sparta serves a similar function in some Euripidean plays dating to the Peloponnesian War.

92. Saïd 1993, 188–89. See further Vidal-Naquet 1997, 113; Grethlein 2003, 52.

93. By contrast, Taplin (1986) demonstrates the centrality of metatheater to ancient comedy.

94. The methodology of Thucydides in his *Archaeology* (1.1–21) is not so dissimilar. Both men relied on comparisons with their own time and place to flesh out the mythic bones of the past. That the son of Euphorion did so less consciously and explicitly than the son of Olorus should not obscure a feature of his artistry that is as important as his grand diction, striking metaphor, and sublime theodicy.

95. On this function of tragedy see Meier 1993. Although Easterling (1985, 1) employs a more nuanced formulation, she arrives at a similar conclusion: "the tragedians had a strong sense, based on their knowledge of Homer, Cyclic epic, and lyric poetry, of the kind of world the heroes inhabited, and this they tried carefully to recreate, at the same time as dramatising the issues, problems, and attitudes of their own contemporary society."

96. Wohl 1998, xxvi.

97. Garvie (2006, 187–90) argues that the title of the play was likely *Sons of Aegyptus* rather than *Wedding Chamber Builders* (Θαλαμοποιοί). He further

demonstrates (200–202) that the evidence is too slender to securely assign Oxyrhynchus Papyrus 2251 to this play.

98. Garvie (2006, 187) argues that the name *Danaides* did double duty, applying both to the third play individually and to the trilogy as a whole.

99. Garvie 2006, 233: "Our entire discussion [of the trilogy's reconstruction] has dealt with uncertainties and possibilities, and at hardly any stage have definite conclusions been possible. Many theories have been developed, some more plausible than others, but none which could not be demolished by a single fortunate papyrus find."

100. The *Oresteia* is the only extant, connected tragic trilogy. Garvie (2006, 183) provides a salutary *caveat* about relying on it too heavily as a model.

101. The most significant attempts at reconstructing the trilogy are von Fritz 1936; Winnington-Ingram 1961; FJW 1980, 1.47–55; Zeitlin 1992; Rösler 1993; Sommerstein 1995; Garvie 2006, 163–233.

102. Garvie 2006, 199: "The death of Pelasgus in battle is the most plausible solution, and has been accepted as such by the majority of scholars."

103. Garvie (2006, 197) notes that any compromise over the Danaids is unlikely; "much more plausible is the view that there was war between the Egyptians and the Argives, and that the latter were defeated or at least reduced to accepting their opponents' terms."

104. See ch. 3.

105. Griffith 1986, 323.

106. Whitehead 1977, 140.

Chapter 1. Charter Myth for Metoikia

1. Themes: Sommerstein 1977, 74–77; Ostwald 1986, 144–45; Farenga 2006, 346–423. Characters: Grossmann (1970, 148) claims that Pelasgus represents "ein ausgesprochen athenisches Ideal." Language: Podlecki 1966, 45–50.

2. On the date see the Introduction.

3. Hurwit (1999, 141) discusses the historical difficulties involved in accepting an "Oath of Plataea" forbidding the rebuilding of the Acropolis.

4. The Tholos on the south side of the Agora was constructed in the second quarter of the fifth century; assembly meetings were transferred from the Agora to the Pnyx (a low hill to its southwest) ca. 460. On the Tholos see H. Thompson 1940; Miller 1978, 54–65; on the Pnyx see H. Thompson 1982, 136–37. According to [Aristotle] *AthPol* 43.3, by the fourth century the *boule* met daily except for holidays, while the assembly had roughly forty scheduled meetings per year. On meetings of the assembly see Hansen 1999, 132–34.

5. Boegehold (1995, 21) notes that jurisdiction in some matters was shifted from the Areopagus to the *heliaia*. He takes the latter term to mean "the entire system of popular courts" (18).

6. Hansen (1999, 188) links the introduction of pay for jurors to the reforms of Ephialtes in 462. On the introduction of pay for military service by the late 460s, see Bakewell 2007, 128.

7. See Whitehead 1977, 152.

8. Manville (1990, 140) suggests that some of the considerable diversity of burial rites in Geometric Attica is attributable to immigrants. He likewise reads (81–82) Draco's homicide law as a sign that "by the end of the seventh century, an awareness in the community between 'insiders' and 'outsiders' was starting to come into legal focus." On the ceramic evidence for the immigration of potters see Papadopoulos and Smithson 2002. And Plutarch (*Solon* 24.4) records a tradition that the lawgiver attempted to attract craftsmen and their families to Athens. See below ch. 4.

9. On this rendering of ἐφυλέτευσε see Whitehead (1977, 144), who follows Kagan 1963.

10. Thus Wilamowitz (1887, 224n3).

11. See Bakewell 1997, 220n62.

12. Bakewell 1997, 220.

13. As Whitehead notes (1977, 144), "Aristotle thought he was providing an example of post-revolutionary enfranchisement."

14. Sealey (1983, 117) links the Athenian military successes recorded at Hdt. 5.77 to an increase in available manpower resulting from the reforms of Cleisthenes.

15. Davies 1977, 117. Manville (1990, 191) argues that Cleisthenes's "'enrollment' did not import and enfranchise aliens and slaves in some deliberate parliamentary manner. Rather, in one stroke, the reforms embraced all Athenians of any defensible status, even the many accused of 'impure birth,' and made them all part of the polis."

16. Whitehead 1984, 57–58.

17. See below ch. 2.

18. Hansen 1999, 53. His figure is on the high end: see Manville 1990, 19n65.

19. Various estimates cited at Stewart 1995, 588. See below ch. 2.

20. See below ch. 4.

21. On immigration from e.g. the Cyclades see Papadopoulos and Smithson 2002.

22. On accents and dialects see [Xenophon] *AthPol* 2 8; Plato *Apology* 17d–18a. According to Halliwell (1990, 73), "a common view of the dialect scenes in Aristophanes . . . sees them in much the same light as barbarian babble or garbled Greek: i.e. as representing sounds intrinsically jarring and laughable to Athenians. Why, in that case, does Aristophanes show his Athenian characters accepting and understanding the dialects without difficulty? Might it not rather be that the scenes are linguistically realistic?" In other words, foreign accents and dialects were conspicuous yet intelligible. By contrast, Halliwell

claims (77) that Aristophanes betrays "only a slight concern with features of speech and pronunciation which might accompany . . . personal and social diversity [among citizen subgroups]."

23. Schuck (1998) provides a comparativist perspective. According to him (23), the emergence of classical immigration law in the United States in the late nineteenth and early twentieth centuries proceeded from: the dramatically changing "ethnic, cultural, and class composition of the immigrant population" (i.e. the shift from northern and western Europeans to southern and eastern Europeans and Asians); America's growing "sense of autonomy and leadership on the international stage"; and the legal system's commitment "to a very broad definition of individual and government sovereignty."

24. Schuck (1998, 80) analyzes the theoretical dangers posed by large-scale immigration in a modern context. "First, there is a risk that [the migrants] will encourage further social and cultural fragmentation, intergroup hostility, distributional inequities, and intensified political conflict, and that these conditions will at some point degrade the quality of American democracy." Second, excessive immigration "impedes communal attempts at self-definition."

25. Meiggs and Lewis 1988, 48, no. 23, lines 7, 13, 30–31. Line 7 refers to "foreigners living at Athens" ([τοὺς ξένο]υς τοὺς οἰκοῦντας Ἀθήνησι), while lines 30–31 refer to "foreigners inscribed with the polemarch" ([τοὺς] δὲ ξ[έν]ους ἐκ τῶν ἀπογεγραμμένων πα-[ρ]ὰ τῶι [πολε]μ[άρχ]ω[ι]). Bakewell (1997, 221) argues that these passages refer to foreigners, not metics per se. On the authenticity of the decree see Chambers 1967. Bäbler (1998, 46n211) claims that in the fifth century ξένοι usually denotes non-Athenian foreigners from allied Greek cities. By the fourth century the word is frequently used of mercenaries as well: see Gauthier 1971.

26. A grave monument dated to ca. 506 (*IG* i[3] 1357) refers to Anaxilas the Naxian as a μετάοικος, but does so in a non-technical way: see Whitehead 1977, 64n44. Similarly, in Aeschylus's *Persians*, produced in 472, the term μέτοικος cannot have a technical meaning when applied to Artabes at line 319: see Bakewell 1997, 221n70.

27. Lewis 1981, 214.

28. The Erinyes become the Semnae, shift their residence to Athens, refer to their own μετοικία (1018), and are called μέτοικοι by Athena (1011). See the conclusion.

29. Conacher (1996, 116) notes that Aeschylus expresses many of his dramatic ideas via important imagery. See also Lebeck (1971), who argues that in the playwright's works the metaphorical regularly becomes visible.

30. To Taplin's (1989, 193–94) arguments for the presence of Danaus here one might add the Danaids' invocation of Zeus as "household protector" (οἰκοφύλαξ, 26).

31. Schlesinger (1933, 32) notes that, etymologically and historically, the word "suppliant" (ἱκέτης) "hängt mit dem Verbum ἱκνέομαι zusammen."

32. Sandin (2003, 38) posits that Danaus brings up the rear "to cover [the Danaids'] backs from the pursuing enemy and to accentuate his subordinate role in the drama." The first mention of him at line 11 may correspond with his becoming visible to the majority of the audience. See Mastronarde 1979, 20.

33. In the formulation of Mitchell (2006, 206), "the daughters of Danaus are both 'insiders' and 'outsiders.'" See further Zeitlin 1992, 211.

34. Rehm (1988, 301) argues that the altar was located in the orchestra rather than on stage.

35. On supplication in general see Naiden 2006.

36. In addition, some information about the content of the play doubtless circulated publicly in advance. On the *proagon* see Csapo and Slater 1994, 105, 109–10.

37. See Grethlein 2003, 48. Other suppliant plays include Sophocles's *Oedipus at Colonus* and Euripides's *Children of Heracles* and *Suppliant Women*.

38. Taplin (1989, 211) calls these two moments "the twin poles of the play." Although the production of the *Oresteia* in 458 is commonly taken as the first occurrence of the scene building in Greek tragedy, a rough *skene* could perhaps make for an admirable hill in *Suppliant Women*.

39. Van Effenterre and van Effenterre 1990, 252: "la marque de l'étranger, c'est d'abord son aspect physique, taille, traits, couleur de peau, d'yeux ou de cheveux. . . . C'est aussi son accoutrement."

40. FJW (1980, 2.190) comment that their robes "are not woolen, like those of Greek women, but of fine linen." This distinction might have been lost on all but the closest spectators. Lee (2004, 253) notes that the *peplos* "was not a garment in common use during the Classical period."

41. They apparently describe themselves as a "race struck black by the sun" (μελανθές / ἡλιόκτυπον γένος) at lines 154–55; see FJW 1980, 2.128. For the contrast between the black limbs and white garments of the Egyptians see lines 719–20. See further Grethlein 2003, 53n37.

42. *Poetics* 1450a, 1454a.

43. E.g. Clytemnestra and Agamemnon and the red carpet in *Agamemnon*, Orestes and his father's robe in *Libation Bearers*, the challengers and their shields in *Seven against Thebes*.

44. According to Gödde (2000, 234), "die Geste der Hand bezeichnet in diesem Drama sowohl autoritäre und gewaltsame Verhältnisse als auch produktive und zivilisatorische Handlungen."

45. On his companions see Taplin 1989, 216–17.

46. "You there, what are you doing?" (οὗτος, τί ποιεῖς;). In commenting on the use of the demonstrative pronouns ἐκεῖνος and οὗτος, Glazebrook (2005, 167) notes that "in the case of men, οὗτος is typical. It indicates the individual's reputation in the community or among a particular group, and can also imply notoriety and infamy. . . . In oratory specifically, the speaker's use of emphatic demonstratives to point out his opponent connotes contempt. They can also be

combined with an aggressive physical gesture when appropriate to indicate further the speaker's ill will."

47. Like Zeus, whose gentle ways once conciliated Io and begat Epaphus, Lynceus will win over Hypermestra with his manner and touch. By contrast, the right hands of her sisters will dispatch their husbands.

48. Paradoxically, their hand movements become less and less "Greek" as the plot progresses. At first the women lay down their branches; later they threaten to disrobe; and still later in the trilogy, they may reach for their daggers.

49. Taplin 1989, 216.

50. Gödde (2000, 29) claims that there was a "ritualisierter Verhaltenskodex" for supplication, "[wobei] spielt der physische Kontakt zwischen dem *hiketes* und dem Angesprochenen eine zentrale Rolle."

51. Cf. Euripides *Suppliant Women* 272–85.

52. Gödde 2000, 219: "In Aischylos' *Hiketiden* markieren Kontakt und Berührung entscheidende Momente der Handlung."

53. Sicherl (1986, 82) comments that "diese Frage wird in den Hiketiden mehrfach aufgeworfen, aber nicht beantwortet."

54. On the motivations of e.g. Cephalos and his family see Gifford 2001. In playing to a jury of Athenian citizens, the prosecutor in Lysias 22 (*Against the Grain Dealers*) insinuates that metics come to Athens to do as they please (5).

55. E.g. *Agamemnon* 381–84, 750–56, 774–82.

56. See e.g. Oedipus's insinuations at *Oedipus the King* 386–89.

57. Seaford 1998, 119. See also Wohl (1998), who argues that tragedy is concerned with the conflict between more aristocratic systems of exchange (such as barter and gift-exchange) and more democratic ones linked to a monetary economy. She focuses in particular on how this conflict intersects with gender relations.

58. The sources are collected by Waser (1901, 2095).

59. On the significance of the Argives as "landholders" (γαμόροι) see ch. 4.

60. Möller (2000, 187–88) summarizes the archaeological evidence. Hdt. 2.178 lists the poleis subsequently involved in setting up the Hellenion as Ionian (Chios, Teos, Phocaea, Clazomenae), Dorian (Rhodes, Cnidus, Halicarnassus, Phaselis) and Aeolian (Mytilene).

61. Möller (2000, 202) notes the artificiality of the inhabitant/trader distinction.

62. Hdt. 2.179–80.

63. Naucratis was famous for its resident courtesans, including the redoubtable Rhodopis from Thrace. Möller notes (2000, 34 with n. 65) that Greeks interested in more lasting unions could marry or live with the locals.

64. According to an ancient scholion to line 3, the Danaids made their flight from the Heracliote mouth of the Nile (Smith 1976, 66).

65. Möller 2000, 211–12.

66. *Phaedrus* 275c5.

67. *Anecdota Graeca* 2.783.7, 786.4–5 Bekker.

68. Lines 179 (αἰνῶ φυλάξαι τἄμ' ἔπη δελτουμένας, "I urge you to guard my words, writing them down") and 991–92 (καὶ ταῦθ' ἅμ' ἐγγράψασθε πρὸς γεγραμμένοις / πολλοῖσιν ἄλλοις σωφρονίσμασιν πατρός, "also write down these things, in addition to the many other wise sayings of your father").

69. Line 463: νέοις πίναξιν βρέτεα κοσμῆσαι τάδε. See also line 709.

70. FJW (1980, 3.251) understand the phrase ἐν πτυχαῖς βύβλων κατεσφραγισμένα as "an allusion to the oriental practice of issuing commands in sealed letters."

71. Vasunia 2001, 145.

72. See also Thomas (1989, 35), who notes that "it is not clear that Athenians actually read inscriptions much. . . . There are important oral or unwritten elements in the classical methods of proof or of disseminating information even where a written version did exist."

73. FJW 1980, 3.250.

74. See further ch. 2.

75. Vasunia 2001, 138.

76. LSJ s.v. ξυνέμποροι.

77. His clinical description of the Danaids as τἄμ' ὀλαλόθ' here recalls the description of Helen as "booty" (τοῦ ῥυσίου) at *Agamemnon* 535, on which see Daube 1938, 109; Fraenkel 1950, 2.270–71.

78. In Lucian's parody *Assembly of Gods*, Dionysus is mocked as being unfit for citizenship given his foreign parentage and the fact that his maternal grandfather, Cadmus, was a trader (ἐμπόρου, 4). On the relevance of Lucian's text to fifth-century metoikia see Ogden 1996, 59.

79. The revolt is generally dated to 460–454. Grethlein (2003, 103) discusses possible links between the play and military action. On the details of the Athenian expedition to Egypt see Kahn 2008.

80. *IG* ii[2] 9984.

81. Garland 1987, 108.

82. Ammon, Isis, Sarapis, Zeus Ammon. See Garland 1987, 109.

83. According to Parker (1997, 196–97), "the common supposition that the last quarter of the fifth century saw a sudden outburst of interest in barbarian gods is simply false. What really changes in the last quarter of the century is the character of our evidence. . . . It remains plausible that Athens became more open to foreign gods in the fifth century, because she became in every sense a city with wider horizons; but we cannot argue that she yielded to eastern temptations only when demoralized by plague and a weary war. Scenes of oriental cult perhaps first appear on vases around 450, and possibly we should recognize a special influx of foreign gods around the middle of the century, a little-acknowledged, if, on reflection, quite comprehensible aspect of those golden Periclean years."

84. Gödde (2000, 145) notes the importance of "Entgrenzung und Grenzziehung" to the play.

85. τόνδ' is the reading of Turnebus; West (1990) prints τῶνδ'.

86. Sandin (2003, 18) claims that "it seems more plausible that the gods were situated on an elevation of some kind at the rear of the orchestra, and that the altar stood on the level ground in front of this elevation—or possibly on the elevation itself."

87. According to Cole (2004, 16), "the first sacred places were simple, open areas, used for communal worship in the form of sacrifices on temporary altars, ritual meals, and deposits of gifts to the gods. Eventually, however, the more significant of these places would be embellished with boundary markers, fences, or walls, permanent altars, and elaborate temple structures."

88. The phrase ἀγωνίων θεῶν recurs at *Agamemnon* 513. Fraenkel (1950, 2.260–61) there translates it as "gods in assembly," i.e. together. He further claims that given its location outside the walled city in *Suppliant Women*, the shrine should not be connected with the agora and its gods. Cf. FJW 1980, 2.166–7. Cole (2004, 67–68) notes that "territories with a single major population center—the feature that typically defined a *polis*—tended to focus on a regional sanctuary near a territorial border."

89. E.g. washing at *perirrhanteria*, which frequently marked the entrances to sanctuaries and, according to Cole (2004, 43), were widespread throughout Greece by the sixth century.

90. On the political and erotic significance of the *exeunt* see ch. 3 and Conclusion below.

91. Comparison with Sophocles's *Oedipus at Colonus* is helpful. There the intruder is the elderly Oedipus, who is Greek and therefore expected to understand the sacred nature of the space in which he sits. The chorus's anger at his presence in large part reflects his failure to observe the appropriate cultural norms. The dramatic particulars suggest, however, that the shrine may not have been delimited with boundary markers (*horoi*). The site of Oedipus's departure at the end of the play, although likewise a place of power and sanctity, is clearly left unmarked.

92. Lines 19–20.

93. On the broad similarities between their positions see Zeitlin 1992, 227.

94. Io's path through Asia (as described by the chorus) touches on the homelands of many metics (546–55).

95. Farenga 2006, 351.

96. Hansen 1999, 96–97.

97. *AthPol* 42.1–2. Etymologically, LSJ connect the verb δοκιμάζω ("to scrutinize") with δέχομαι ("to accept, receive") rather than δοκέω.

98. *AthPol* 42.1, 42.2.

99. Farenga (2006, 358n21) lists references to *dokimasiai* in the orators.

100. Hansen 1999, 219. Aristophanes *Wasps* 578 suggests that candidates for citizenship (παίδων δοκιμαζομένων) underwent physical as well as verbal scrutiny.

101. Farenga 2006, 396–97.

102. West 1990, 142: "desunt personarum notae; 298–307 distributio inter chorum et regem minus certa."

103. Mastronarde 1979, 45.

104. E.g. the encounter between Diomedes and Glaucus at *Iliad* 6.123–231.

105. Patterson 1986. Blok (2005, 9) notes that "male and female members of the *polis* had far more in common than is usually assumed."

106. In the courts, for instance, women mentioned in lawsuits are normally identified only by their relationships to other men, not by name. According to Glazebrook (2005, 166), when women are called by their names, it is often meant as an insult.

107. On the *lexiarchika grammateia* see Whitehead 1986, 35n130.

108. Farenga himself (2006, 393) acknowledges the cumulative force of potential objections, countering that "if [the Danaids] strike us as hardly resembling an ephebe confronting a demarch at this ceremony, it's worth recalling Vidal-Naquet's characterization of the ephebe as a 'temporary alien' and a 'temporary woman.'" The invocation of Vidal-Naquet notwithstanding, this is precisely the point. In the course of the play, the Danaids do not cease being either women or metics. These are lasting aspects of their characterization, not temporary ones. Nor does it help Farenga to claim (398) that metoikia is a kind of "quasi-citizenship" when Whitehead (1977, 70) has demonstrated the contrary: that "a more apt soubriquet [for metics] than 'quasi-citizen' would be *anti*-citizen, the negative image."

109. On *AthPol*'s use of the same term in describing Pericles's citizenship law of 451/50 see ch. 2. Blok (2005, 15) has demonstrated that "until the fifth century the most current word for 'those belonging to the city' was not *politai* but *astoi*. Like *politai*, *astoi* occurs almost exclusively in the plural until the second half of the fifth century: again, the inhabitants are pictured as a group, not as a sum of individuals." In this she has corrected Cohen, who argued (2000, 70–78) that ἀστοί is an antonym for ξένοι, denoting local residents rather than citizens. See further R. Osborne 2002.

110. Significantly, these uses occur both before and after the assembly's grant of metoikia (described at 605–24). As Whitehead notes (1977, 61), "evidence upholds probability in the view that *metoikoi* were an opposite, not a component, of *astoi*."

111. On its later, more precise meaning of "foreigners connected by race with the city" see FJW 1980, 2.235. See also Zeitlin 1992, 245n49. The intriguing term ἀστυπολίτης (perhaps a corruption of ἀστοπολίτης?) is contained in the Suda's definition of δημοποίητος; see Patterson 1981, 6n4.

112. Cole (2004, 76) notes that Greek poleis were typically "bounded by fringe areas, *eschatiai*, or edge zones—the mountains shared with neighbors or the sea that defined the shore. . . . Beyond such *eschatiai*, a city's lands ended in the transitional space marking the borders between the territory of one polis and the next."

113. Zeitlin 1992, 204.

114. See *Odyssey* 7.133–85. On a possible parallel between the Danaids and the exiled Themistocles see ch. 4.

115. Cole (2004, 63) notes the historical displacement of supplication ritual from the ruler's body to an altar or sacred space during the classical period.

116. Podlecki 1966, 49–50, 57. This and the following paragraph are a slightly reworked version of Bakewell 1997, 212–13.

117. The use of this term is particularly appropriate, given that it often refers to a polis-wide muster of citizens for military action. Later in the trilogy the Argives were likely summoned πανδημίαι to fight the Egyptians. The second-century CE traveler Pausanias claims (1.22.3) that the Athenians began the worship of Aphrodite Πάνδημος and of Persuasion (Πειθώ) following the *synoikism* of Theseus.

118. Bakewell 1997, 210n5.

119. Cf. FJW 1980, 2.510.

120. FJW (1980, 2.488) further claim that ψήφισματα are measures "carried not by balloting but by show of hands."

121. See FJW 1980, 2.490.

122. FJW (1980, 2.487) note that the formula ἔδοξε τῶι δήμωι is inscriptionally attested at Athens from ca. 500. See e.g. *IG* i^3 1 line 1.

123. E.g. *IG* i^3 9 line 4. Danaus's failure to mention any specific sponsor may be intended to emphasize the unity of the Argives in this matter; in effect, all citizens move the measure, just as all vote to approve it.

124. The assembly's decree would, of course, not have contained a first-person pronoun. Danaus is offering a close paraphrase, in which his ἡμᾶς replaces e.g. the speaker's original αὐτούς.

125. Petre (1986, 27) claims that the protections awarded to Acheloion in *IG* i^3 19 lines 2–5 served as a model for the decree in *Suppliant Women*. See further Bakewell 1997, 213.

126. At line 728 Danaus fears that the Egyptians will arrive ἄγειν θέλοντες, ῥυσίων ἐφάπτορες.

127. LSJ s.v. ἀρρυσίαστος. See also FJW 1980, 2.498–99; Fraenkel 1950, 2.270–72 s.v. τοῦ ῥυσίου ἥμαρτε. At line 424 the Danaids envision themselves being dragged away, ῥυσιασθεῖσαν.

128. Bakewell 1997, 212n22.

129. On the *asylon* as a physical location see Cole 2004, 16.

130. Tucker 1889, 123. See also *IG* i^3 72.34; *IG* i^3 104.37–38 (restoration based on Demosthenes 23.60).

131. FJW 1980, 2.499.

132. See ch. 4.

133. Zeitlin (1992, 211) notes that much of the play is concerned with the newcomers' "education into the rules of this 'civilized' society into which they will be incorporated." See ch. 2.

134. On the educational aspect of the tragedies of Euripides, see Gregory 1991.

135. One of the shocking features of the Danaids' arrival in Argos was their lack of *proxenoi*—i.e. formalized versions of "local guest-friends." See line 239.

136. Gould 1973, 90. See also Zeitlin 1992, 211: "Historically, the suppliant transaction is one of the earliest forms of foreign relations (along with heralds) and the means of mediation between two cultures, a way of importing or adopting alien others into one's society."

137. Unusually, Danaus does not depart at the end of the preceding act. See Taplin 1989, 209–11.

138. According to FJW (1980, 3.171), lines 825–902 "appea[r] to have suffered severe and multifarious corruption already at an early stage of transmission, and as is natural with an already partly unintelligible text, to have deteriorated further later on."

139. West (1990) prints φίλαις at line 954. On the gender of the attendants, and the question of whether to read the masculine φίλοις or the feminine φίλαις, see Garvie 2006, 195.

140. Whitehead 1986, 26.

141. Whitehead 1986, 83.

142. Taplin 1989, 239.

143. See ch. 3. Most scholars now hold that this secondary chorus was composed of Argives. See FJW 1980, 3.306–9; Taplin 1989, 232; Rösler 1993, 14–15; Sommerstein 1995, 120. On analogy with the end of Aeschylus's *Seven against Thebes*, Sommerstein further argues (1995, 120n46) that lines 977–79, which contain the only clear reference to any maids of the Danaids, "were inserted by a later producer in order to validate the presence on stage of these supernumerary performers."

144. According to Neils (2001, 186), the Panathenaic Frieze on the Parthenon contains depictions of metics participating in the procession.

145. The tableau is a visual reminder of Goldhill's claim (2007, 130) that "the story of the Athenian citizen is constantly interwoven with the normative construction of the insider and the outsider, and the myth or ideology of the polis inevitably makes walls a charged space of definition." The linkage between insiders and outsiders is emphasized at lines 1022–23, where the Danaids call to their Argive counterparts ὑποδέξασθε ⟨δ'⟩ ὀπαδοὶ / μέλος. FJW (1980, 3.312) claim that the imperative ὑποδέξασθε here means "'accept,' 'give ear to'" and not "take up the song." However, in the subsequent *strophae* and *antistrophae* the two groups do seem to respond to each other. And the theatrical potential of some sort of hand gesture (or even touch) linking the two groups should not be discounted. After all, the prayer to Zeus at lines 1064–68 dwells on his power to "make [sexual] violence kind" (εὐμενῆ βίαν κτίσας, 1067) with his "victorious touch" (χειρὶ παιωνίαι, 1066).

146. Blok (2009, 147) notes that at Athens, metoikia involved "participation

in several *polis* festivals, first of all the Panathenaia." In contrast to the Danaids, the herald retains his allegiance to the gods of the Nile (922).

Chapter 2. Spoken Like a Metic

1. According to FJW (1980, 2.104), the ἰλέομαι of Turnebus and Page is an unattested form.

2. FJW 1980, 2.106.

3. The women's use of the verb φασί ("they say") at line 291 suggests an acquaintance with Io's story.

4. The situation is analogous to that of those Athenians (and their descendants) sold abroad or driven into exile and brought back to Athens by Solon at the start of the sixth century. In his poetry the great lawgiver claimed (quoted at *AthPol* 12.4, lines 11–15):

I brought back to Athens, their divinely founded homeland,
many who had been sold, some justly,
others not, and still others in exile for debt, who no longer
spoke the Attic dialect because of their many wanderings.

πολλοὺς δ' Ἀθήνας, πατρίδ' εἰς θεόκτιτον,
ἀνήγαγον πραθέντας, ἄλλον ἐκδίκως,
ἄλλον δικαίως, τοὺς δ' ἀναγκαίας ὑπὸ
χρειοῦς φυγόντας, γλῶσσαν οὐκέτ' Ἀττικὴν
ἱέντας, ὡς ἂν πολλαχῇ πλανωμένους.

5. FJW 1980, 2.107.

6. FJW (1980, 2.106) note Kretschmer's suggestion that it may derive from the Egyptian toponym Qarbana.

7. Sandin 2003, 60.

8. J. Hall 1997, 177: "language and dialect . . . cannot be regarded as criteria of ethnicity. That does not, however, prevent them from occasionally acting as indicia of ethnicity; in other words, the relationship between language and ethnicity is unidirectional."

9. FJW 1980, 2.107.

10. δήμιον is the reading offered by M; West (1990) adopts Dindorf's δάμιον.

11. Easterling 1985, 2.

12. Cf. Grethlein, who notes (2003, 59): "dieser Ausspruch zeigt für Barbaren typische Vorstellungen von Herrschaft, die in Widerspruch zum griechischen Polisverständnis stehen."

13. LSJ s.v. I.

14. LSJ s.v. II.

15. *AthPol* 43.4 notes that the *prytaneis* set the agenda for the *boule*, which in turn set the agenda for the *ekklesia*. Likewise, according to *AthPol* 43.6, her-

alds (κήρυκες), emissaries (πρέσβεις), and those bearing letters (οἱ τὰς ἐπιστολὰς φέροντες) reported first to the Athenian *prytaneis*.

16. LSJ s.v. ἄκριτος.

17. Easterling 1985, 2. Κρίνω, the verb to which ἄκριτος is etymologically related, appears in a political context at *AthPol* 25.3. Here the leader Themistocles is described as preparing to respond to a charge of Medizing (ἔμελλε δὲ κρίνεσθαι μηδισμοῦ).

18. This was an important feature distinguishing Athens from other poleis and political entities. In *Persians*, for instance, Aeschylus has the Persian queen describe her son Xerxes as not accountable, οὐχ ὑπεύθυνος πόληι (213).

19. LSJ s.v. I.2.

20. On the importance to democracy of ruling and being ruled in turn see Aristotle *Politics* 1317a40, 1332b25.

21. *AthPol* 62.3. See further Hansen 1985, 51.

22. Hansen (1985, 52) notes that a man could preside over the *prytaneis* (ἐπιστατὴς τῶν πρυτανῶν) but once in his life, and even then for only twenty-four hours.

23. E.g. *Iliad* 1.528.

24. Boegehold (personal correspondence) suggests that the use of the phrase ψῆφον τυράννων at Sophocles *Antigone* 60 (describing Creon's edict forbidding the burial of Polyneices) may be similar in tone.

25. Metaphorically speaking, he is thus well qualified to handle the brassy Danaids, whom he describes (282–83) as coins struck with a Cypriote die. For further analysis of the metaphor see ch. 3.

26. The generals are a primary example. Bakewell (2007) argues that these men took care to track their income and expenses, precisely because of their independence and legal vulnerability.

27. For the scepter as symbol see e.g. *Iliad* 1.234–39.

28. At lines 695–700 the Danaids reprise some of the key terms from lines 370–75, now claiming that it is τὸ δήμιον that directs the city (τὸ πτόλιν κρατύνει, 695). But these lines are not a political palinode. FJW (1980, 3.60) note that "the vagueness of [their] abstractions avoids the particularization of persons or groups of persons as invested with that power." And in any event the Danaids continue to prefer *oikos* to *polis*. As Sommerstein (1977, 76) observes, for the newcomers "family solidarity is everything . . . [while] a Greek state, and particularly a democratic state, must put family solidarity in its proper place."

29. See Sicherl 1986. No city would knowingly connive to thwart the divine will; the potential consequences were too dangerous.

30. Naiden (2006) emphasizes the fact that a *supplicandus* is generally free to reject suppliants, while Turner (2001) notes the lack of social sanction for the Danaids' claim. According to the latter (28), "the suppliant may be in the right by virtue of striving toward a socially accepted goal . . . or, more vaguely, by simply suffering hardship from a position of weakness. . . . The Danaids fail to

meet either of these criteria. Consequently, their assumption of the suppliant's role is invalid."

31. For this rendering of στρόφους ζώνας τε see FJW 1980, 2.361–62.

32. Bednarowski (2010, 193) argues that "the Danaids' suicide threat contributes to the ambiguous portrayal of them in *Suppliants*."

33. Buxton 1982, 62–64.

34. Turner 2001.

35. Zeitlin 1992, 244n36. Buxton (1982, 49) argues that the Greeks understood persuasion as "get[ting] (someone) to acquiesce." On his understanding *peitho* embraced gifts, bribery, and threats, in addition to convincing language.

36. Bachvarova (2009, 299) claims that the Danaids' riddles "paralle[l] the *stichomuthia* with Pelasgus in which they established their right to Argive protection through a series of questions and answers that confirmed each party's knowledge of Io's history."

37. Naiden (2006, 84) notes that in general suppliants' "threats are rare and almost always fail."

38. See Gödde 2000, 216: "die Schutzflehenden drohen auch die ihnen zugedachte Demutshaltung in offene Aggression zu wenden—eine Aggression, die zunächst ihnen selbst, aber in letzter Instanz auch demjenigen gilt dessen Schutz und Autorität sie sich überantwortet haben." For other instances where suppliants threaten or commit suicide in a sanctuary see Thuc. 3.81.3 (Corcyraeans); Euripides *Helen* 980–87 (Menelaus).

39. FJW (1980, 2.369) state that the accusative singular μαστικτῆρα, a correction for the manuscripts' μακιστῆρα, is elsewhere unattested but "virtually certain." Pindar uses the oxymoronic phrase μάστιγι Πειθοῦς to good effect in his description of Medea at Pythian 4.390.

40. According to E. Hall (1996, 136) "unpleasant physical punishments are hallmarks of the barbarian tyrant in Greek thought." See e.g. Hdt. 7.56.

41. Burkert (1985, 201) notes that chthonic deities were sometimes depicted as snakes. He adds that "in Argos the setting up of an image of Zeus Meilichios signified purification after a bloody civil war. The god is represented either as a paternal seated figure or simply as a snake."

42. See ch. 4.

43. FJW (1980, 2.157) note that the conjecture σεσωφρονισμένων (printed by West 1990) "is by no means implausible, though impossible to substantiate."

44. West (1990) treats the ξένη as a vocative, setting it off with commas.

45. In Euripides's *Suppliant Women*, the metic Parthenopaeus is praised precisely because he is not "given to disputatious speech" (ἐξεριστὴς τῶν λόγων, 894).

46. FJW (1980, 2.155) rightly call lines 197–99 "a massive elaboration of a simple notion." Danaus could hold his own with subsequent Sicilian sophists like Tisias and Gorgias, who "through their force of language" not only made "small things appear great and great things appear small," but also "invented rhetorical shortcuts and endless disquisitions about all things" (Plato *Phaedrus* 267a7–b2).

47. Gödde 2000, 25–26: "begründet . . . einen spezifischen Modus des Sprechens, mittels dessen der Schutzflehende seinen Fall vorbringt und die Aufnahme zu erwirken sucht."

48. Gödde 2000, 143. She adds that "die Hikesie dient . . . häufig dazu, einen Raum zu schaffen, aus dem heraus derjenige, der bereits dem Tod anheim gegeben ist, noch zu sprechen vermag."

49. Hence Danaus's present reminder that they are needy exiles (χρεῖος εἶ ξένη φυγάς, 202).

50. On ancient supplication in general see Naiden 2006.

51. E.g. Cylon at Athens, on whom see Hdt. 5.71.1.

52. LSJ s.v. ἔπηλυς. Etymologically the noun derives from ἐπέρχομαι, "to come upon, approach."

53. McClure 1999a, 6.

54. In Lucian's *Assembly of Gods*, one of Momus's main arguments against the (to his mind) spurious divinities is their uncouth speech. According to him, these polyglot pretenders are disturbing to heavenly symposia (καὶ θεοὶ δόξαντες ἐμπεπλήκασι μὲν τὸν οὐρανὸν ὡς μεστὸν εἶναι τὸ συμπόσιον ὄχλου ταραχώδους πολυγλώσσων τινῶν, "those seeming to be gods have so filled heaven that our symposium is disturbed by the disruptive rabble with their many foreign tongues," 14). Mithras the Mede is so ignorant of Greek that he doesn't even understand it if someone makes a toast in his honor (οὐδὲ ἑλληνίζων τῇ φωνῇ, ὥστε οὐδ' ἤν προπίῃ τις ξυνίησι, 9).

55. These linguistic expectations are reinforced elsewhere in the play; at line 273, for instance, the women receive a reminder from Pelasgus: μακράν γε μὲν δὴ ῥῆσιν οὐ στέργει πόλις ("the city does not like a long speech").

56. FJW 1980, 3.277; Sommerstein 1996a, 148.

57. The remainder of this section is a revised version of Bakewell 2008a.

58. LSJ s.v. βούλαρχος and στασίαρχος.

59. The history of Danaus's family resembles that of board games themselves. Once known in Greece, they subsequently vanished, only to be reintroduced from Egypt after a hiatus. See Vermeule 1979, 77–80.

60. Crates Comicus 7.

61. LSJ s.v. πεσσοί.

62. See FJW 1980, 2.17–18. There may be an additional allusion to a race-type game (on which see Austin 1940, 259): Danaus has gotten his daughters safely off the board before the Egyptians can catch them.

63. FJW 1980, 2.16.

64. On the details of the quarrel see Garvie 2006, 164–66.

65. Sommerstein (1977, 67) supports his claim by noting that Danaus makes a total of three entrances in the play (here with the Danaids, and again at lines 600 and 980). "Just before his second entrance we hear the words ἀρχᾷ (595) and βούλιος (599)"; he is again described as βούλαρχος shortly before the third entrance (970).

66. On Danaus as tyrant see Turner 2001, 36–38.

67. Sommerstein 1977, 67. On βούλευσις see Todd 1993, 274; Rhodes 1992, 643.

68. Wilson 2000, 315n42. He also emphasizes the relationship between "social divisions and their ritual-festival counterparts in *khoroi*."

69. Taplin and Wilson 1993.

70. Taplin and Wilson (1993, 172) cite the Erinyes' description as a χορός at *Agamemnon* 1186 and e.g. *Eumenides* 307, and their link with στάσις at *Agamemnon* 1117 and *Eumenides* 311.

71. Sommerstein 1977, 67. Herodotus (1.59.3) explicitly calls the beginning of Peisistratid rule a time of στάσις (referring to the followers of Megacles and Lycurgus with the participle στασιαζόντων). Peisistratus himself is said to lead one of the city's factions: ἤγειρε τρίτην στάσιν, συλλέξας δὲ στασιώτας . . . ("he raised up a third faction, and having collected his partisans . . .").

72. On the basis of Plato *Republic* 566b and Aristotle *Rhetoric* 1357b30–36, FJW (1980, 3.277) claim that such a request was "a routine step towards making oneself a tyrant."

73. Whether *Suppliant Women* was the first or second play of the trilogy does not materially affect the views advanced here. For the claim that *Aegyptioi* came first see Rösler 1993, 7–10.

74. Kurke 1999, 254–55.

75. For instance, a passage from Euripides's *Erechtheus* (fr. 360, lines 7–13, in Collard 1995, 158) twice draws an explicit comparison between *pessoi* and inhabitants of cities who move there from elsewhere—i.e. metics:

First of all, we are a people not led here from elsewhere,
but autochthonous. Other cities have been founded
as if by movements of *pessoi*,
with various cities being led up from various places.
But whoever lives in one city coming from another,
just like a poorly fitting peg in wood,
is a citizen in name, but not in his deeds.

ἧι πρῶτα μὲν λεὼς οὐκ ἐπακτὸς ἄλλοθεν,
αὐτόχθονες δ' ἔφυμεν· αἱ δ' ἄλλαι πόλεις
πεσσῶν ὁμοίως διαφοραῖς ἐκτισμέναι
ἄλλαι παρ' ἄλλων εἰσὶν εἰσαγώγιμοι.
ὅστις δ' ἀπ' ἄλλης πόλεος οἰκήσῃ πόλιν,
ἁρμὸς πονηρὸς ὥσπερ ἐν ξύλῳ παγείς,
λόγῳ πολίτης ἐστί, τοῖς δ' ἔργοισιν οὔ.

See also Kurke 1999, 251.

76. Lines 6–7, 640, 942–43. See Bakewell 2008a, 304–5. On ψῆφος as a synonym for πεσσός see LSJ s.v. II.2.

77. B 52 (Diels and Kranz 1968, 162): αἰὼν παῖς ἐστι παίζων, πεσσεύων· παιδὸς ἡ

βασιληίη ("Life is a boy playing, moving pieces: his is the kingdom"). See further Kurke 1999, 260–63.

78. Archaeological evidence suggests that board games were a prime source of entertainment for ephebes in training on the frontier. Munn (1993, 78–79) discusses several game boards incised on clay roof tiles that were found in connection with the Dema Tower located in the Aigaleon-Parnes gap.

79. Kurke 1999, 265.

80. Vasunia (2001, 141) suggests that at lines 942–49 Pelasgus "is reiterating the Argives' decree orally, and that he is not just speaking out but reading out a public notice of that decree."

81. Kurke (1999, 261) notes that in the game of *polis* "an isolated man brought danger to himself and to his side."

82. Kurke 1999, 265.

83. The term κύριος has a suggestively wide range of meanings; see LSJ s.v. At lines 188–89 Danaus tells the women to climb a hill and enter a rural sanctuary; at lines 1009–11 he directs their movements into the *asty* proper and specifies where they should lodge. On the latter issue see ch. 4.

84. Kurke (1999, 265) suggests that "the 'holy line' as the mid-most of five lines may evoke the temples and sanctuaries that tend to occupy the acropolis at the center of the city."

85. According to Eustathius, "move from the holy line" was a proverbial expression for the actions of those in desperate straits. See Kurke 1999, 262.

86. For possible scenarios see Winnington-Ingram 1961, 145.

87. Welcker's comparison of Pelasgus and Danaus (1861, 105) is succinct: "jener ist ganz der Mann ein Reich zu verlieren, dieser eins zu erwerben."

88. Grethlein (2003, 82–83) also notes the contrast between Pelasgus's initial encounter with the Danaids and his subsequent meeting with the herald.

89. Grethlein 2003, 38: "kennzeichnend ist für [die Szene] der Rekurs auf die eigene Identität, der durch das Aufeinandertreffen mit dem Fremden ausgelöst wird. Zentrale Felder dieser Identität sind neben Recht und Brauch . . . die Religion und die politische Verfassung."

90. On the assembly as a primary locus for citizen speech see McClure 1999a, 8.

91. The sentence may also allude to the τύχη πρακτήριος Pelasgus prayed for earlier at line 523.

92. FJW (1980, 3.252) note that the phrase is "better rendered 'd' une bouche libre' . . . than 'free-spoken.'"

93. Raaflaub 1980, 14: "Fähigkeit der Meinungsaüsserung." See further FJW 1980, 2.252.

94. Raaflaub 1980, 14: "der Sinnzusammenhang bleibt ganz unpolitisch: Das Wort eines freien Mannes ist wahr und zuverlässig."

95. It is the herald's task to provide his Aegyptid masters with an accurate account of the interchange: see lines 930–33.

96. Raaflaub 1980, 24–28.

97. Ober 1989, 296: "the central freedom that the Athenians cherished, therefore, was *isegoria*: the right of the citizen to address the sovereign Assembly of the people. This important right was reiterated at every assembly, when after a motion had been made, the 'president' of the Assembly asked who among those present had advice to give to the Athenians."

98. Raaflaub 1980, 31–32.

99. Monoson (1994, 179) notes that Athenian *isegoria* lent credibility "to the claim that individual citizens are meaningfully implicated in the decisions of the Assembly and therefore morally obligated to obey them."

100. Pelasgus's words recall Hector's remarks at *Iliad* 22.105–7, where the Trojan hero explains why he must fight Achilles:

I fear the Trojans and the Trojan women with their trailing *peploi*,
lest one of them, worse than I, should sometime say:
"Trusting in his own might, Hector destroyed his people."

αἰδέομαι Τρῶας καὶ Τρῳάδας ἑλκεσιπέπλους,
μή ποτέ τις εἴπῃσι κακώτερος ἄλλος ἐμεῖο·
"Ἕκτωρ ἧφι βίηφι πιθήσας ὤλεσε λαόν."

Like the Trojan before him, Pelasgus fears what his countrymen will think of his actions. But significantly, Hector fears the voice of a less worthy individual (τις . . . κακώτερος ἄλλος ἐμεῖο), while Pelasgus fears the sentiment of his people as a whole (λεώς). In addition, Hector's fear drives him out to individual action, while Pelasgus's leads him to consult and heed the Argive assembly.

101. West (1990) adopts Schneidewin's λῷιον, yielding the general sense "if something bad should happen." See further FJW 1980, 2.316.

102. FJW 1980, 2.314.

103. Burian 1974, 7–9. By contrast, West (2006, 37) emphasizes the extent to which Aeschylus was constrained by mythological tradition. See further Podlecki 1986, 82.

104. Rösler (1989, 110) notes that tragedy's interest in the workings of democracy is often at odds with its mythical content. According to him, there are two basic possibilities for depicting kings in tragedy: "die eine Möglichkeit bestand darin, das despotische Regime eines Königs als Gegenbild zu den Verhältnissen in der Demokratie erscheinen zu lassen, die andere darin, den König als auf das Volk hörend, im Extremfall gar als quasidemokratischen Oberbeamten darzustellen. Herausragendes Beispiel für den zweiten Typus sind eben die *Hiketiden*." On the relative frequency with which Aeschylus explores the interactions between ruler and *demos* see West 2006.

105. In Aeschylus's *Seven against Thebes*, Eteocles evinces (6–7) a similar fear of what the people may say should things go wrong during the assault on Thebes. West (2006, 34) notes that their mutterings "will be of the nature of

preludes, φροίμια. Preludes to what? Obviously to active revolt. . . . If the whole city should turn against him, he could hardly hope to remain in power."

106. Carawan 1987, 167.

107. Hdt. 6.136.1–3. Carawan (1987, 194) notes that the charge of deceit (ἀπάτη) is equivalent to a similar phrase used in a later procedure, ἐάν τις ὑποσχόμενός τι τὸν δῆμον ἐξαπατήσῃ ("if anyone deceives the people by promising [them] something," Dem. 20.100). This second formulation calls to mind the wording of Pelasgus's earlier refusal to act on the Danaids' request without consulting all the citizens (ἐγὼ δ' ἂν οὐ κραίνοιμ' ὑπόσχεσιν παρος, 368).

108. Such a dynamic is described at Thuc. 2.13, where on the eve of Sparta's first invasion of Attica Pericles fears ordinary Athenians will think he has cut a private deal with his guest-friend Archidamus.

109. The use of the word λόγος at line 484 may indicate a formal, public dimension to the process. In this regard the Argives of *Suppliant Women* differ from those of *Agamemnon,* who grumble against their leaders, but in secret (e.g. lines 449–51, 457–58, and the watchman's remarks at lines 36–39). The difference stems from the fact that in *Agamemnon* the city is ruled by a tyranny.

110. Pierart (1971, 572) concludes that "la présence d' εὔθυνοι dans la loi du dème des Scambonides, qui est antérieure à 460, permettait d'affirmer à coup sûr que les euthynes existaient déjà dans la constituition d'Athènes à cette époque. L'emploi formulaire de εὐθύνεσθαι permet de remonter, avec certitude, jusqu'en 485/4, peut-être jusqu'à l'extrême fin du VIe siècle."

111. See Bakewell 2007.

112. E.g. Sommerstein 1996b, 75: "Pelasgos is shown as obtaining this decision [the grant of metoikia] by blatant manipulation."

113. Based on the summary of the assembly's proceedings at lines 615–20. Sommerstein 1996b, 75; Farenga 2006, 416.

114. Farenga (2006, 416n102) concedes this last point. Danaus's remarks here resemble a formal staple of tragedy, the messenger's speech.

115. The suppression of the conspiracy of Cylon in 632 had given the Athenians first-hand experience with the pollution accruing from bloodshed in a city sanctuary (*AthPol* 1.1). Two centuries later, the notion of the curse remained sufficiently strong for the Spartans to try to exploit it against Pericles (Thuc. 1.26–27).

116. See Pelasgus's taunt at line 952: ἀλλ' ἄρσενάς τοι τῆσδε γῆς οἰκήτορας / εὑρήσετ', οὐ πίνοντας ἐκ κριθῶν μέθυ.

117. West (1990) reads εὐπειθεῖς, not εὐπειθής. The latter was first proposed by Bothe and accepted by FJW (1980, 2.510). See below n. 128.

118. Sommerstein 1996b, 76. Farenga (2006, 416) more cautiously translates it as "the orator's highly persuasive moves."

119. LSJ s.v. offer no etymology. Δημήγορος has an admittedly negative cast at *Hecuba* 254, where the queen exchanges harsh words with Odysseus and faults those who strive after δημηγόρους τιμάς ("crowd-pleasing honors"). But

Euripides's play likely dates to ca. 424 and reflects the stresses of the Archidamian War following the death of Pericles. Comparison with the similar term δημαγωγός ("popular leader") is instructive. According to Connor (1992, 110), "when the word first came into use it was not pejorative, unless it was spoken among a group that was agreed and united in its hatred of the *demos*."

120. E.g. Aristophanes *Acharnians* 45.

121. FJW 1980, 2.511.

122. Farenga 2006, 417, with n103. He prefers the reading εὐπειθεῖς.

123. Johnstone 1996, 114–26.

124. Johnstone 1996, 122.

125. Johnstone 1996, 126.

126. The noun στροφαί is also used of the back-and-forth movements employed by dramatic choruses in delivering their songs.

127. In *Nicias* 8 Plutarch claims that "Cleon destroyed decorum on the *bema* and was the first to shout aloud while speaking and to pace at the same time he spoke" (καὶ τὸν ἐπὶ τοῦ βήματος κόσμον ἀνελὼν καὶ πρῶτος ἐν τῷ δημηγορεῖν ἀνακραγὼν . . . καὶ δρόμῳ μετὰ τοῦ λέγειν ἅμα χρησάμενος). For a similar claim see *AthPol*. 28.3. Connor, however, suggests (1992, 134) that Cleon "drew upon many of the techniques of Perikles and other earlier politicians."

128. FJW (1980, 2.512) note that Bothe's correction of the manuscripts' εὐπειθεῖς is metrically and orthographically acceptable. It is also aesthetically desirable, permitting proportionate assignment of adjectives to nouns in an interlocking arrangement: δημηγόρους (A) εὐπειθής (B) στροφάς (A) δῆμος (B).

129. LSJ s.v. εὐπειθής.

130. FJW 1980, 2.512.

131. Heath 2005, 6.

132. For a schematic overview of the options available to individual poleis see Whitehead 1984.

133. Patterson 1981, 134.

134. *AthPol* 26.4. [Aristotle] here offers what has been traditionally viewed as the standard formulation of the law. Blok (2009) has recently argued that the precise terminology of the law was slightly different. She notes (144–45) that "all other occurrences of μετέχειν τῆς πόλεως date to the fourth century" and claims that (145) "the most common way of referring to a citizen in the mid-fifth century was . . . by using the *ethnicon*." She therefore argues (146) that "the text of the law probably included μὴ Ἀθηναῖον εἶναι ὅς ἂν μὴ ἐξ ἀμφοῖν ἀστοῖν ᾖ γεγονως." Whether she is correct in this regard has little effect on the argument presented here.

135. According to Patterson (1981, 136), "it is striking that we hear of no debate or objections, such as were raised over the building of the Parthenon . . . and actually very little about this law at all."

136. This accords with broad statements in the *Politics* (1278A 26–34), where Aristotle connects generous definitions of citizenship with manpower concerns.

137. *Pericles* 37.2.

138. The issue treated by Plutarch is the Athenians' decision to permit Pericles to enroll his son by his non-Athenian concubine Aspasia as a citizen following the deaths of his two legitimate sons in the plague. According to Ogden (1996, 60–62), the biographer has borrowed from a comic source to personalize the issue: the fact that Pericles must seek the relaxation of his own citizenship law provides an instance of Nemesis in action. Carawan (2008) ascribes a more sweeping character to the decision, arguing that in 430/29 the Athenians amended the law of 451/50 to allow others in similar circumstances to enroll their *nothoi* as well.

139. Ogden (1996, 64–69) and Podlecki (1998, 159–61) offer recent overviews of the question.

140. LSJ s.v. πλῆθος.

141. Boegehold 1994.

142. Boegehold (1994, 65) contends that Pericles may simply have been acting like a good politician: he "did not anticipate some pressing need: he could instead have been confirming a manifest consensus." Blok (2009, 149) is skeptical, arguing that "the archaeological record shows that throughout the fifth and fourth centuries, Athens continued to fill in its arable land and increased its production." Yet the archaeological record, incomplete as it is, does not necessarily contradict Boegehold's view: more intensive cultivation and the citizenship law could both be expressions of land shortage, as could the foundations of cleruchies and colonies Blok further cites to support her argument.

143. Patterson (1981, 105) suggests a connection between food scarcity and Athenian military activities in Egypt and Boeotia during the 450s and 440s.

144. Philochorus (*FGH* 328 F 119); Plutarch *Pericles* 37.4.

145. Rhodes (1992, 333) is incredulous: "it is wholly implausible that as many as 4,760 were deprived of citizenship or exposed as non-citizens."

146. See, however, Ogden (1996, 59), who notes that in Lucian's parody *Assembly of Gods*, one of Momus's arguments for conducting a divine διαψηφισμός is that the ambrosia and nectar have begun to run low διὰ τὸ πλῆθος τῶν πινόντων ("because of the number of [heavenly] drinkers," 14).

147. On the concomitant rise of draft evasion at Athens, see Christ 2006, 88–142.

148. Although the date for the beginning of the *patrios nomos* is contested, the best evidence puts it in the 470s or 460s. See Hornblower 1991, 292–93. On the custom in general see Clairmont 1983. Bakewell (1997, 128) offers a literary argument for 458 as a *terminus ante quem*. On the funeral oration see Loraux 1986. On casualty lists see Bradeen 1967, 1969.

149. *AthPol* 24.3 lists such payments (i.e. ὀρφανοί) among Athens's expenditures in the period prior to 462. On the complexities involved in interpreting this section of the treatise see Rhodes 1993, 300–309. An inscription dated by Lewis to before 460 (*IG* i^3 6) may also refer to the practice (C 40–41).

150. *AthPol* 24.3; on his death see Plutarch *Aristides* 26.

151. Σ Dem. 13 (*Peri Syntaxeos*) in Dilts 1983, 167.24–25.

152. Podlecki (1998, 11–16) suggests that Pericles's performance as *choregus* for Aeschylus's *Persians*, produced in 472, marked his appearance on the political scene and signaled his "sympathy with Themistocles" (15).

153. Pritchett 1971, 12–13; Rhodes 1992, 306; Loomis 1998, 36–37. While Pritchett relies heavily on the literary evidence, Loomis surveys the relevant inscriptions as well.

154. Plutarch *Pericles* 12.4.

155. Hansen 1999, 38.

156. Sources collected at Hansen 1999, 38n151. *IG* i^3 82 is securely dated to 421/20, and the restoration of line 20 would seem to provide a *terminus ante quem* for the payment of wages to βουλευταί. The opening of the archonship to *zeugitae* in 457/56 made the post accessible to those of somewhat lesser means.

157. Thuc. 2.13.6–7: "And so he was encouraging them thus about money, and that there were 13,000 hoplites apart from the 16,000 in the forts and on garrison duty. For this many men were protecting the city at first, whenever the enemy invaded, and were drawn from the oldest and the youngest, and the metic hoplites" (χρήμασι μὲν οὖν οὕτως ἐθάρσυνεν αὐτούς, ὁπλίτας δὲ τρισχιλίους καὶ μυρίους εἶναι ἄνευ τῶν ἐν τοῖς φρουρίοις καὶ τῶν παρ' ἔπαλξιν ἑξακισχιλίων καὶ μυρίων. τοσοῦτοι γὰρ ἐφύλασσον τὸ πρῶτον ὁπότε οἱ πολέμιοι ἐσβάλοιεν, ἀπό τε τῶν πρεσβυτάτων καὶ τῶν νεωτάτων, καὶ μετοίκων ὅσοι ὁπλῖται ἦσαν). Duncan-Jones (1980) offers a mainstream reading of the passage and its difficulties; Winton (2007) suggests a repunctuation with radical consequences.

158. Beloch 1923, 386–88.

159. For a survey of the problems involved see Hansen 1985, 8–16. For other theoretical approaches see Hansen 1988, 2006a, and 2006b.

160. I.e. the census underwritten by Demetrius of Phaleron in the years 317–307 (preserved in Athenaeus 272c), which gives figures of 21,000 adult male Athenians, 10,000 metics, and 400,000 slaves. See Hansen 1985, 29–36.

161. Patterson 1981, 48–49.

162. Hdt. 9.28.

163. Patterson 1981, 65. She adds that the 440s saw Athens send out numerous colonies and cleruchies, in part to relieve population pressure in Attica.

164. Patterson 1981, 68. She further notes that this growth in population occurred despite the significant dislocation caused by the Persian destruction of 480 and the unhygienic consequences of increasing urbanization.

165. See further Watson 2009, 262–63.

166. Patterson 1981, 42. Hansen (1985, 11) suggests a "natural" growth rate of 0–0.5 percent per annum.

167. Patterson 1981, 28: "Through the early fifth century citizenship was determined by one's neighbors and kin on a traditional and familial basis."

168. Patterson 1981, 103–4.

169. Her basic scenario has found wide acceptance: see e.g. Carawan 2008, 389–90.

170. Duncan-Jones 1980, 101–3.

171. Duncan-Jones 1980, 102.

172. See also Watson 2009, 264n21. French (1994) claims Pericles's law was directed primarily against metics.

173. Rhodes further argues (1992, 333–34) that the law would "limit citizens in their choice of wives but would not reduce the number of sons born in wedlock to citizen fathers." Note that (as preserved) Pericles's law did not directly regulate marriage; any effect in this regard will have been indirect.

174. Rhodes 1992, 334.

175. Ogden (1996, 66) also links this explanation to older formulations emphasizing Athenian concerns about "racial purity." Boegehold (1994, 58) offers a critique of the latter formulation.

176. Blok (2009, 169) understands the law as a morale booster: "by emulating the *gene*, who guarded their inherited *timai* of *polis* priesthood by claiming uninterrupted, exclusively Athenian descent, Perikles sought to gentrify the *demos* to the same status. Such a higher consciousness of one's identity as a citizen would lift the spirits at a moment when countless citizens had perished due to prolonged warfare."

177. The verb μετέχω is also used in contexts related to citizenship three times (1, 3, 3) in Lucian's spoof *Assembly of Gods*. On the relevance of this second-century CE text to Pericles's citizenship law see Ogden 1996, 59.

178. Pausanias (1.22.3) says that Theseus instituted a shrine to her and to Aphrodite Pandemos. The depiction of both goddesses on the south frieze of the classical temple of Athena Nike above their own sanctuary (Hurwit 1999, 212) suggests that the worship of Peitho there predates 425.

179. Ober (1994, 157) notes that "Athenian political ideology and significant aspects of Athenian social practice were formulated through, maintained by, and revealed in the processes of public speech."

180. Christ 2006, 15: "Although bad citizenship could arise from a wide range of motivations, it was rooted in the individual's pursuit of self-interest."

181. On the trope see Whitehead 2006.

182. At Thuc. 6.92, Alcibiades seeks to forestall the deployment of this sort of argument against himself at Sparta in 414.

183. According to Todd (2000, 237–38), while the procedure was an *eisangelia* to a *dikasterion* for profiteering, the precise charge is "obscure in detail."

184. Monoson 1994, 181. See also Ober 1989, 297.

185. Monoson 1994, 182.

186. Ps.-Xenophon claims (1.12) that the need for metics to serve as sailors and craftsmen led the city to countenance a certain degree of outspokenness in them. But his tract is polemical, and he is surely exaggerating when he says that the city awarded them *isegoria* vis-à-vis the citizens (ἰσηγορίαν . . . ἐποιήσαμεν, καὶ

τοῖς μετοίκοις πρὸς τοὺς ἀστούς). First of all, metics never possessed the formal right of *isegoria*; on the contrary, they were barred from most political venues. Second, the author's main point of comparison is Sparta's harsh treatment of its slaves (1.11). Athens's metics were indeed treated better than this group, but that is not saying much, and does not properly amount to *isegoria*.

187. Zeitlin 1992, 211.

188. See Scafuro 1994.

189. E.g. Thuc. 1.2. See ch. 4 below.

190. See e.g. lines 547–55.

191. Grethlein (2003, 69) notes that "die Danaiden sind vor allem in zwei Aspekten als barbarisch charakterisiert: Das entscheidende Merkmal ist nebem dem Aussehen und der Kleidung das Verständnis des politischen Lebens."

Chapter 3. The Cypriote Stamp

1. Grethlein 2003, 78: "Das Problem der Integration von Fremden wird noch verschärft durch die Stellung von Frauen, die nicht durch die Ehe ihren festen Platz in der Polis haben." See further 106–7.

2. FJW (1980, 1.30) claim that "the most fundamental question posed by [the play is] that of the Danaids' justification, and so motivation, for refusing to marry." Garvie (2006, 211–23) and MacKinnon (1978) provide comprehensive surveys of existing opinion on the issue.

3. Wilamowitz 1914, 15: "aus angeborener Männerfeindschaft." On the interpretation of the women's infamous phrase αὐτογενῆ φυξανορίαν ("innate avoidance of [the] men," 8), see FJW 1980, 2.13–14. FJW claim elsewhere (1980, 1.132) that "there is, in fact, not one passage in *Supp.* where the Danaids clearly express an attitude of general aversion to the institution of marriage, or to sexuality, or to the male sex as such."

4. MacKinnon 1978, 79–80. On the *hybris* of the Aegyptids in general see H. G. Robertson 1936.

5. References collected at Garvie 2006, 216n3.

6. Thomson 1941, 298–309. MacKinnon (1978, 78–79) explores the related possibility that the audience might have understood the Danaids as *epikleroi*, marriageable heiresses.

7. Sicherl (1986) has argued that Danaus received an oracle prophesying his death at the hands of a son-in-law, and thus urges his daughters not to marry.

8. Murnaghan 2005, 184.

9. Seaford 1987, 110.

10. Zeitlin 1992. Seaford (1987, 115–16) also explores the idea.

11. Zeitlin 1992, 236.

12. Zeitlin (1992, 235) counters that "the Danaids' connection with the Thesmophoria might be understood therefore as a compensatory shift in model from the father-daughter dyad to that of mother and daughter, which in the

relation of Demeter and Kore assumes a beneficent reciprocity, even a perennial circularity, between the two." Evidence for such a compensatory shift is lacking.

13. At lines 315–24 the Danaids trace only their patrilineal descent; Pelasgus responds with a reference to their "paternal houses" (πατρῷια δώματα, 326).

14. Seaford (1987, 116) concludes that "no evidence survives for a substantial connection between the Thesmophoria and marriage."

15. Zeitlin 1992, 237. Winnington-Ingram, although more cautious, makes the same assumption, claiming (1961, 142n9) that the women "presumably cease to be μέτοικοι . . . and become full citizens."

16. According to Tzanetou (2002, 331), participation in the Thesmophoria was restricted to citizen wives.

17. If we look to Aeschylean comparanda, the *Oresteia* offers a caution. This connected trilogy also ends with powerful females transformed and taking up residence in a new city. Yet *Eumenides* stresses that the Erinyes move to Athens as metaphorical metics, not citizens. The fact that the final scene depicts a procession *in Athens*, from the Areopagus to beneath the Acropolis, suggests that the play offers a best-case scenario. (While tragedies set in Athens turn out well, other locales are less conducive to happy endings.) See Bakewell 1999a, 52–53.

18. This is particularly true given its Argive setting. See Grossmann 1970, 118–19.

19. Patterson (1994, 211) notes that "to the Athenian audience, whether in the theater or the law court, marriage represented the first political bond of the polis and was a potent symbol of the political order."

20. Dawe (1965, 59) lists three conjectures for completing the line: <στυγερόν τε> (Jurenka), <διάνοιαν> (Weil, followed by Wilamowitz), <παράνοιαν> (Mazon). All three are compatible with the argument advanced here.

21. Bachvarova (2009) offers a reading of Aeschylus's Danaids as nymphs who at first oppose marriage and childbirth before later bringing moisture and fertility to Argos.

22. E.g., in the Homeric *Hymn to Demeter*, Zeus gives his daughter to his brother Hades without consulting her or her mother. Foley (1994, 105) argues that "Zeus attempts to impose on Persephone a form of marriage new to Olympus, the divine equivalent of a mortal institution familiar in Homer: in modern terms we would categorize it as patriarchal and virilocal exogamy."

23. On κυριεία in general see Todd 1993, 207–10.

24. The ἄκουσαν ἄκοντος reading is transmitted by M and accepted by FJW (1980, 2.183); West (1990) prints ἑκουσαν ἄκοντος.

25. FJW 1980, 2.183.

26. E.g. lines 223–25.

27. ἄδμητος ἀδμήται is the reading of Pauw; West (1990) prints ἀδμῆτος ἀδμήτα.

28. On Artemis's association with topographic (as well as developmental) turning points see Cole 2004, 186.

29. In Aeschylus's *Agamemnon*, for instance, the sacrifice of Iphigenia is described partly in the language of wedding rites (e.g. προτέλεια, 227) and partly in the language of taming animals (e.g. βίαι χαλινῶν, 238).

30. Von Fritz 1936, 259; Garvie (2006, 223) notes that "they reject a marriage that is in itself perfectly legitimate and conventional." The Danaids' prayer to Artemis nevertheless also hints ironically at the future awaiting them. For while the goddess is a *parthenos* sympathetic to the sufferings of innocent animals, she also presides over the Arcteia at Brauron. According to Foley (1994, 104), in this festival "Attic girls . . . were probably initiated into adulthood and marriage."

31. Sommerstein (1977, 72) earlier argued that "there is no convincing interpretation of 339 that can allow it to be spoken by the chorus leader. Therefore it must be spoken by the king." He now (2008) assigns it to the chorus leader instead. West (1990) prints the entire passage as a stichomythia.

32. West (1990) prints φιλοῦσ'.

33. M's reading ὥνοιτο must be replaced. Turnebus offers ὠνοῖτο, Robortello ὄνοιτο, and Casaubon οἴοιτο.

34. See MacKinnon 1978, 76–77.

35. Sommerstein (1977, 81n28) objects that ὄνοιτο "is not otherwise found in tragedy (or even lyric) or in any Attic writer." His preference for ὠνοῖτο is, however, linked with dowries, which have not been mentioned in the play thus far. By Aeschylus's time dowries were generally regarded not as a means of "purchasing" husbands but as a way of protecting the interests and well-being of wives and their natal families. On the possibility that lines 977–79 (which mention a dowry, φερνή) are interpolated see Taplin (1989, 228–38) and Sommerstein (1996a, 140n5).

36. FJW (1980, 2.272) claim that "the implicit rejection of Pelasgus' disjunction reflects the habitual tendency of the Danaids and Danaus to assimilate θέμις and similar objective standards to their own personal feelings, cf. 9–10."

37. See also MacKinnon 1978, 79.

38. Seaford (1987, 117) cites the presence of the adjective ἔχθραν at line 336 and adds that "φίλοι, 'kin,' . . . would normally also be 'dear.'"

39. On this understanding of ἀπαλλαγή see Seaford 1987, 117. Sommerstein (1977, 72) explains that "a bad marriage can easily be ended on the initiative of the wife or her family." Although distributing line 339 to Pelasgus gives him three lines in a row and interrupts the strict stichomythia, Sommerstein notes that Aeschylus does the same thing elsewhere: i.e. *Libation Bearers* 766–78.

40. FJW 1980, 2.306–7; MacKinnon 1978, 79.

41. Taplin (1989, 205) notes that the manner of Danaus's exit at line 503 is a strong indication of "how his role is deliberately made secondary and unenterprising." While departing characters ordinarily speak their own exit lines, in this instance Pelasgus has the final say (500–503).

42. The use of the terms πέπλοι (*peploi*, 235) and γυναικῶν ("women," 237) earlier in the play suggests that Pelasgus speaks only to women here.

43. According to Turner (2001, 46), "the Aegyptids alone pursue a marriage that a contemporary audience would have regarded as quite proper."

44. FJW 1980, 1.34–36.

45. Cf. the later Catullan *epithalamion* 62, whose chorus of girls is hostile to the evening star Hesperus because of his role in removing the bride from her natal home. See further Swift 2006, 135.

46. According to Sourvinou-Inwood (1987, 137), on vase paintings the act of grabbing a fleeing girl "denotes capture, and carries connotations of violence, defined by the context as sexual."

47. Jenkins 1983, 140: "Whether married by betrothal or taken by force, the bride had no power to decide her own destiny."

48. Jenkins 1983, 140.

49. See Sandin 2003, 48–49.

50. Lee 2004, 275.

51. King 1983, 120. She further notes (119) that "strangulation can . . . be culturally opposed to unwanted sex."

52. Zeitlin 1992, 229, with n. 97.

53. Cf. the scene with Candaules, his wife, and Gyges at Hdt. 1.11.

54. Taplin 1989, 211.

55. Taplin 1989, 213.

56. In the remainder of the trilogy we see his lack of control writ large. At first he apparently persuades, rather than forces, his daughters to marry the Aegyptids. He is, however, powerless to stop the growing love between Hypermestra and Lynceus. When he urges the women to kill their cousin-husbands, Hypermestra's disobedience trumps her sisters' obedience. And if Sicherl (1986) is correct about the oracle, Hypermestra's marital independence leads directly to Danaus's death.

57. Aeschylus is aware of the potential titillation involved in having the audience imagine the deaths of scantily clad young virgins; the chorus of *Agamemnon* describe the sacrifice of Iphigenia in voyeuristic fashion. They tell how her robe flows to the ground (239) before breaking off at the climactic moment: τὰ δ' ἔνθεν οὔτ' εἶδον οὔτ' ἐννέπω ("what happened next I neither saw nor say," 248).

58. On this translation of φυτόν see FJW 1980, 2.223.

59. FJW 1980, 2.220.

60. FJW 1980, 2.220.

61. For our purposes, the historical accuracy of these ethnographic claims is less important than the fact that Herodotus and other Greeks apparently believed them.

62. Vasunia 2001, 92: "[The historian] writes from an Hellenocentric perspective, regardless of the identity of the ethnic group he is describing and . . . uses symmetry and inversion to point to cultural difference."

63. Michelini 1978; McMahon 1996. According to Glazebrook (2005, 168), in the orators the adjective τοιοῦτον often implies "extreme behavior and is used of

an individual who is excessive in some way." She further notes that it is often used to characterize the wayward erotic behavior of *hetaerae*.

64. Hdt. 3.98.

65. Davidson 1997, 78. Simply drinking and dining among men who were not their relatives earned Greek women a bad reputation: see e.g. [Demosthenes] 59.22–40.

66. E.g. Aeschylus *Eumenides* 680–90; Lysias *Funeral Oration* 2.4–7.

67. On their representation on the Stoa Poikile see Castriota 2005. Stewart (1985, 582) notes that during the same period vases emphasize "large-scale panoramic battles" in which sexually mature women are shown locked in hand-to-hand combat with Greek men. In this guise the Amazons represent a challenge to "the cultural stereotype of a docile femininity by exhibiting not only an independent sexuality but also a vigorous and resourceful courage in battle" (584).

68. Stewart 1995, 578.

69. Stewart 1995, 586.

70. Stewart 1995, 589.

71. Stewart 1995, 587–89.

72. Mitchell (2006, 213n23) follows Ruth Veness in claiming that Amazons "represent a complex and shifting exploration of the dangers of women, and especially those women who have been brought as wives into the household."

73. FJW 1980, 2.223.

74. FJW 1980, 2.224. Cf. Hdt. 7.90; Thuc. 1.112.2.

75. FJW 1980, 2.225.

76. Also troubling to Sandin (2003, 156–57) are the placement of τ' after noun and attribute in line 282 and the lack of a dative for εἰκώς (283).

77. Sommerstein 1977, 71.

78. FJW (1980, 2.223) do not categorically reject the possibility of a link to coinage.

79. Sandin 2003, 157. He concedes that the use of the noun χαρακτήρ to mean "letter" or "symbol" is unattested prior to the second century BCE.

80. Sommerstein 1977, 69–70.

81. LSJ s.v. I.3.

82. LSJ (s.v. I.2) claim references to metalworkers occur rarely despite Euripides *Alcestis* 5. *Suppliant Women*'s subsequent description of Zeus as φυτουργὸς αὐτόχειρ ἄναξ, / γένους παλαιόφρων μέγας / τέκτων (592–94) associates the god with the realms of gardening and craftsmanship.

83. LSJ s.v. πλήσσω I.3.

84. Sommerstein 1977, 70.

85. Sommerstein 1977, 70.

86. Aeschylus's coinage metaphor likely derived from first-hand familiarity with specific issues. Kraay (1976, 301–2) notes that several Cypriote poleis minted coins with likenesses of Aphrodite during the fifth and fourth centuries. For instance, the so-called Citium hoard, discovered in 1933, contains a number

of staters from Lapethus with a head of Aphrodite on the obverse. The ca. 480 deposit date of this hoard suggests that such coins were circulating in the Athenian sphere of interest during the second half of the 460s.

87. LSJ (s.v. I.2) claim that ἡ Κυπρία is equivalent to ἡ Κύπρις. Gantz (1978, 281) finds it "hard to believe that Κύπριος does not represent in some fashion an Aeschylean pun on the presence of Kypris within the Danaids."

88. Sommerstein (1977, 71) suggests that the places of εἰκώς and Κύπριος be exchanged and that the latter be emended to the dative Κυπρίοις; these changes seem unnecessary.

89. In this regard εἰκώς functions as an antonym of coinage that is κίβδηλος, "adulterated." On the latter see Rhodes 1993, 576.

90. Wohl 1998, xxvi–xxviii.

91. Kurke 1999, 181–82.

92. On the connection between apples, courtship, and marriage in ancient Greece see Winkler 1990a, 173, 185.

93. On the stereotype linking foreignness and promiscuity in women see Glazebrook 2005, 163. Although Athenian women could certainly divorce and remarry without being termed promiscuous, they normally did so at the behest of male relatives rather than of their own volition. By contrast, Helen's agency in departing for Troy makes her the object of innuendo at e.g. Aeschylus *Agamemnon* 448 (ἀλλοτρίας διαὶ γυναικός).

94. According to Henderson (1991, 8), sexual metaphors in tragedy (as opposed to Old Comedy) tend toward the oblique. In the women-as-furrows conceit at Sophocles *Oedipus the King* 1211 and Euripides *Phoenician Women* 18, for instance, "the respectable nature of agricultural terminology, and the remoteness of the image, save it [from obscenity]."

95. Garvie (2006, 233) suggests a number of thematic connections between the trilogy and the satyr play.

96. Hose (2006) offers a cogent discussion of the order of the plays, concluding that the evidence does not establish whether *Suppliant Women* came first or second. See also Mitchell 2006, 208–9.

97. Garvie 2006, 164.

98. Garvie 2006, 164.

99. Radt 2009, 158. On the textual issues see Garvie 2006, 228.

100. Garvie 2006, 228–29.

101. Garvie 2006, 229–30.

102. Radt 2009, 159–60. The fragment is preserved at Athenaeus 13.600b.

103. For bibliography see Garvie 2006, 205–6 with nn.

104. While Pausanias gives no motive for her disobedience, other accounts say either that she fell in love with Lynceus or that he did not attempt to consummate the marriage. For the sources see Garvie 2006, 165.

105. E.g. Diamantopoulos 1957, 222. Aphrodite's action might thus resemble Apollo's defense of Orestes in *Eumenides*. Yet it is dangerous to rely

too heavily on the *Oresteia* to reconstruct the Danaid trilogy: see Garvie 2006, 184, 210.

106. The prosecution of Orestes in *Eumenides* results from his murder of his mother, not his disagreement with her. Föllinger (2007) notes the prominence of father-daughter conflict in Aeschylus, concluding (21) that although his dramas demonstrate "daß die Affirmation der väterlichen Macht keineswegs mit positiven Folgen verbunden sein muß, weisen sie auf die prekäre Balance im Machtgefälle der Generationen hin."

107. LSJ (s.v. I) define it as an "adventure, enterprise, daring or shameless act."

108. See Bakewell 2008a, 304.

109. Garvie 2006, 206.

110. D. S. Robertson 1924, 52.

111. Garvie 2006, 208–9.

112. The Furies assume this function in *Eumenides* because Clytemnestra has no surviving kin willing to perform the task.

113. On the question of whether Aeschylus brought Aegyptus to Argos at any point in the trilogy see Garvie 2006, 180, 209.

114. Gruppe (cited by Garvie [2006, 203]) suggests that the second play of the trilogy may have ended with a wedding song (ὑμέναιος κατακοιμητικός) leading the newlyweds to their chamber; this would correspond to the song (ὑμέναιος διεγερτικός, fr. 43) meant to rouse them at the start of *Danaids*.

115. Athenaeus 13.600b: "Aeschylus in *Danaids* leads in Aphrodite saying . . ." (ὁ σεμνότατος Αἰσχύλος ἐν ταῖς Δαναίσιν αὐτὴν παράγει τὴν Ἀφροδίτην λέγουσαν . . .).

116. Garvie 2006, 170.

117. Garvie 2006, 170.

118. Auffarth (1995) has shown that the Danaids' importance for subsequent Argive genealogy is not incompatible with their status as dangerous outsiders. As he puts it (43), "The myth of the Danaides stands in sharp contrast to the principles of the *polis*. . . . Their attitude would lead to the death of the *polis* in the next generation, i.e. they would kill the *polis*."

119. Winnington-Ingram 1961, 143.

120. E.g. Hyginus *Fabulae* 168, 170. Cf. Ovid *Heroides* 14; Servius *ad Aeneid* 10.497. See further Keuls 1974.

121. On the separate possibility that Aeschylus likened the Danaids to nymphs, and on their subsequent connection with the streams of Argos, see, however, Bachvarova 2009.

122. While Garvie (2006, 210) adds that "it is possible that the final Exodus takes them out to their death," he offers no conjecture as to how this might happen.

123. Von Fritz 1936, 265: "Bleiben nur zwei Möglichkeiten des Abschlusses

übrig: entweder völliger Untergang der Danaiden . . . oder Wiederherstellung der göttlichen Ordnungen durch Entsühnung." See also Winnington-Ingram 1961, 143.

124. On the forty-ninth daughter Amymone (who is sometimes twinned with Hypermestra) see Sommerstein 1996a, 151–52.

125. Lines 112–16.

126. Von Fritz (1936, 131) notes, "Daß bei Pindar von der Entsühnung nichts steht, ist kein Beweis dagegen, daß sie von alters her dazu gehörte. Denn es entspricht dem Stil des Chorliedes, daß nur ein ganz kleiner Ausschnitt aus der Sage andeutend erwähnt wird."

127. Lines 1–4.

128. Sommerstein 2008, 282.

129. Murnaghan (2005) provides an overview of the relationship between the Danaids and the choral songs of Greek *parthenoi*.

130. LSJ s.v. ὀπαδοί. Sophocles uses the word of the goddess Artemis (*Oedipus at Colonus* 1093), while Euripides applies it to both male (*Medea* 53) and female (*Alcestis* 136) slaves. In the passage most like that of *Suppliant Women*, Hyllus combines an address to his male retainers as ὀπαδοί with the plural imperative αἴρετ' ("raise up").

131. FJW 1980, 3.306–7.

132. FJW 1980, 3.306–8. Sommerstein, who once (1977, 76–80) took the side of the maids, now concedes (1996a, 140) that "assign[ing] it to the Argives probably requires less special pleading."

133. Garvie (2006, 195) discusses the problems with emending the masculine adjective φίλοις to the feminine φίλαις to modify ὀπάοσιν at line 954.

134. Taplin 1989, 228–30. The main difficulties (from the point of view of stagecraft) are that no song marks the maids' entry and that no notice is taken of them until line 977. According to Taplin, it is (233) "impossible for a group of extras the same size as the chorus to remain inconspicuously out of the way for 975 lines. . . . Twelve actors, let alone fifty, cannot simply retire inconspicuously and sit or stand still 'conveniently grouped' for the best part of the play. . . . It is incredible that a chorus of desperate fugitive exiles should be the only chorus in all of surviving Greek tragedy to trail around a crowd of permanent attendants."

135. Taplin 1989, 200, 220.

136. On the meaning of the imperative ὑποδέξασθε (1022) see FJW 1980, 3.312–13.

137. Bachvarova (2009, 304) notes that "the ionic meter of the first three strophic pairs of the song [lines 1018–61], the one extended passage of ionics in the play, fits traditional marriage and love songs as we know them from Sappho and Alcaeus."

138. Bachvarova 2009, 303.

139. Following Henri Weil, FJW (1980, 3.317) note that M's reading γάμος may have arisen as a gloss on τέλος . . . Κυθερείας.

140. With Weil's emendation of line 1034 (ἀμελὴς ἐσμός), the sense is that "this kindly swarm is not heedless of Aphrodite" (Κύπριδος ⟨δ'⟩ οὐκ ἀμελὴς ἐσμὸς ὅδε εὔφρων). Seaford (1987, 114) notes that the noun phrase ἐσμὸς ὅδε may refer to the Danaids as well.

141. The noun τρίβοι may also have a more frankly erotic dimension ("rubbings"). As Tyrrell (1980, 45) notes, the etymologically related word ἱστοτρίβης at *Agamemnon* 1443 "was most likely coined by Aeschylus and from elements having recognizably obscene connotations."

142. On the personification see FJW 1980, 3.327.

143. Lines 1050–51: μετὰ πολλᾶν δὲ γάμων ἅδε τελευτά / προτερᾶν πέλοι γυναικῶν.

144. FJW 1980, 3.333.

145. On the various possible permutations see FJW 1980, 3.335–36.

146. Seaford 1987, 114. His n. 93 lists several Sapphic fragments deriving from similar songs.

147. For the reading δίκαι Δίκαν see FJW 1980, 3.344–45.

148. *Eumenides* 1031 refers to the εὐάνδροι συμφοραί attendant on the Erinyes' presence in Athens.

149. FJW 1980, 3.339. Zeitlin (1992, 227) concludes that "the story of Io . . . reads like a more extravagant symbolic version than the story of the Danaids of the precarious circumstances surrounding the transition of the virgin into matrimony."

150. Vernant (1990, 39) holds that "an inquiry into the true nature of *kratos*" is one of the play's main themes.

151. On implications of Argos as the dramatic locale see Grossmann 1970, 118–19.

152. Von Fritz 1936, 259: "Daß der freie Entschluß der Danaiden Anlaß und Ausgangspunkt der ganzen Handlung ist, gibt diesen zweifellos in gewissem Sinn etwas Männliches oder hebt sie zum mindesten über das Weibliche, wie es die Zeit Aeschlus zu sehen pflegte, hinaus."

153. Even women relatively accepting of the *status quo* create difficulties. On e.g. Sophocles's *Trachiniae* see Wohl 1998. According to her (36), "Deianira's struggle for subject status thus both questions and ultimately reaffirms the categories within which the self is formulated. It reasserts the hegemony of the aristocratic and male; Deianira can be a valid subject only to the degree to which she can approximate these qualities, and, as her death shows, she can never approximate them fully."

154. Griffith 1999, 1–2. Scullion (2002, 85–86) places it somewhat earlier, perhaps ca. 450.

155. At line 806 she addresses the chorus as citizens of her native land, ὦ γᾶς πατρίας πολῖται.

156. Murnaghan (1986, 198–200) traces Antigone's rejection of the institutions forming the basis for polis life. Cf. Lysias 22.5, where the prosecutor implies that metics reject the city's *nomoi* in favor of self-interest. See above ch. 2.

157. Rehm 1994, 63, 182n16.

158. For the reflection of their differences in their speech see Griffith 2001, 127.

159. Griffith (1999, 215) notes that this term refers not only to care for the dead, but also to the guardianship of a female or minor relative.

160. E.g. lines 458–59, 469–70, 509, 942.

161. The text cited below is Griffith 1999.

162. E.g. Rehm 1994, 64.

163. Griffith 1999, 272.

164. Whitehead (1977, 36) claims that "pathos is the keynote of this cluster of three metic metaphors." On his reading the passages are akin to other metic references evoking death and grief, such as *Agamemnon* 57 and *Persians* 319.

165. See lines 773–76. Following line 943 Antigone departs via an *eisodos*; this type of exit was often associated with a move outside the city. On such symbolic use of *eisodoi* see Padel 1990, 343.

166. E.g. Rehm 1994, 63. On the similarity of marriage and death for women see further Rehm 1994, 29; Foley 1994, 104.

167. Rehm 1994, 65.

168. On this reversal see Ormand 1999, 82.

169. Ormand (1999, 92) notes the similarity of their match to those marriages deplored by the speaker of Isaeus 3 (*On the Estate of Pyrrhos*). In both instances men pick women of questionable worth; they act based on *eros* rather than more practical considerations; they do so despite disapproval from relatives, and to the detriment of their *oikoi*.

170. Dougherty (1993, 66) notes that in colonization myths, "the narrative pattern depends on the tendency to associate the female with elements of nature, particularly with the land itself."

171. On attempts to assign Helen a value in *Agamemnon* see Wohl 1998, 83–99.

172. Known from e.g. Menander *Perikeiromene* 1013–14.

173. Bakewell (2008b) argues that the fourth-century law banning mixed-status marriages cited at *Neaera* 16 derives from just such a fear.

174. The text of *Medea* used here is Mastronarde 2002. At the outset of the play, the nurse describes her mistress as "inhabiting this Corinthian land" (κατῴκει τήνδε γῆν Κορινθίαν, 10), and says her sojourn there delights the citizens among whom she has arrived (ἁνδάνουσα μὲν / φυγὰς πολίταις ὧν ἀφίκετο χθόνα, 11–12). Rehm (1994, 97) notes that "her position mirrors that faced by foreign wives after the enactment of Perikles' Citizenship Law." See also McClure 1999b, 379–80. On the text of line 12 see Mastronarde 2002, 165. One of the play's recurring themes is the different sort of behavior expected from

foreigners and citizens; see e.g. lines 222–24. Pace Cohen (2000, 51n13), Mastronarde (2002, 207) rightly regards ἀστός and πολίτης as equivalent here.

175. The tradition that Medea murdered her brother takes on added significance in this regard.

176. See e.g. his remarks at lines 547–50.

177. When Aegeus enters from Delphi (669), he does so with marriage on his mind. On the chorus see lines 638–44. Mastronarde (2002, 279) claims that "the chorus is asking that [Aphrodite] recognize (as the chorus themselves do) the superior value of peaceful unions and determine her appointment of sexual experience intelligently, in accordance with that recognition."

178. Lines 235–36: κἀν τῶιδ' ἀγὼν μέγιστος, ἢ κακὸν λαβεῖν / ἢ χρηστόν ("And the greatest competition lies in this, whether one takes a bad or a good [husband]").

179. Foley 2001, 259. She also notes Medea's use of the active (as opposed to middle) participle γαμοῦσα at line 606.

180. At line 8 the chorus describe Medea as ἔρωτι θυμὸν ἐκπλαγεῖς' Ἰάσονος ("struck in her heart by love of Jason") when she departed Iolchis.

181. Lines 548–49.

182. Note his purpose clause at lines 559–60: ἀλλ' ὡς, τὸ μὲν μέγιστον, οἰκοῖμεν καλῶς / καὶ μὴ σπανιζοίμεσθα ("So that, most importantly, our household may fare well, and we may lack for nothing"). Significantly, he expects his second marriage to produce new children.

183. Boedeker 1997, 142.

184. Forms of ὀνίημι: 254, 533, 567, 618, 1025. Forms of λύω with the meaning of λυσιτελεῖ, "to profit, gain": 566, 1112, 1362.

185. Boedeker 1997, 144–45.

186. Boedeker 1997, 147.

187. Dunkle 1969.

188. For the tradition see the fragments of Sophocles's *Aegeus* and Knox 1979, 295. At *Medea* 714–15 Medea urges Aegeus to accept her at his hearth, praying that the gods will grant him a childbearing love and prosperity. Two lines later she promises to see to these matters personally: παύσω γέ σ' ὄντ' ἄπαιδα καὶ παίδων γονὰς / σπεῖραί σε θήσω ("I will put an end to your childlessness, and will establish you in a position to sow descendants"). As she departs in the chariot of the Sun, she says she goes to Athens "to dwell with Aegeus the son of Pandion" (Αἰγεῖ συνοικήσουσα τῶι Πανδίονος, 1385). According to Mastronarde (2002, 384), the future participle συνοικήσουσα "suggest[s] to the audience a future in which Medea becomes Aegeus' wife."

189. Persistent Athenian unease about the implications of marriages between citizens and metics crops up throughout the fifth and fourth centuries, surfacing most visibly in the prosecution of Neaera on a *graphe xenias* in the 340s. See Bakewell 2008b.

190. Maitland (1992, 26) argues that Greek tragedies often present a discrepancy between "the objectives and behaviour of the great aristocratic clans

and of those families which were neither so wealthy nor so politically influential. A dichotomy is thus presented between dynastic interests and the interests of the ordinary family as a well-regulated part of the Athenian city-state." See also Griffith 1995.

191. Stewart 1995, 588.

192. Rhodes 1993, 334.

193. In this regard they resemble the fourth-century courtesan Neaera, who was depicted as having sex in public with different men, accumulating wealth in various forms, and scheming to establish her own family at Athens with herself as its head. According to Patterson (1994, 199–200), "Apollodoros presents Neaira, and her infiltration into one Athenian oikos, as a threat to (or violation of) the collective identity of all Athenian oikoi."

194. Stewart 1995, 580.

Chapter 4. Sons of Earth

1. Grethlein 2003, 89; Rosivach 1987, 298n15.

2. Cohen (2000, 79–103) rejects the idea that Athenians actually thought they were descended from the earth. According to him (83), "no fifth-century author deals explicitly with Athenian self-perception, except for Thucydides, who rejects the mythological tradition of autochthony." Yet Thucydides regularly takes pains (e.g. 1.20) to distinguish his views from those of the many. Moreover, Cohen neglects the possibility of finding Athenian self-perceptions refracted in sources such as tragedy. His entire discussion of autochthony makes no reference to Aeschylus's *Suppliant Women*. Ultimately, Cohen must engage in a bit of slippage to make his case: he concludes (103) not that Athenians didn't *believe* they were autochthonous, but that this belief was (by our lights) incredible and untrue.

3. Taken together, they constitute an ancient instance of the "deep mapping" described by Pearson and Shanks (2001, 64–65).

4. Pelasgus's memorialization of Apis calls to mind the genre of the *epitaphios*, in which the achievements of previous generations are used to challenge the living to a similar display of virtue.

5. See Manville (1990), who poses a hypothetical question (101): "If one day a stranger appears in a rural neighborhood, where and under what conditions can he begin to dig with his spade, and raise crops for himself? Where and under what conditions can he not? In most agrarian communities, the distinction between 'insiders' and 'outsiders,' critical to the concept of citizenship, depends on rights and access to land."

6. Taplin (1989, 204) claims that Aeschylus intentionally "put[s] [Danaus] in the background and pay[s] no attention to him."

7. Should they arrive in chariots (see Taplin 1989, 201), they would have an even more martial appearance.

8. On the *proagon* see Csapo and Slater 1994, 105, 109–10.

9. See lines 917, 919.
10. See ch. 2.
11. Legitimate authority: *Iliad* 1.234–39; practical force: *Iliad* 2.2.65.
12. Podlecki 1966, 46.
13. LSJ (s.v.) note that while in Homer ἔτης is always used in the plural to denote "clansmen," in classical times it assumes the meaning (II) of "citizen," especially (in the singular) "a private citizen, [as] opp[osed] to those who hold office." A scholion to the Aeschylus passage (Smith 1976, 71) glosses ἐτῆς as equivalent to "demesman" (δημότης). See also Aeschylus fr. 281a, line 28 (Radt 2009, 381).
14. FJW (1980, 2.200) translate τηρὸν ἱερόρραβδον as "warden with sacred staff."
15. Fraenkel (1950, 2.329), citing Pfeiffer, notes that in Aeschylus the adverbs ὀρθῶς, ἐτητύμως, ἀληθῶς, and εὐλόγως are often used in connection with names denoting "character, action, or destiny."
16. The deictic words were perhaps accompanied by bold hand gestures.
17. E.g. *Iliad* 2.681; Euripides *Phoenissae* 256; *Orestes* 692. See also Sandin 2003, 147–48; J. Hall 1997, 72.
18. E. Hall 1989, 171–72.
19. Thus Plato *Politicus* 269b; Aristotle *De generatione animalium* 762b29.
20. The contrast with another "earthborn" ruler, γηγενὴς Ἐριχθόνιος (Euripides *Ion* 21), is suggestive. The Athenian's proper name is derived from an adjective (χθόνιος); the Argive's from the noun itself (χθών).
21. FJW (1980, 2.204) note that according to other sources and traditions, Pelasgus himself is "earth-born" (αὐτόχθων).
22. On the complicated relationship between Erechtheus and Erichthonius see Loraux 1993, 46–47.
23. Loraux (1993, 54–55), discussing the representations of eponymous heroes in vase painting.
24. J. Hall (1997, 77) notes that "while eponymous ethnic ancestors could serve to explain origins and the kin-ties that gradually came to be recognized between geographically distant populations in Greece, their universal applicability was expedited by the fact that they were rather shallow personalities to whom few, if any, mythological adventures could be attached."
25. Loraux (1993, 64) argues that "the masculine dream of the Greeks" was "to have a child outside the limits of procreative activity."
26. Loraux 1993, 66. See further Saxonhouse 1986, 259.
27. In ancient Greek, land was ordinarily gendered female. *Suppliant Women*'s depiction of Argos as male is thus anomalous, and may go beyond the customary elision of women's role in procreation. Cf. Apollo's argument at *Eumenides* 657–61, and Athena's subsequent endorsement (736–38) of his claim.
28. *Suppliant Women* leaves unclear the relationships (temporal and otherwise) between Io's return to human form, her impregnation, and her son's birth.

29. The priestesses of Hera at Argos were important enough figures to be used as chronographic markers. The fifth-century writer Hellanicus of Lesbos compiled a list of them (Jacoby *FGH* 4 F 74), and Thucydides uses Chrysis's tenure in the office to help date the start of the Peloponnesian War (2.2.1).

30. *Eumenides* begins in similar fashion, with the Pythia reciting competing female and male claims to the shrine at Delphi.

31. Rosivach 1987, 301–5.

32. While Saxonhouse (1986, 256) rightly argues that "an autochthonous society . . . must . . . be xenophobic," she wrongly claims that it must also be "aristocratic." Her basic contention is that the myth's emphasis on land ignored the sea, which was historically speaking the source of Athens's imperial power and the reason for the political rise of the thetes. But the myth is not aristocratic, insofar as it makes even the lowliest Athenians sharers in the land. A laudatory epigram describing the honors bestowed on the supporters of Thrasyboulus refers to the entire δῆμος as παλαίχθων (Aeschines *Against Ctesiphon* 190). Even democrats fiercely opposed to oligarchy could clearly be praised as autochthonous.

33. See ch. 2.

34. Loraux 1993, 45.

35. The duty is often described as a debt that must be repaid; see e.g. Aeschylus *Seven against Thebes* 20.

36. J. Harrison (1977, 267) claims that eponymous heroes often received their names from their peoples, rather than vice versa.

37. Sandin 2003, 148.

38. Sandin 2003, 148.

39. Grethlein (2003, 56) comments that "dieser Exkurs . . . zeugt von der Bedeutung von Territorium und Geschichte, besonders der 'charter myths,' für die kollektive Identität." It may also have been intended to remind the audience that the Argos of the play was not coterminous with the contemporary polis of the Argolid.

40. As does Prometheus's prophecy of Io's wanderings in *Prometheus Bound* (786–819).

41. E. Hall 1989, 75–76.

42. Many spectators will have had first-hand experience of foreign cities and lands (though not Epirus) from their service on Delian League campaigns. Kennedy (2006) assigns greater thematic significance to Aeschylus's geographical excursuses, arguing that in *Eumenides* they map and justify an Athenian sphere of influence. Her tentative attempt (38) to extend this analysis to *Suppliant Women* is less convincing; the Argives are concerned with safeguarding their own land against encroachment, not extending their dominion over others. While the chorus of *Eumenides* salute the war god as one of the patron deities of Athens, the Danaids describe him as "undancing, unmusical, [and] tear-begetting" (ἄχορον, ἀκίθαριν, δακρυογόνον Ἄρη, 681).

43. Sandin 2003, 150.

44. FJW (1980, 2.212) read ἃ δή, "ones which . . ."

45. Sandin 2003, 150. FJW (1980 2.210) express the same view more obliquely: "this excursus into local history is less obviously relevant to the Coryphaeus' question (247–8) than the preceding description of Pelasgus and his empire (250–9) by which it is balanced."

46. Hdt. 3.27–8. See Sandin 2003, 66–67, 105.

47. Sandin (2003, 150) notes the resemblance of Pelasgus's Apis to Asclepius.

48. See e.g. the analysis of lines 370–75 in ch. 2 above.

49. Bakewell 1997, 218.

50. FJW 1980, 2.201–2. On the way Aeschylus interweaves medical imagery and political themes in the *Oresteia*, see Irby-Massie 2008, 142n31.

51. The fact that the Danaids are violently pursued means that the Argive plain may be soaked with blood (αἱμάξαι πέδον, 477) in another way as well. Later in the play the Egyptian pursuers are described as serpents with evil intent (δρακόντων δυσφρόνων, 511). See FJW 1980, 2.201–2.

52. The parallel between the Danaids and the serpents is not exact. The serpents may resemble the Argives in their autochthony; see lines 265–66.

53. Sandin 2003, 151.

54. Sandin 2003, 152.

55. Taplin (1989, 221) notes that "insults, threats, and taunts provide the most common use of [lines cast at a departing back]."

56. On the possibility that choruses were ordinarily composed of ephebes and that their dancing resembled military maneuvers, see Winkler 1990b.

57. Aristophanes *Frogs* 1021. The shadow combat ends more favorably for the Argives than does the subsequent combat occurring (off-stage?) in the remainder of the trilogy.

58. Hdt. 1.2.2: "The Persians say Io arrived in Egypt thus (the Greeks disagree), and this first began the injustices."

59. Thuc. 1.135.3: πέμπουσι μετὰ τῶν Λαδεδαιμονίων ἑτοίμων ὄντων ξυνδιώκειν ἄνδρας οἷς εἴρητο ἄγειν ὅπου ἂν περιτύχωσιν.

60. Podlecki 1966, 55.

61. On the antitheses see E. Hall 1989.

62. I.e. traveling in a covered women's coach (Plutarch *Themistocles* 26).

63. Thuc. 1.138.1.

64. Plutarch *Themistocles* 28.1.

65. The contrast between Themistocles and the Danaids grows stronger: (1) the earlier in the 460s we date his arrival at the Persian court; and (2) the later in the 460s we date *Suppliant Women*. On the date of the play see the introduction.

66. The phrase λοιμὸς ἀνδρῶν may not be a reference to actual disease, but rather a metaphorical extension of the subject of the verb αἱματίσαι, to which it stands in apposition.

67. Dawe 1965, 70. Cf. *Eumenides* 976–83, where the Furies pray that *sta-*

sis, "insatiate of evils," may never stain the land with the blood of citizens. On the broader similarities between *Suppliant Women* and *Eumenides* see the conclusion.

68. FJW 1980, 3.32.

69. Thuc. 3.82.1. See also 3.83.1.

70. Thus FJW 1980, 3.48. West (1990) prints M's βοάν.

71. Cf. line 401.

72. Ch. 2.

73. The *demos*'s insistence on accountability affected *inter alia* military recordkeeping. See Bakewell 2007.

74. Later in the fifth century, generals were frequently deposed via *apocheirotonia*, and often brought to trial. If Hansen (1999, 217) is correct, between 432 and 355 "in every board of ten generals there were probably at least two who, in the course of their military careers, would be denounced . . . and the first *eisangelia* was usually their last, for it usually ended with a condemnation and the death sentence."

75. Here the adjective δημοκράντου contains a possible link to *Suppliant Women*. On the prominence of -κραίνω verbs in the play see Bakewell 2008a, 304–5.

76. Prior to the development of Hellenistic siege weaponry and tactics, one of the surest ways to capture a walled city was to rely on help from within. Given their uncertain loyalties, metics were suspect in this regard. It is no coincidence that in recording Athenian garrison numbers at the start of the war, Thucydides (2.13.7) has Pericles list older citizens together with metics, as it is improbable that the latter would have been left alone to guard the fortifications. See further Goldhill 2007, 146–47.

77. On Danaus as a tyrant-in-waiting, see ch.2.

78. Taplin 1989, 201.

79. On the importance of what happens off-stage in tragedy see Padel 1990.

80. Burford (1993, 30) notes the conceptual opposition between ἀτιμία and γαμόρος.

81. LSJ s.v. γαμόροι.

82. *AthPol* fr. 2.; the term used is actually γεωμόροι, which LSJ equate with γαμόροι (I.2).

83. The emendation proposed by Dobree for *Eumenides* 890 refers to the Erinyes (in the dative singular) as τῇσδε γαμόρωι χθονός. But Athena's use of the noun here appears, if not deceptive, at least calculated to win over her opponents. Sommerstein (1989, 256) notes that "the word suggests . . . that the Erinyes are to become part of the Athenian civic body. . . . Only at the end . . . do we learn that they are to be μέτοικοι, honoured residents in the πόλις but not members of it."

84. Pelasgus says (253), "the Pelasgian people reap the harvest of this soil" (γένος Πελασγῶν τήνδε καρποῦται χθόνα).

85. Extrapolating from e.g. the fate foretold for Eteocles and Polyneices at *Seven against Thebes* 820.

86. According to Todd (1993, 143), at Athens *atimia* "was regularly lifelong." It was often accompanied by various forms of shaming: e.g., exclusion from the Agora and temples (Aeschines *Against Ctesiphon* 176). Thomas (1989, 65) claims that "the list of public debtors in the Acropolis, probably a wooden tablet, was—and was meant to be—frequently consulted."

87. Cf. the speaker's attack on Philon at Lysias 31.6. See further Thucydides 6.92, where the exiled Alcibiades puts a new spin on the familiar tropes in his remarks to the Spartan assembly.

88. On the debate over when democracy actually begins at Athens see e.g. Morris and Raaflaub 1998.

89. Manville 1990, 145–46.

90. Plutarch's account (*Solon* 18.1–2) adds little of value.

91. Hansen 1999, 43: "Wealth is measured in produce, not in capital. . . . The only relevant produce is crops." See also Rhodes 1993, 142.

92. E.g. fr. 13 West 43–62.

93. Pace e.g. Waters 1960, 183. Rhodes (1993, 142) notes although "it has been widely assumed that later generations applied a new means of classification, with a monetary basis . . . there is no evidence that it was ever made."

94. De Ste. Croix 2004, 33.

95. De Ste. Croix 2004, 34–35.

96. De Ste. Croix 1956.

97. For a sympathetic survey of the difficulties besetting Greek farmers see Hanson 1995, 127–78.

98. French 1961, 511.

99. Rosivach 2002, 38.

100. De Ste. Croix 2004, 42.

101. According to Foxhall (1997, 129), "partaking in the *polis* and its power structures was entangled with land ownership from the start."

102. LSJ s.v. ἱπποτροφέω.

103. Whitehead 1981, 284.

104. Whitehead 1981; Van Wees 2006; Raaflaub 2007, 128–36.

105. Rhodes (1993, 138) sees the *pentecosiomedimnoi* as a later graft onto a preexisting tripartite social structure consisting of *hippeis*, *zeugitae*, and *thetes*. According to him *pentecosiomedimnoi* were superwealthy cavalrymen grouped into a class all their own.

106. Whitehead (1981, 285–86) has argued that the nominal suffix (-ιτης) in the term *zeugites* refers to one who is himself yoked—i.e. to those beside him in the phalanx.

107. For comparison with the *comitia centuriata* in ancient Rome see Raaflaub 2007, 128–29.

108. See e.g. Bugh 1988, 33–34; de Ste. Croix 2004, 15.

109. Hdt. 7.144.

110. See Raaflaub 2007, 130.

111. Hanson 1995, 112.

112. Hanson 1995, 114–15.

113. Significantly, *Suppliant Women* depicts its Argives as either cavalrymen or hoplites. At lines 182–83 Danaus describes the approaching host as "a crowd bearing shields and waving spears . . . with horses and curving chariots" (ὄχλον δ' ὑπασπιστῆρα καὶ δορυσσόον / . . . ξὺν ἵπποις καμπύλοις τ' ὀχήμασιν). On the possibility that they make a mounted entrance see Taplin 1989, 201.

114. For the view that *hektemoroi* were sharecroppers rather than landowners see e.g. Forsdyke 2006, 338.

115. Forsdyke (2006, 338) suggests that they resembled migrant workers who tilled others' fields for wages rather than produce.

116. *Rhetoric* 1361a21.

117. Burford 1993, 19.

118. Manville 1990, 106.

119. Manville 1990, 108.

120. By contrast, those who were ostracized lost neither their membership in the community nor their possessions.

121. On the *antidosis* procedure see Todd 1993, 120; MacDowell 2009, 38–40, 148–50.

122. Sickinger 1998, 55. On the registers themselves see Whitehead 1986, 35n130.

123. E.g. Thomas 1989.

124. Hansen 1985, 83–89; see further Christ 2001, 416.

125. Rosivach 2002, 42–43.

126. Rhodes (1993, 144–45) defends the traditional understanding of the accompanying inscription—namely, that Anthemion was celebrating his change in status.

127. She suggests (personal correspondence) that the couplet cited by *Ath-Pol* includes "a fragment of satirical elegiac verse, mistakenly associated with an Acropolis dedication by either the author or one of his sources."

128. Scafuro 1994.

129. On the conceptual underpinning of *horoi* see Cole 2004, 45–46. See also Ober, who claims (2006, 477) that "the base-line meaning of *horos*, the meaning with which Solon and his archaic contemporaries were working, was 'marker of distinction between this and that.'"

130. Finley 1981, 63.

131. Fr. 36.3–7.

132. Rhodes 2006, 252–53.

133. By contrast, Bintliff (2006, 329) argues that peasants in Solon's time were required to work their masters' fields and to yield much of the produce from their own as well. As he puts it, "By taking away the markers of tied

tenancy on the peasants' *own* plots, Solon 'freed' them to be worked purely for the benefit of the peasants, leaving the personal estates of the upper class as they were, but perhaps still with the peasant duty to work on these, left in place."

134. In fr. 36, the repatriation follows directly upon the *seisachtheia* (lines 8–15).

135. Solon also claims to have freed a number of Athenians enslaved at home. The similarity of the phrasing is noteworthy. The earth (Γῆ) is described as πρόσθεν δὲ δουλεύουσα, νῦν ἐλευθέρη ("formerly a slave, now free," 36.7). As for the people, Solon claims τοὺς δ' ἐνθάδ' αὐτοῦ δουλίην ἀεικέα / ἔχοντας . . . ἐλευθέρους ἔθηκα ("those holding shameful slavery here I set free," 36.13–15).

136. In this regard, they bore a resemblance to Aeschylus's Danaids, whose foreign speech stands out upon their arrival in Argos. See ch. 2.

137. Fr. 37.9–10. According to Manville (1990, 126), "the metaphor of the boundary stone was certainly apt. For a general theme in all of Solon's reforms was the creation of boundaries—spatial, legal, and even psychological."

138. Ch. 1.

139. LSJ s.v. 2. See e.g. Laius in Sophocles *Oedipus the King* 751.

140. LSJ s.v. I. The word is frequently used of eponymous heroes.

141. Other snake-killers with a comparable function include Apollo at Delphi, Cadmus at Thebes, and Heracles at Lerna.

142. Graham 1983, 59: "the principle that the colonists should participate on equal terms had definite practical force even among oligarchic peoples."

143. An inscription describing the foundation of Cyrene (Meiggs and Lewis 1988, no. 5) refers to both Apollo (line 11) and Battos (line 26) as ἀρχαγέτας.

144. Note the phrases ἐπὶ πολύ and οἱ πλείους in the Greek original.

145. Habash 1995, 559, 567.

146. Ostwald 1986, 505.

147. Whitehead 1984, 57–58.

148. According to Bakewell (1999b), Lysias exploits the contrast between bad citizens and good metics.

149. Thucydides (1.2.2) links early migrations in Greece to people's belief that they could obtain the necessities of life anywhere (τῆς τε καθ' ἡμέραν ἀναγκαίου τροφῆς πανταχοῦ ἂν ἡγούμενοι ἐπικρατεῖν).

150. Jones 2004, 14.

151. Papadopoulos (2002, 193) claims that "potters like the Parian Ad Painter and the Ram Jug Painter, among others, provide a potential glimpse of Cycladic immigrants working in Athens generations before the reforms of Solon."

152. Plutarch *Solon* 24.

153. On the Peisistratid reshaping of the Agora see Anderson 2003, 88–92.

154. Dunbabin (1950) published a Corinthianizing bowl made of Athenian clay and likely dating to the second quarter of the sixth century.

155. Demosthenes (*Against Eubulides* 30–31) implies that working in the Agora could be a source of reproach for citizens. See Loomis 2003, 293, 298.

156. Bäbler 1998, 48n223.

157. Randall 1953, 201. Of the remaining 41 men, 20 (i.e. 19 percent of the total) are slaves. The social status of the final 21 is unknown.

158. Randall (1953, 202) claims that this fact stems in part from the particular phase of the Erechtheum's construction described by the inscriptions, which required more skilled labor. He further argues (203) that citizen casualties suffered by Athens during the Peloponnesian War had thrown the labor market somewhat out of balance.

159. Face B, col. 1, lines 1, 9, 11; col. 2, lines 2, 5.

160. κηπορ(ός) (Face B, col. 1, line 6); ἐλαιογ(-) (Face B, col. 1, line 8); καρυο(-) (Face B, col. 1, line 10).

161. E.g. Manes the metic, described as a γεωργός at *IG* ii^2 1553 l.30.

162. Hennig 1994, 305; Manville 1990, 94. Pritchett (1956, 261–76) categorizes and analyzes the various types of property confiscated from the Hermocopidae and profaners of the Mysteries in 415/14.

163. Casson 1976.

164. Hennig 1994, 310–11.

165. Pecirka 1966, 147. *IG* ii^2 53 dates to ca. 430 and awards *enktesis* of a house (line 3) to Philytus and his descendants at Athens.

166. Gauthier 1976, 66–68.

167. On this type of property see Gabrielsen 1986. The Attic Stelae provide a revealing look at the assets confiscated from various individuals. The only possessions of the metic Cephisodorus recorded on the extant portions of Stele I (lines 33–49) are slaves. See Pritchett 1953, 242. The fear that metic wealth might prove too dangerous for the city even with these limitations may lie behind a passage in Plato's *Laws* (915b). Here the dialogue's nameless Athenian recommends the expulsion of all metics after twenty years of residence.

168. Leiwo and Remes 1999.

169. Leiwo and Remes 1999, 166.

170. FJW 1980, 3.258.

171. Thus also Garvie 2006, 143.

172. Garvie 2006, 182.

173. At *Libation Bearers* 581–82, Orestes asks the chorus to stay silent or speak opportunely (τὰ καίρια) to aid his plans for revenge. The women in turn (766–73) involve the nurse in the logistical preparations for Aegisthus's murder.

174. Bakewell 1997, 213–15.

175. Ch. 1.

176. On metics as habitual lodgers see Whitehead 1977, 71; Hennig 1994, 305.

177. LSJ s.v. δήμιος.

178. See also Danaus's use of the word πόλις at line 1010. FJW suggest (1980, 3.258), less plausibly, that the phrase might also apply to other "prominent Argives whom Pelasgus could rely upon to entertain his and the city's proteges as their private guests."

179. For instance, *IG* i³ 44, dated by Lewis to 450–445, records the terms of a lease on a piece of property. Note in particular the mention of γες (line 7) and [τ]ο χορ[ι]ο (10). And *IG* i³ 252, dated by him ca. 450 and found on the south slope of the Acropolis, seems to concern the leasing of property belonging to a tribe. See [τ]ελουμε (1), ἐκ τες φυ[λες] (3), and ΟΩΣΛΜ (15); of the last cluster of letters Lewis notes (224), "[μισ]⟨θ⟩ως⟨α⟩μ—subesse iure suspicias."

180. R. Osborne 1988, 285. See further Cohen 2000, 124–27.

181. The offer of public housing was not necessarily a selfless gesture on the part of the Argives. See R. Osborne 1988, 288. On the less ambiguous honor of board at the Prytaneion see W. Thompson 1971.

182. By opening his own doors to the Danaids, Pelasgus is apparently reversing his earlier course; see lines 365–66: οὔτοι κάθησθε δωμάτων ἐφέστιοι / ἐμῶν.

183. Rösler 1989, 109n4. Cf. FJW (1980, 3.258), who take the clause as modifying both the δώματ' . . . δήμια and the dwellings of Pelasgus.

184. FJW 1980, 3.260.

185. The difficulty of interpreting this line is increased by the claim of Demosthenes (3.25) that following the Persian Wars, Athenian leaders contented themselves with modest houses no more impressive than those of their neighbors. The orator had ample scope for rhetorical exaggeration, however. The phrase "if any of you knows what the houses of Aristides and Miltiades and the other leaders then were like" (ὥστε τὴν Ἀριστείδου καὶ τὴν Μιλτιάδου καὶ τῶν τότε λαμπρῶν οἰκίαν εἴ τις ἄρ' οἶδεν ὑμῶν ὁποία ποτ' ἐστίν, 3.26) reminds us that his audience likely possessed little real knowledge about such matters more than a century after the fact.

186. On the γραφὴ ἀπροστασίου see Lipsius 1966, 369–72.

187. A. Harrison 1998, 1.165. Meyer (2009) argues persuasively that *phialai exeleutherikai* represent dedications by metics acquitted of this charge.

188. Wilamowitz 1887, 223–33.

189. Thür 1989, 120.

190. Taplin (1989, 222) places the departure at line 974.

191. FJW (1980, 3.302) understand the verb διδοῖ as an Ionic form of the present indicative.

192. LSJ s.v. μισθός.

193. Hennig 1994, 337: "Schaffet die Enktesis die rechtliche Basis zum legalen Immobilienerwerb für Nichtbürger, konnten darüber hinaus besonders verdienten Wohltätern unter ihnen . . . ein Haus and Grundstücke verschiedener Art und Nutzungsmöglichkeit zum Geschenk gemacht werden." On the potential income from rental properties see Athenaeus 12.542.

194. FJW 1980, 3.258.

195. Rösler 1989, 110: "die Offerte des Königs hat also folgenden chiastischen Aufbau: Angebot, in δώματ᾽ . . . δήμια zu wohnen—Angebot, im Palast zu wohnen—Erläuterung der letztgennanten Möglichkeit—Erläuterung der erstgenannten Möglichkeit."

196. Rösler 1989, 110: "Häuser von einheitlicher Form."

197. In the period between 480 and *Suppliant Women*'s performance in the latter half of the 460s, the fabric of urban life was rapidly transformed. H. Thompson (1981, 344) notes that "when the Persians finally withdrew from Athens they left behind a thoroughly ruinous city: the Acropolis looted and burned, the lower city also burned; the fortification walls, sanctuaries and houses demolished; there remained only a few short stretches of the city walls and some of the houses in which high-ranking Persians had been quartered."

198. Burns 1976, 417. See also Gorman 1995.

199. Hoepfner and Schwandner 1994, 24. Cahill (2002, 5) notes that "this type of hierarchical divisive planning, with wide streets defining 'major rectangles' which are then subdivided into blocks, is a method quite different from that of cities like Olynthus, where streets of equal width divide the city into blocks, without larger arteries or clearly divided sectors."

200. Castagnoli 1971, 129. See also Hoepfner and Schwandner 1994, 24–30, who conclude (29–30) that "nur mit einer normierten Insulagröße gerechnet werden kann."

201. Rösler 1989, 111: "Das von Hippodamos von Milet entwickelte Konzept einer Wohnbebauung . . . für die ein einheitlicher Typus der Bürgerhauses konstitutiv war."

202. *Politics* 1330b21–24: ἡ δὲ τῶν ἰδίων οἰκήσεων διάθεσις ἡδίων μὲν νομίζεται καὶ χρησιμωτέρα πρὸς τὰς ἄλλας πράξεις, ἂν εὔτομος ᾖ καὶ κατὰ τὸν νεώτερον καὶ τὸν Ἱπποδάμειον τρόπον.

203. Tzakirgis 2005, 69: "Classical Athenians did not take advantage of the post-Persian clean-up to rebuild in regular blocks with uniform house lots."

204. Tzakirgis 2005.

205. Burns 1976, 417–18; Cahill 2002, 4.

206. Kraounaki (in Hoepfner and Schwandner 1994, 32–38) describes the remains of an early classical house uncovered in 1988.

207. Hoepfner and Schwandner (1994, 38–42) offer a reconstruction of a hypothetical Piraeus *insula* composed of eight uniform adjoining houses.

208. E.g. Olynthus. Cahill (2002, 82) acknowledges the "general similarity among many houses at Olynthus," but adds (84) "the houses at Olynthus are a diverse group. Some adhere to the 'standard plan' while others never did."

209. Cited by Rösler 1989, 113: "Wir stellen uns das so vor, daß man in solchen Fällen von einem Musterhaus ein Modell gebaut hat, das von einem Gremium und wohl auch von der Volksversammlung beschlossen wurde. Dieses Modell bot dann die Möglichkeit, über einen längeren Zeitraum die Maße abzunehmen, um sie in Wirklichkeit zu übertragen."

210. Whitehead 1986, 83. See further Garland 1987, 61; [Xenophon] *Constitution of the Athenians* 1.12.

211. Lysias 23.6 provides some evidence for the tight-knit nature of metic communities. (The Plataeans are admittedly a special case, given the circumstances of their mass escape to Athens.)

212. Garland 1987, 101. The worship of the Egyptian gods was particularly distinctive and increased after the fourth century. Von Reden (1995, 31–32) cautions that the proliferation of foreign cults was not necessarily a sign of increasing Athenian tolerance.

213. The presence of the infinitive σωφρονεῖν is significant. Glazebrook (2006) notes that in the Attic orators σωφροσύνη is the foremost virtue associated with citizen women; those lacking it are marked as foreign and potentially promiscuous. FJW (1980, 3.303) observe that "τὸ σωφρονεῖν . . . is synonymous with the metrically unsuitable σωφροσύνην."

214. FJW 1980, 3.303.

215. The only choice many tragic protagonists have is whether to don the "yoke-strap of necessity" (ἀνάγκας . . . λέπαδνον, *Agamemnon* 218).

216. The punctuation employed in line 92 is that of FJW (1980) and Page (1972).

217. Sandin 2003, 92.

218. FJW 1980, 2.421. On the significance of Io more generally see Murray 1958.

219. Their father may even exit at this point. Although no other characters comment on Danaus's departure, Apollo's exit in *Eumenides* is unremarked; see Taplin 1989, 403.

220. Thuc. 1.2.

Conclusion

1. Macleod 1983, 25.

2. See Taplin 1989, 410.

3. Orestes's reference to the jurors as σύ . . . πολισσοῦχος λεώς at line 775 is picked up by Athena's address to the πρόπομποι at line 1010. See further Taplin 1989, 411.

4. A few lines later the goddesses refer to their sojourn in Athens as "my metoikia" (μετοικίαν δ' ἐμάν, 1018).

5. The reciprocity of the polyptoton ἀγαθῶν / ἀγαθή at lines 1012–13 implies that the two groups' fortunes are already linked. In *Suppliant Women*, the chorus wish Pelasgus well in similar terms: ἀλλ' ἀντ' ἀγαθῶν ἀγαθοῖσ⟨ι⟩ βρύοις / δῖε Πελασγῶν ("may you abound in good things in return for good, godlike one of the Pelasgians," 966–67). The mention of his eponymous people suggests that the blessing extends to them as well.

6. Sommerstein 1989, 251. He also notes (281–82) that the goddesses' crim-

son apparel (φοινικοβάπτοις ἐνδυτοῖς ἐσθήμασι, 1028) resembles that worn by metics in the parade. According to Neils (2001, 146–50), the *scaphephoroi* (N13–15, S119–21) and perhaps the *hydriaphoroi* (N16–19, S115–18) represented on the Parthenon frieze were metics.

7. Sommerstein 1989, 260. The idea that the cast is saying a fond farewell to its audience acquires even more significance if metics made up a significant proportion of those in attendance (thus Sommerstein 1996b, 67).

8. On this fundamental opposition see Buxton 1982, 58.

9. Rösler (1993, 21) notes that "in beiden Trilogien gelingt die Konfliktbewältigung, weil sie in institutionellen Bahnen verläuft, auf der Basis von Argumentation und Abstimmung."

10. Bachvarova (2009, 296) observes that "in the *Eumenides* it is those from whom the suppliant desires protection who move from cursing to blessing, not the suppliant."

11. Although Athena reminds the Furies she has access to her father's thunderbolts (*Eumenides* 827–28), she stresses that is not her preferred approach. On the contrary, she says she will never tire of talking about the benefits of reconciliation (οὔτοι καμοῦμαί σοι λέγουσα τἀγαθά, 881) and urges the goddesses to respect the power of *Peitho* (ἀλλ' εἰ μὲν ἁγνόν ἐστί σοι Πειθοῦς σέβας, 885).

12. Though they did on occasion amend or overlook it. See Carawan 2008.

13. Davies (1977, 106) stresses "the care which was continuously taken to ensure that out-groups remained out-groups." For instance (107), the enfranchisement of the Samians was more a case of "*isopoliteia* . . . than . . . true integration."

14. M. Osborne 1983, 3/4.205.

15. For evidence of metics among the supporters of Thrasyboulus see e.g. *IG* ii^2 10.

16. On the political context see Ostwald 1986, 507–8.

17. Grethlein 2003, 99: "Es läßt sich vermuten, daß die Wahl eines demokratischen Argos die Darstellung einer Niederlage eines demokratischen Staates ermöglichte, die mit Athen als Handlungsort zu brisant gewesen wäre."

References

Abbreviations

FJW Friis Johansen, H., and E. Whittle. 1980. *Aeschylus: The Suppliants*. 3 vols. Copenhagen.

IG i³ Lewis, D. 1981. *Inscriptiones Graecae*, vol. 1: *Inscriptiones Atticae Euclidis Anno Anteriores*. 3rd ed. Berlin.

IG ii² Kirchner, I. 1913. *Inscriptiones Graecae*, vols. 2 and 3: *Inscriptiones Atticae Euclidis Anno Posteriores*. 2nd ed. Berlin.

LSJ Liddell, H., R. Scott, and H. Jones. 1940. *A Greek-English Lexicon*. 9th ed. Oxford.

Adak, M. 2003. *Metöken als Wohltäter Athens: Untersuchungen zum sozialen Austausch zwischen ortsansässigen Fremden und der Bürgergemeinde in klassischer und hellenistischer Zeit (ca. 500–150 v. Chr.)*. Munich.

Anderson, G. 2003. *The Athenian Experiment: Building an Imagined Political Community in Ancient Attica, 508–490 B.C.* Ann Arbor.

Auffarth, C. 1995. "Constructing the Identity of the *Polis*: The Danaides as 'Ancestors.'" In *Ancient Greek Hero Cult*, ed. R. Hägg, 39–48. Stockholm.

Ault, B. 2005. "Housing the Poor and Homeless in Ancient Greece." In *Ancient Greek Houses and Households: Chronological, Regional, and Social Diversity*, ed. B. Ault and L. Nevett, 140–59. Philadelphia.

Austin, R. G. 1940. "Greek Board-Games." *Antiquity* 14:257–71.

Bäbler, B. 1998. *Fleißige Thrakerinnen und wehrhafte Skythen: Nichtgriechen im klassischen Athen und ihre archäologische Hinterlassenschaft*. Stuttgart.

Bachvarova, M. 2009. "Suppliant Danaids and Argive Nymphs in Aeschylus." *Classical Journal* 104:289–310.

Bakewell, G. 1997. "Μετοικία in the *Supplices* of Aeschylus." *Classical Antiquity* 16:209–28.

———. 1999a. "Εὔνους καὶ πόλει σωτήριος / μέτοικος: Metics, Tragedy, and Civic Ideology." *Syllecta Classica* 10:43–64.

———. 1999b. "Lysias 12 and Lysias 31: Metics and Athenian Citizenship in the Aftermath of the Thirty." *Greek, Roman, and Byzantine Studies* 40:5–22.

———. 2007. "Written Lists of Military Personnel in Classical Athens." In *Politics of Orality*, ed. Craig Cooper, 89–102. Orality and Literacy in Ancient Greece 6. Leiden.

———. 2008a. "Aeschylus' *Supplices* 11–12: Danaus as Πεσσονομῶν." *Classical Quarterly* 58:303–7.

———. 2008b. "Forbidding Marriage: *Neaira* 16 and Metic Spouses at Athens." *Classical Journal* 104:97–109.

Bednarowski, P. 2010. "The Danaids' Threat: Obscurity, Suspense, and the Shedding of Tradition in Aeschylus' *Suppliants*." *Classical Journal* 105:193–212.

Beloch, K. J. 1923. *Griechische Geschichte*, vol. 3.2. 2nd ed. Berlin.

Bintliff, J. 2006. "Solon's Reforms: An Archaeological Perspective." In *Solon of Athens: New Historical and Philological Approaches*, ed. J. Blok and A. Lardinois, 321–33. Leiden.

Blok, J. 2005. "Becoming Citizens: Some Notes on the Semantics of 'Citizen' in Archaic Greece and Classical Athens." *Klio* 87:7–40.

———. 2009. "Perikles' Citizenship Law: A New Perspective." *Historia: Zeitschrift für alte Geschichte* 58:141–70.

Boedeker, D. 1997. "Becoming Medea: Assimilation in Euripides." In *Essays on Medea in Myth, Literature, Philosophy, and Art*, ed. J. Clauss and S. Johnston, 127–48. Princeton.

Boegehold, A. L. 1994. "Perikles' Citizenship Law of 451/0 B.C." In *Athenian Identity and Civic Ideology*, ed. A. L. Boegehold and A. Scafuro, 57–66. Baltimore.

———. 1995. *The Lawcourts at Athens: Sites, Buildings, Equipment, Procedure, and Testimonia*. Athenian Agora 28. Princeton.

Bradeen, D. 1967. "The Athenian Casualty List of 464 B.C." *Hesperia* 36:321–28.

———. 1969. "The Athenian Casualty Lists." *Classical Quarterly* 19:145–59.

Bugh, G. 1988. *The Horsemen of Athens*. Princeton.

Burford, A. 1993. *Land and Labor in the Greek World*. Baltimore.

Burian, P. 1974. "Pelasgus and Politics in Aeschylus' Danaid Trilogy." *Wiener Studien* 8:5–14.

Burkert, W. 1985. *Greek Religion*. Tr. J. Raffan. Cambridge, MA.

Burns, A. 1976. "Hippodamos and the Planned City." *Historia* 25:414–28.

Buxton, R. 1982. *Persuasion in Greek Tragedy: A Study of "Peitho."* Cambridge.

Cahill, N. 2002. *Household and City Organization at Olynthus*. New Haven.

Carawan, E. 1987. "*Eisangelia* and *Euthyna*." *Greek, Roman and Byzantine Studies* 28:167–208.

———. 2008. "Pericles the Younger and the Citizenship Law." *Classical Journal* 103:383–406.

Casson, L. 1976. "The Athenian Upper Class and New Comedy." *Transactions of the American Philological Association* 106:29–59.

Castagnoli, F. 1971. *Orthogonal Town Planning in Antiquity*. Cambridge, MA.

Castriota, D. 2005. "Feminizing the Barbarian and Barbarizing the Feminine: Amazons, Trojans, and Persians in the Stoa Poikile." In *Periklean Athens and Its Legacy: Problems and Perspectives*, ed. J. Barringer and J. Hurwit, 89–102. Austin.

Cawkwell, G. L. 1984. "Athenian Naval Power in the Fourth Century." *Classical Quarterly* 34:334–45.

Chambers, M. 1967. "The Significance of the Themistocles Decree." *Philologus* 3:166–69.

Christ, M. 2001. "Conscription of Hoplites in Classical Athens." *Classical Quarterly* 51:398–422.

———. 2006. *The Bad Citizen in Classical Athens*. Cambridge.

Clairmont, C. 1983. *Patrios Nomos: Public Burial in Athens during the Fifth and Fourth Centuries B.C.* British Archaeological Reports, International Series 161. Oxford.

Clerc, M. 1893. *Les métèques athéniens*. Paris.

Cohen, E. 2000. *The Athenian Nation*. Princeton.

———. 2006. "Free and Unfree Sexual Work: An Economic Analysis of Athenian Prostitution." In *Prostitutes and Courtesans in the Ancient World*, ed. C. Faraone and L. McClure, 95–124. Madison.

Cole, S. G. 2004. *Landscapes, Gender, and Ritual Space: The Ancient Greek Experience*. Berkeley.

Collard, C., M. Cropp, and J. Gibert. 1995. *Euripides: Selected Fragmentary Plays*, vol. 1. Warminster.

Conacher, D. J. 1996. *Aeschylus: The Earlier Plays and Related Studies*. Toronto.

Connor, W. R. 1992. *The New Politicians of Fifth-Century Athens*. Indianapolis.

Csapo, E., and W. Slater. 1994. *The Context of Ancient Drama*. Ann Arbor.

Daube, B. 1938. *Zu den Rechtsproblemen in Aischylos' "Agamemnon."* Zürich.

Davidson, J. 1997. *Courtesans and Fishcakes: The Consuming Passions of Classical Athens*. New York.

Davies, J. K. 1977. "Athenian Citizenship: The Descent Group and the Alternatives." *Classical Journal* 73:105–21.

Dawe, R. D. 1965. *Repertory of Conjectures on Aeschylus*. Leiden.

De Ste. Croix, G. E. M. 1956. "Greek and Roman Accounting." In *Studies in the History of Accounting*, ed. A. C. Littleton and B. S. Yamey, 14–74. Homewood.

———. 2004. *Athenian Democratic Origins and Other Essays*. Ed. D. Harvey and R. Parker. Oxford.

Diamantopoulos, A. 1957. "The Danaid Trilogy of Aeschylus." *Journal of Hellenic Studies* 77:220–29.

Diels, H., and W. Kranz. 1952. *Die Fragmente der Vorsokratiker*, vol. 1. 6th ed. Berlin.

Dilts, M. 1983. *Scholia Demosthenica*. Leipzig.

Dougherty, C. 1993. *The Poetics of Colonization: From City to Text in Archaic Greece*. New York.

Dunbabin, T. J. 1950. "An Attic Bowl." *Annals of the British School at Athens* 45:193–202.

Duncan-Jones, R. P. 1980. "Metic Numbers in Periclean Athens." *Chiron* 10: 101–9.

Dunkle, R. 1969. "The Aegeus Episode and the Theme of Euripides' *Medea*." *Transactions of the American Philological Association* 100:97–107.

Easterling, P. 1985. "Anachronism in Greek Tragedy." *Journal of Hellenic Studies* 105:1–10.

Effenterre, H. van, and M. van Effenterre. 1990. "Le contrôle des étrangers dans la cité grecque." In *Symposion 1988: Vortraege zur griechischen und hellenistischen Rechtsgeschichte*, ed. G. Nenci and G. Thür, 251–59. Köln.

Farenga, V. 2006. *Citizen and Self in Ancient Greece: Individuals Performing Justice and the Law*. Cambridge.

Finley, M. 1981. *Economy and Society in Ancient Greece*. Ed. B. Shaw and R. Saller. New York.

Foley, H. 1994. *The Homeric Hymn to Demeter: Translation, Commentary, and Interpretive Essays*. Princeton.

———. 2001. *Female Acts in Greek Tragedy*. Princeton.

Föllinger, S. 2007. "Väter und Töchter bei Aischylos." In *Generationenkonflikte auf der Bühne: Perspektiven im antiken und mittelalterlichen Drama*, ed. T. Baier, 11–22. Tübingen.

Forrest, W. 1960. "Themistokles and Argos." *Classical Quarterly* 10:221–41.

Forsdyke, S. 2006. "Land, Labor and Economy in Solonian Athens: Breaking the Impasse between Archaeology and History." In *Solon of Athens: New Historical and Philological Approaches*, ed. J. Blok and A. Lardinois, 334–50. Leiden.

Foxhall, L. 1997. "A View from the Top: Evaluating the Solonian Property Classes." In *The Development of the* Polis *in Archaic Greece*, ed. L. Mitchell and P. J. Rhodes, 113–36. London.

Fraenkel, E. 1950. *Aeschylus "Agamemnon."* 3 vols. Oxford.

French, A. 1961. "Solon's Hoplite Assessment." *Historia: Zeitschrift für alte Geschichte* 10:510–12.

———. 1994. "Pericles' Citizenship Law." *Ancient History Bulletin* 8:71–75.

Fritz, K. von. 1936. "Die Danaidentrilogie des Aeschylus." *Philologus* 91:121–36, 249–69.

Gabrielsen, V. 1986. "Φανερά and Ἀφανὴς Οὐσία in Classical Athens." *Classica et Mediaevalia* 37:99–114.

Gantz, T. 1978. "Love and Death in the *Suppliants* of Aeschylus." *Phoenix* 32:279–87.

Garland, R. 1987. *The Piraeus*. London.

Garvie, A. 2006. *Aeschylus' "Supplices": Play and Trilogy*. 2nd ed. Bristol.

Gauthier, P. 1971. "Les xenoi dans les textes athéniens de la seconde moitié du Ve siècle av. J-C." *Revue des Études Grecques* 84:44–79.

———. 1972. *SYMBOLA: Les étrangers et la justice dans les cités grecques*. Paris.

———. 1976. *Un commentaire historique des "Poroi" de Xénophon*. Geneva.

Gifford, M. 2001. "Dramatic Dialectic in *Republic* Book I." In *Oxford Studies in Ancient Philosophy XX*, ed. D. Sedley, 35–106. Oxford.

Glazebrook, A. 2005. "The Making of a Prostitute: Apollodoros's Portrait of Neaira." *Arethusa* 38:161–87.

———. 2006. "The Bad Girls of Athens: The Image and Function of *Hetairai* in Judicial Oratory." In *Prostitutes and Courtesans in the Ancient World*, ed. C. Faraone and L. McClure, 125–38. Madison.

———. 2007. "Porneion: Prostitution in Athenian Civic Space." Paper presented at the Annual Meeting, Archaeological Institute of America.

Gödde, S. 2000. *Das Drama der Hikesie: Ritual und Rhetorik in Aischylos' "Hiketiden."* Münster.

Goldhill, S. 1987. "The Great Dionysia and Civic Ideology." *Journal of Hellenic Studies* 107:58–76.

———. 2007. "What's in a Wall?" In *Visualizing the Tragic: Drama, Myth, and Ritual in Greek Art and Literature*, ed. C. Kraus, S. Goldhill, H. Foley, and J. Elsner, 127–47. Oxford.

Gorman, V. 1995. "Aristotle's Hippodamos (*Politics* 2.1267b22–30)." *Historia* 44:385–95.

Gould, J. 1973. *"HIKETEIA." Journal of Hellenic Studies* 93:74–103.

Graham, A. J. 1983. *Colony and Mother City in Ancient Greece*. 2nd ed. Chicago.

Gregory, J. 1991. *Euripides and the Instruction of the Athenians*. Ann Arbor.

Grethlein, J. 2003. *Asyl und Athen: Die Konstruktion kollektiver Identität in der griechischen Tragödie*. Stuttgart

Griffith, M. 1986. Review of FJW 1980. *Phoenix* 40:323–40

———. 1995. "Brilliant Dynasts: Power and Politics in the *Oresteia*." *Classical Antiquity* 14:62–129.

———. 1999. *Sophocles "Antigone."* Cambridge.

———. 2001. "Antigone and Her Sister(s): Embodying Women in Greek Tragedy." In *Making Silence Speak. Women's Voices in Greek Literature and Society*, ed. A. Lardinois and L. McClure, 117–36. Princeton.

Grossmann, G. 1970. *Promethie und Orestie: Attischer Geist in der attischen Tragoedie*. Heidelberg.

Habash, M. 1995. "Two Complementary Festivals in Aristophanes' *Acharnians*." *American Journal of Philology* 116:559–77.

Hall, E. 1989. *Inventing the Barbarian*. Oxford.

———. 1996. *Aeschylus "Persians."* Warminster.

Hall, J. 1997. *Ethnic Identity in Greek Antiquity*. Cambridge.

———. 2002. *Hellenicity: Between Ethnicity and Culture*. Chicago.

Halliwell, S. 1990. "The Sounds of the Voice in Old Comedy." In *Owls to Athens:*

Essays on Classical Subjects Presented to Sir Kenneth Dover, ed. E. M. Craik, 69–79. Oxford.

Hansen, M. H. 1985. *Demography and Democracy*. Herning.

———. 1988. *Three Studies in Athenian Demography*. Copenhagen.

———. 1999. *The Athenian Democracy in the Age of Demosthenes*. Norman.

———. 2006a. *The Shotgun Method: The Demography of the Ancient Greek City-State Culture*. Columbia.

———. 2006b. *Studies in the Population of Aigina, Athens, and Eretria*. Copenhagen.

Hanson, V. 1995. *The Other Greeks: The Family Farm and the Agrarian Roots of Western Civilization*. New York.

Harrison, A. 1998. *The Law of Athens*. 2nd ed. Indianapolis.

Harrison, J. 1977. *Themis: A Study of the Social Origins of Greek Religion*. 2nd ed. London.

Heath, J. 2005. *The Talking Greeks: Speech, Animals, and the Other in Homer, Aeschylus, and Plato*. Cambridge.

Henderson, J. 1991. *The Maculate Muse: Obscene Language in Attic Comedy*. New York.

Hennig, D. 1994. "Immobilienerwerb durch Nichtbürger in der klassischen und hellenistischen Polis." *Chiron* 24:305–44.

Hoepfner, W., and E.-L. Schwandner. 1994. *Haus und Stadt im klassischen Griechenland*. Munich.

Hornblower, S. 1991. *A Commentary on Thucydides*, vol. 1: *Books I–III*. Oxford.

Hose, M. 2006. "*Vaticinium Post Eventum* and the Position of the *Supplices* in the Danaid Trilogy." In *Dionysalexandros: Essays on Aeschylus and His Fellow Tragedians in Honour of Alexander F. Garvie*, ed. D. Cairns and V. Liapis, 91–98. Swansea.

Humphreys, S. 1977. "Public and Private Interests in Classical Athens." *Classical Journal* 73:97–104.

Hurwit, J. 1999. *The Athenian Acropolis: History, Mythology, and Archaeology from the Neolithic Era to the Present*. Cambridge.

Irby-Massie, G. 2008. "*Prometheus Bound* and Contemporary Trends in Greek Natural Philosophy." *Greek, Roman and Byzantine Studies* 48:133–57.

Jenkins, I. 1983. "Is There Life after Marriage? A Study of the Abduction Motif in Vase Paintings of the Athenian Wedding Ceremony." *Bulletin of the Institute of Classical Studies* 30:137–45.

Johnstone, C. 1996. "Greek Oratorical Settings and the Problem of the Pnyx: Rethinking the Athenian Political Process." In *Theory, Text, Context: Issues in Greek Rhetoric and Oratory*, ed. C. Johnstone, 97–128. Albany.

Jones, N. F. 2004. *Rural Athens under the Democracy*. Philadelphia.

Kagan, D. 1963. "The Enfranchisement of Aliens by Cleisthenes." *Historia* 12:41–46.

Kahn, D. 2008. "Inaros' Rebellion against Artaxerxes I and the Athenian Disaster in Egypt." *Classical Quarterly* 58:424–40.

Kennedy, R. 2006. "Justice, Geography, and Empire in Aeschylus' *Eumenides.*" *Classical Antiquity* 25:35–72.

Keuls, E. 1974. *The Water-Carriers in Hades: A Study of Catharsis through Toil in Classical Antiquity*. Amsterdam.

King, H. 1983. "Bound to Bleed: Artemis and Greek Women." In *Images of Women in Antiquity*, ed. A. Cameron and A. Kuhrt, 109–27. Detroit.

Knox, B. 1979. *Word and Action: Essays on the Ancient Theater*. Baltimore.

Kraay, C. 1976. *Archaic and Classical Greek Coins*. Berkeley.

Kurke, L. 1999. *Coins, Bodies, Games, and Gold: The Politics of Meaning in Archaic Greece*. Princeton.

Lebeck, A. 1971. *The Oresteia: A Study in Language and Structure*. 1971. Cambridge, MA.

Lee, M. 2004. "Evil Wealth of Raiment: Deadly Πέπλοι in Greek Tragedy." *Classical Journal* 99:253–79.

Leiwo, M., and P. Remes. 1999. "Partnership of Citizens and Metics: The Will of Epicurus." *Classical Quarterly* 49:161–66.

Lipsius, J. H. 1966. *Das attische Recht und Rechtsverfahren*. Darmstadt.

Loomis, W. 1998. *Wages, Welfare Costs and Inflation in Classical Athens*. Ann Arbor.

———. 2003. "Athenian Slander: A Common Law Perspective." In *Gestures: Essays in Ancient History, Literature and Philosophy Presented to Alan L. Boegehold*, ed. G. Bakewell and J. Sickinger, 287–300. Oxford.

Loraux, N. 1986. *The Invention of Athens: The Funeral Oration in the Classical City*. Tr. Alan Sheridan. Cambridge, MA.

———. 1993. *The Children of Athena: Athenian Ideas about Citizenship and the Division between the Sexes*. Tr. C. Levine. Princeton.

MacDowell, D. M. 2009. *Demosthenes the Orator*. Oxford.

MacKinnon, J. K. 1978. "The Reasons for the Danaids' Flight." *Classical Quarterly* 28:74–82.

Macleod, C. 1983. *Collected Essays*. Oxford.

Maitland, J. 1992. "Dynasty and Family in the Athenian City State: A View from Attic Tragedy." *Classical Quarterly* 42:26–40.

Manville, P. 1990. *The Origins of Citizenship in Ancient Athens*. Princeton.

Mastronarde, D. 1979. *Contact and Discontinuity: Some Conventions of Speech and Action on the Greek Tragic Stage*. Berkeley.

———. 2002. *Euripides "Medea."* Cambridge.

McClure, L. 1999a. *Spoken Like a Woman: Speech and Gender in Athenian Drama*. Princeton.

———. 1999b. "'The Worst Husband': Discourses of Praise and Blame in Euripides' *Medea*." *Classical Philology* 94:373–94.

McMahon, J. 1996. "Cultivating Passion: Vegetables, Belief, and Sexuality." *Newsletter of the Classical Association of the Empire State* 31.2.

Meier, C. 1993. *The Political Art of Greek Tragedy*. Tr. Andrew Webber. Baltimore.

Meiggs, R., and D. Lewis. 1988. *A Selection of Greek Historical Inscriptions to the End of the Fifth Century B.C.* Rev. ed. Oxford.
Meyer, E. 2009. *Metics and the Athenian "Phialai"-Inscriptions.* Historia Einzelschriften 208. Stuttgart.
Michelini, A. 1978. "Ὕβρις and Plants." *Harvard Studies in Classical Philology* 82:35–44.
Miller, S. 1978. *The Athenian Prytaneion.* Berkeley.
Mitchell, L. 2006. "Greeks, Barbarians, and Aeschylus' *Suppliants.*" *Greece and Rome* 53:205–23.
Möller, A. 2000. *Naukratis: Trade in Archaic Greece.* Oxford.
Monoson, S. 1994. "Frank Speech, Democracy, and Philosophy: Plato's Debt to a Democratic Strategy of Civic Discourse." In *Athenian Political Thought and the Reconstruction of American Democracy,* ed. P. Burian, J. Wallach, and J. Ober, 172–97. Ithaca.
Morris, I., and K. Raaflaub. 1998. *Democracy 2500? Questions and Challenges.* Dubuque.
Munn, M. 1993. *The Defense of Attica: The Dema Wall and the Boiotian War of 378–375 B.C.* Berkeley.
Murnaghan, S. 1986. "Sophocles, *Antigone* 904–920 and the Institution of Marriage." *American Journal of Philology* 107:192–207.
———. 2005. "Women in Groups: Aeschylus' *Suppliants* and the Female Choruses of Greek Tragedy." In *The Soul of Tragedy: Essays on Athenian Drama,* ed. V. Pedrick and S. Oberhelm, 183–98. Chicago.
Murray, R. 1958. *The Motif of Io in Aeschylus' "Suppliants."* Princeton.
Naiden, F. S. 2006. *Ancient Supplication.* Oxford.
Neils, J. 2001. *The Parthenon Frieze.* Cambridge.
Niku, M. 2007. *The Official Status of the Foreign Residents in Athens, 322–120 B.C.* Helsinki.
Ober, J. 1989. *Mass and Elite in Democratic Athens: Rhetoric, Ideology, and the Power of the People.* Princeton.
———. 1994. "How to Criticize Democracy in Late Fifth- and Fourth-Century Athens." In *Athenian Political Thought and the Reconstruction of American Democracy,* ed. J. P. Euben, J. R. Wallach, and J. Ober, 149–71. Ithaca.
———. 1995. "Greek *Horoi:* Artifactual Texts and the Contingency of Meaning." In *Methods in the Mediterranean,* ed. D. Small, 91–123. Leiden.
———. 2006. "Solon and the *Horoi*: Facts on the Ground in Archaic Athens." In *Solon of Athens: New Historical and Philological Approaches,* ed. J. Blok and A. Lardinois, 441–56. Leiden.
Ogden, D. 1996. *Greek Bastardy in the Classical and Hellenistic Periods.* Oxford.
Ormand, K. 1999. *Exchange and the Maiden: Marriage in Sophoclean Tragedy.* Austin.
Osborne, M. 1981–83. *Naturalization in Athens.* 4 vols. Brussels.
Osborne, R. 1988. "Social and Economic Implications of the Leasing of Land and Property in Classical and Hellenistic Greece." *Chiron* 18:279–323.

———. 2002. Review of Cohen 2000. *Classical Philology* 97:93–98.

Ostwald, M. 1986. *From Popular Sovereignty to the Sovereignty of Law: Law, Society, and Politics in Fifth-Century Athens*. Berkeley.

Padel, R. 1990. "Making Space Speak." In *Nothing to Do with Dionysos? Athenian Drama in Its Social Context*, ed. J. Winkler and F. Zeitlin, 336–65. Princeton.

Page, D. 1972. *Aeschyli septem quae supersunt tragoedias*. Oxford.

Papadopoulos, J., and E. Smithson. 2002. "The Cultural Biography of a Cycladic Geometric Amphora: Islanders in Athens and the Prehistory of Metics." *Hesperia* 71:149–99.

Parker, R. 1997. *Athenian Religion: A History*. Oxford.

Patterson, C. 1981. *Pericles' Citizenship Law of 451/0*. New York.

———. 1986. "*Hai Attikai*: The Other Athenians." *Helios* 13:49–67.

———. 1994. "The Case against Neaira and the Public Ideology of the Athenian Family." In *Athenian Identity and Civic Ideology*, ed. A. Boegehold and A. Scafuro, 199–216. Baltimore.

———. 2001. "The Hospitality of Athenian Justice: The Metic in Court." In *Law and Social Status in Classical Athens*, ed. V. Hunter and J. Edmondson, 93–112. Oxford.

Pearson, M., and M. Shanks. 2001. *Theatre/Archaeology*. London.

Pecirka, J. 1966. *The Formula for the Grant of Enktesis in Attic Inscriptions*. Prague.

Petre, Z. 1986. "Le décret des *Suppliants* d'Eschyle." *Studii Clasice* 24:25–32.

Pierart, M. 1971. "Les EYΘYNOI athéniens." *L'Antiquité Classique* 40:526–73.

Podlecki, A. 1966. *The Political Background of Aeschylean Tragedy*. Ann Arbor.

———. 1986. "*Polis* and Monarch in Early Greek Tragedy." In *Greek Tragedy and Political Theory*, ed. J. P. Euben, 76–100. Berkeley.

———. 1998. *Perikles and His Circle*. London.

Pritchett, W. K. 1953. "The Attic Stelai, Part I." *Hesperia* 22:225–99.

———. 1956. "The Attic Stelai, Part II." *Hesperia* 25:178–317.

———. 1971. *The Greek State at War: Part I*. Berkeley.

Raaflaub, K. A. 1980. "Des freien Bürgers Recht der freien Rede." In *Studien zur antiken Sozialgeschichte: Festschrift Friedrich Vittinghoff*, ed. W. Eck, H. Galsterer, and H. Wolff, 7–57. Köln.

———. 2007. "The Breakthrough of *Demokratia* in Mid-Fifth-Century Athens." In *Origins of Democracy in Ancient Greece*, ed. K. A. Raaflaub, J. Ober, and R. Wallace, 105–54. Berkeley.

Radt, S. 2009. *Tragicorum Graecorum Fragmenta*, vol. 3: *Aeschylus*. 2nd ed. Göttingen.

Randall, R. 1953. "The Erechtheum Workmen." *American Journal of Archaeology* 57:199–210.

Reden, S. von. 1995. "The Piraeus: A World Apart." *Greece and Rome* 42:24–37.

Rehm, R. 1988. "The Staging of Suppliant Plays." *Greek, Roman and Byzantine Studies* 29:263–307.

———. 1994. *Marriage to Death: The Conflation of Wedding and Funeral Rituals in Greek Tragedy*. Princeton.

Rhodes, P. J. 1993. *A Commentary on the Aristotelian Athenaion Politeia*. 2nd ed. Oxford.

———. 2006. "The Reforms and Laws of Solon: An Optimistic View." In *Solon of Athens: New Historical and Philological Approaches*, ed. J. Blok and A. Lardinois, 248–60. Leiden.

Robertson, D. S. 1924. "The End of the *Supplices* Trilogy of Aeschylus." *Classical Review* 38:51–53.

Robertson, H. G. 1936. "Δίκη and Ὕβρις in Aeschylus' *Suppliants*." *Classical Review* 50:104–9.

Robinson, E. 1997. *The First Democracies: Early Popular Government outside Athens*. Stuttgart.

Rosivach, V. 1987. "Autochthony and the Athenians." *Classical Quarterly* 37: 294–306.

———. 2002. "The Requirements for the Solonic Classes in Aristotle, *AP* 7.4." *Hermes* 130:36–47.

Rösler, W. 1989. "Typenhäuser bei Aischylos?" in *Demokratie und Architektur: Wohnen in der klassischen Polis II*, ed. W. Schuller, W. Hoepfner, and E. Schwandner, 109–14. Munich.

———. 1993. "Der Schluß der 'Hiketiden' und die Danaiden-Trilogie des Aischylos." *Rheinisches Museum* 136:1–22.

Saïd, S. 1993. "Tragic Argos." In *Tragedy, Comedy and the Polis*, ed. A. Sommerstein, S. Halliwell, J. Henderson, and B. Zimmerman, 167–89. Bari.

Sandin, P. 2003. *Aeschylus' "Supplices": Introduction and Commentary on Vv. 1–523*. Göteborg.

Saxonhouse, A. 1986. "Myths and the Origins of Cities: Reflections on the Autochthony Theme in Euripides' *Ion*." In *Greek Tragedy and Political Theory*, ed. J. P. Euben, 252–73. Berkeley.

Scafuro, A. 1994. "Witnessing and False Witnessing: Proving Citizenship and Kin Identity in Fourth-Century Athens." In *Athenian Identity and Civic Ideology*, ed. A. Boegehold and A. Scafuro, 156–98. Baltimore.

Schlesinger, E. 1933. *Die griechische Asylie*. Giessen.

Schuck, P. 1998. *Citizens, Strangers, and In-Betweens: Essays on Immigration and Citizenship*. Boulder.

Scullion, S. 2002. "Tragic Dates." *Classical Quarterly* 52:81–101.

Seaford, R. 1987. "The Tragic Wedding." *Journal of Hellenic Studies* 107:106–30.

———. 1998. "Tragic Money." *Journal of Hellenic Studies* 118:119–39.

Sealey, R. 1983. "How Citizenship and the City Began in Athens." *American Journal of Ancient History* 8:97–129.

Segal, E. 1987. *Roman Laughter: The Comedy of Plautus*. 2nd ed. Oxford.

Sicherl, M. 1986. "Die Tragik der Danaiden." *Museum Helveticum* 43:81–110.

Sickinger, J. 1998. *Public Records and Archives in Classical Athens*. Chapel Hill.

Smith, O. L. 1976. *Scholia Graeca in Aeschylum Quae Exstant Omnia, Pars I: Scholia in "Agamemnonem Choephoros Eumenides Supplices" Continens*. Stuttgart.

Sommerstein, A. 1977. "Notes on Aeschylus' *Suppliants.*" *Bulletin of the Institute of Classical Studies* 24:67–82.

———. 1989. *Aeschylus "Eumenides."* Cambridge.

———. 1995. "The Beginning and the End of Aeschylus' Danaid Trilogy." In *Griechisch-römische Komödie und Tragödie*, vol. 3, ed. B. Zimmermann, 111–34. Stuttgart.

———. 1996a. *Aeschylean Tragedy*. Bari.

———. 1996b. "The Theatre Audience, the *Demos*, and the *Suppliants* of Aeschylus." In *Greek Tragedy and the Historian*, ed. C. Pelling, 63–79. Oxford.

———. 2008. *Aeschylus I: Persians, Seven against Thebes, Suppliants, Prometheus Bound*. Cambridge, MA.

Sourvinou-Inwood, C. 1987. "A Series of Erotic Pursuits: Images and Meanings." *Journal of Hellenic Studies* 107:131–53.

Stewart, A. 1995. "Imag(in)ing the Other: Amazons and Ethnicity in Fifth-Century Athens." *Poetics Today* 16:571–97.

Swift, L. 2006. "Mixed Choruses and Marriage Songs: A New Interpretation of the Third Stasimon of the *Hippolytos.*" *Journal of Hellenic Studies* 126:125–40.

Taplin, O. 1986. "Fifth-Century Tragedy and Comedy: A Synkrisis." *Journal of Hellenic Studies* 106:163–74.

———. 1989. *The Stagecraft of Aeschylus: The Dramatic Use of Exits and Entrances in Greek Tragedy*. Corrected ed. Oxford.

Taplin, O., and P. Wilson. 1993. "The 'Aetiology' of Tragedy in the *Oresteia.*" *Proceedings of the Cambridge Philological Society* 39:169–80.

Thomas, R. 1989. *Oral Tradition and Written Record in Classical Athens*. Cambridge.

Thomson, G. D. 1941. *Aeschylus and Athens: A Study in the Social Origins of Drama*. London.

Thompson, H. 1940. *The Tholos of Athens and Its Predecessors. Hesperia* Supplement 4. Princeton.

———. 1981. "Athens Faces Adversity." *Hesperia* 50:343–55.

———. 1982. "The Pnyx in Models." *Hesperia* 19:133–47.

Thompson, W. 1971. "The Prytaneion Decree." *American Journal of Philology* 92:226–37.

Thür, G. 1989. "Wo wohnen die Metöken?" In *Demokratie und Architektur: Wohnen in der klassischen Polis II*, ed. W. Schuller, W. Hoepfner, and E. Schwandner, 117–21. Munich.

Todd, S. 1993. *The Shape of Athenian Law*. Oxford.

———. 2000. *Lysias*. Austin.

Turner, C. 2001. "Perverted Supplication and Other Inversions in Aeschylus' Danaid Trilogy." *Classical Journal* 97:27–50.

Tyrrell, W. 1980. "An Obscene Word in Aeschylus: II." *American Journal of Philology* 101:44–46.

Tzakirgis, B. 2005. "Living and Working around the Athenian Agora: A Preliminary Case Study of Three Houses." In *Ancient Greek Houses and Households:*

Chronological, Regional, and Social Diversity, ed. B. Ault and L. Nevett, 67–82. Philadelphia.

Tzanetou, A. 2002. "Something to Do with Demeter: Ritual and Performance in Aristophanes' *Women at the Thesmophoria*." *American Journal of Philology* 123:329–67.

Vasunia, P. 2001. *The Gift of the Nile: Hellenizing Egypt from Aeschylus to Alexander*. Berkeley.

Vermeule, E. 1979. *Aspects of Death in Early Greek Art and Poetry*. Berkeley.

Vernant, J.-P. 1990. "Tensions and Ambiguities in Greek Tragedy." In *Myth and Tragedy in Ancient Greece*, ed. J.-P. Vernant and P. Vidal-Naquet, tr. J. Lloyd, 29–48. New York.

Vidal-Naquet, P. 1997. "The Place and Status of Foreigners in Athenian Tragedy." In *Greek Tragedy and the Historian*, ed. C. Pelling, 109–19. Oxford.

Waser, O. 1901. "Danaos." In *Pauly's Real-Encyclopädie der classischen Altertumswissenschaft*, vol. 4, s.v. Stuttgart.

Waters, K. H. 1960. "Solon's 'Price-Equalisation.'" *Journal of Hellenic Studies* 80:181–90.

Watson, J. 2009. "The Origin of Metic Status at Athens." *Cambridge Classical Journal* 55:259–78.

Wees, H. van. 2006. "Mass and Elite in Solon's Athens." In *Solon of Athens: New Historical and Philological Approaches*, ed. J. Blok and A. Lardinois, 357–89. Leiden.

Welcker, F. G. 1861. "Des Aeschylus Schutzflehende, Aegypter, und Danaiden." In *Kleine Schriften*, vol. 4, 100–27. Bonn.

West, M. 1990. *Aeschyli Tragoediae cum Incerti Poetae Prometheo*. Stuttgart.

———. 2006. "King and *Demos* in Aeschylus." In *Dionysalexandros: Essays on Aeschylus and His Fellow Tragedians in Honour of Alexander F. Garvie*, ed. D. Cairns and V. Liapis, 31–40. Swansea.

Whitehead, D. 1977. *The Ideology of the Athenian Metic*. Cambridge.

———. 1981. "The Archaic Athenian ZEYΓITAI." *Classical Quarterly* 31:282–86.

———. 1984. "Immigrant Communities in the Classical Polis: Some Principles for a Synoptic Treatment." *L'Antiquité Classique* 53:47–59.

———. 1986. *The Demes of Attica 508/7–ca. 250 B.C.: A Political and Social Study*. Princeton.

———. 2006. "Absentee Athenians: Lysias against Philon and Lycurgus against Leocrates." *Museum Helveticum* 63:132–51.

Wilamowitz-Möllendorff, U. von. 1887. "Demotika der attischen Metöken." *Hermes* 22:107–28, 211–59.

———. 1914. *Aischylos:Interpretationen*. Berlin.

Wilson, P. 2000. *The Athenian Institution of the "Khoregia": The Chorus, the City, and the Stage*. Cambridge.

Winkler, J. 1990a. *The Constraints of Desire: The Anthropology of Sex and Gender in Ancient Greece*. New York.

———. 1990b. "The Ephebes' Song: *Tragoidia* and *Polis*." In *Nothing to Do with Dionysos?*, ed. J. Winkler and F. Zeitlin, 20–62. Princeton.

Winnington-Ingram, R. P. 1961. "The Danaid Trilogy of Aeschylus." *Journal of Hellenic Studies* 81:141–52.

Winton, R. 2007. "Thucydides 2.13.6–7: Oldest, Youngest, Hoplites, Metics." *Classical Quarterly* 57:298–301.

Wohl, V. 1998. *Intimate Commerce: Exchange, Gender, and Subjectivity in Greek Tragedy*. Austin.

Zeitlin, F. 1990. "Thebes: Theater of Self and Society in Athenian Drama." In *Nothing to Do with Dionysos?*, ed. J. Winkler and F. Zeitlin, 130–67. Princeton.

———. 1992. "The Politics of Eros in the Danaid Trilogy of Aeschylus." In *Innovations of Antiquity*, ed. R. Hexter and D. Selden, 203–52. New York.

Index

acculturation. *See* assimilation; civic incorporation

Acharnians (Aristophanes), 109

Acropolis: Diphilus statue on, 107; goddess Peitho on, 55; "Oath of Plataea" and, 132n3; *Oresteia* and, 155n17; Persian looting and burning of, 175n197; public debtor list on, 170n86; restoration of, 18; tyrant's control of, 42

Aegeus (Sophocles), 164n188

Aegyptids. *See* Egyptians

Aeschylus: approach to past, 15; coinage in time of, 153n178; commitment to suppliant tradition, 97; contests of plays and, 10; dowries in time of, 156n35; imagery used by, 134n29; immigration in lifetime of, 3, 17; mythological tradition as constraint on, 148n103; props and gestures as characterizations in, 22–23, 135n43; topographical outlines deployed by, 93–94

—WORKS: *Amymone*, 73, 159n95; *Libation Bearers*, 100, 135n43, 173n173; *Persians*, 93, 134n26, 143n18, 152n152; *Seven against Thebes*, 10, 96, 135n43, 141n143, 148–49n105; *Sons of Aegyptus*, 15–16, 60, 73, 131–32n97. See also *Agamemnon*; *Danaids*; Danaid trilogy; *Eumenides*; *Oresteia*

Aeschylus: The Suppliants (Friis Johansen and Whittle [FJW]): on Argives and marriage, 78–79; on Athenian spending authority, 37; on Bothe's corrections, 150n128; comprehensiveness of, 10; on corrupted lines in play, 141n138; on Danaids' appeal for power, 80; on Danaids' appearance, 135n40; on Danaids' housing, 113, 115, 116, 174n183; on Danaids' language, 36, 143n28, 144n39; on Danaus's bodyguards, 146n72; on Danaus's characteristics, 43, 119; on Danaus's coaching, 144n46; foreign groups compared to Danaids in, 68, 70–71; on invasion of Argos, 99; on Io, 162n149; on local history, 168n45; on marriage issue, 62, 154nn2–3, 156n36; on metic terminology, 5; on Pelasgus, 46, 48, 93; on voting, 140n120

Agamemnon (Aeschylus): bird description in, 128n15; citizens vs. ruler in, 149n109; Helen as "booty" in, 137n77; leader reproached in, 100; props and gestures in, 135n43; sacrifice of Iphigenia in, 156n29; *Suppliant*

Agamemnon (Aeschylus) (*continued*)
Women compared with, 162n141; territorial definitions in, 93; titillating images in, 157n57. See also *Oresteia*
agrarian citizen farmer: census categories of, 103–5; enduring myth of, 109; metic artisans juxtaposed to, 111–12; stereotype of, 87. *See also* autochthony; land
agriculture: centrality of, 110; metics as farmers, 111; yield and acreage in, 103–4. *See also* agrarian citizen farmer; land
Alcibiades, 109, 153n182, 170n87
Amasis (Egyptian king), 24
Amazons: Danaids perceived as, 67–68, 72; gender challenges posed by, 70, 86, 158n67, 158n72
Amymone (Aeschylus), 73, 159n95
Amynomachus, 112
Anaxilas of Naxos, 130n80
Antidotus, 50
Antigone (Sophocles), 61, 81–83, 143n24, 163n156
Aphrodite: Argive worship of, 76, 78–79; Athenian worship of, 140n117; coin images of, 71–72, 153n178; Danaid trial and, 74–76
Apis: Asclepius compared with, 168n47; Pelasgus compared with, 94–96, 108, 120; plague of snakes during rule of, 39–40, 87, 94–95; veneration of, 100
architecture, Athenian self-definition linked to, 6. *See also* Acropolis; housing
archons and archonship, 52, 104, 106–7, 152n156
Areopagus, 52, 70, 122, 123, 132n5, 155n17. See also *Eumenides*; law courts
Argive assembly: fulfillment of promise, 33; leaders held accountable by, 47–48; metoikia granted to Danaids by, 4, 30–32, 34, 101–2; Pelasgus's placing decision before, 13–14, 29–30, 38, 46–48; Pelasgus's speech to, 48–49
Argives: ancestors of, 91; as autochthonous landholders, 108–9; characterization of, 100–102, 171n113; Danaids accompanied by men, 33; as Danaids' second husbands, 77–78; as owners of housing offered to Danaids, 114; as Pelasgians (and Hellenes), 90; Pelasgus's fears of accusations by, 47–48, 100, 148n100, 149n107
Argos: Aphrodite cult in, 76, 78–79; Athenian metoikia in relation to, 14–15; Athens compared, summarized, 120–21; bloodshed on plains of, 168n51; citizens' fears of newcomers' impact on, 34–35; crisis in, 13–14; Danaids as threat to, 35–40, 58, 65, 98–100, 144n32; Danaids' entry into city center of, 32–33; Danaids' residence at, 87–88, 113–19; Danaus as ruler of, 15–16, 44–45; Danaus as threat to, 40, 42–45; defeat of, 15, 46, 160n118; Egyptians' war with, 96–97, 140n117; public shrine of, 26–27; serpents driven from, 39–40, 87, 94–95, 108; territorial definition of, 87, 92–94; as *topos*, 15; trade and commerce unimportant in mythical, 25–26; type of threat and cure for, 95–96. *See also* Apis; Argive assembly; Argives; natives/newcomers/land relationship; Pelasgus
Aristides, 52, 174n185
Aristophanes: use of dialect in, 133–34n22
—WORKS: *Acharnians*, 109; *Birds*, 127n10; *Wasps*, 138n100
Aristophanes of Byzantium, 8
Aristophon, 125
Aristotle: alienable property in time of, 106; on assembly and *boule* meetings, 132n4; on changing census status, 107; citizen defined

by, 54–55; on citizenship and manpower, 150n136; on Cleisthenes, 18, 133n13; on dwelling space, 117; on pay for jurors, 52; on Pericles's law, 150n134; on tragic figures, 22
—*AthPol* topics: *boule*, 132n4; census, 102–3, 104, 107; "citizen," 101; military wage, 52; pay for jurors, 52; Pericles's law, 50–51, 54–55, 139n109; political structure, 142–43n15; would-be citizens, 28, 29
Artemis, 62, 66, 78, 156n30, 161n130
Asclepius, 168n47
assembly (*ekklesia*): citizen's role as assemblyman, 55; metics barred from, 35; proceedings and meetings of, 48–49, 132n4; voting in, 30, 140n120, 140n123. *See also* Argive assembly; *isegoria*; speech norms
Assembly of the Gods (Lucian), 137n78, 145n54, 151n146, 153n177
assimilation: metics viewed as unsuited to, 34–35; as theme of *Suppliant Women*, 127n8. *See also* civic incorporation
astoi, 9, 139n109
Athena: Danaids purified by, 76–77; Erinyes (Semnae) and, 134n28; hope for reconciliation, 123, 177n11; persuasion by, 169n83; shrine for, 153n178
Athenaeus, 74, 75, 160n115
Athenians: attitudes toward Amazons, 70; attitudes toward metics, 12–14, 131n87; bloodshed in city sanctuary remembered by, 149n115; enslaved or exiled, returned under Solon, 107, 128n35, 142n4, 172n135; food supplies for, 51; free vs. slave distinctions, 128n32; literacy of, 107, 137n72; racial concerns of, 153n175; self-interest of, 8. *See also* audience; collective identity
Athenian tragedy. *See* tragedy
Athens: accountability proceedings (*euthunai*) in, 48; Argive metcikia in relation to, 14–15; Argos compared, summarized, 120–21; autochthony as ideology at, 91–93; colonies and cleruchies sent out by, 152n164; constitution of, 6, 13; construction projects in, 111, 132n4, 173nn157–58; divorce in, 159n93; housing in, 117–18; indebtedness in, 107, 170n86; influx of foreign gods in, 26, 137n83; metics in *asty* proper of, 32; metics' participation in festivals of, 141–42n146; as nation and polis, 8–9, 18; population numbers in, 19, 52–53; reshaping historical study of, 6–7; striking of noncitizens banned in, 13; transformation of (480/60), 175n197, 175n203. *See also* Acropolis; Attica; autochthony; citizens; immigration; military; natives/newcomers/land relationship; *polis*
Attica: agriculture as central to, 110; distinctions in, based on economic status, 7; diversity of burial rites in (Geometric Attica), 133n8; land ownership in, 106; people enrolled in demes and, 18; population growth of, 52–53; stone marker (*horoi*) in, 107–8, 171n129, 171–72n133, 172n137; types of inhabitants in, 9
audience: citizen autochthony idea and, 92; education of, 31; expectations of, 135n36; foreign experiences of, 167n42; geography and culture linked for, 68–69; immigration in daily lives of, 3, 17; location and political understandings of, 32; marriage views of, 61–63, 83, 85–86, 130n77, 154n6, 155n19, 157n43; titillating images for, 65–66, 157n57. *See also* Athenians
Auffarth, C., 160n118
autochthony: census linked to, 12, 87, 102–3, 106; concept of, 7, 101; debates on, 165n2; father-son

autochthony (*continued*)
resemblance and, 90–91; implications of, 101–3; myth of, 91–93, 167n32; Pelasgus's and Argive identification with, 12, 87, 89–92, 108–9, 120; Solon and, 121; xenophobic nature of, 167n32. *See also* agrarian citizen farmer; census; land

Bäbler, Balbina, 111, 134n25
Bachvarova, Mary, 10, 144n36, 155n21, 161n137, 177n10
Bamberger (scholar), 99
barbaroi, 127n13
Bednarowski, P., 144n32
Beloch, Karl J., 52–53
bia ("force"), 35–40
Bintliff, J., 171–72n133
Birds (Aristophanes), 127n10
Blok, J. H., 9, 139n105, 139n109, 150n134, 151n142, 153n176
Boedeker, Deborah, 85
Boegehold, Alan L., 51, 132n5, 143n24, 151n142
border crossings: dramaturgy of, 26–29, 88–89; *horoi* at, 107–8, 171n129, 171–72n133, 172n137; in Oedipus at Colonus, 138n91; territorial definitions and, 87, 92–94, 167n42. *See also* immigration
boule. *See* council
Bronze Age migration myth, 3–4, 17, 73. *See also* Danaids; *metoikia* charter myth
Burford, Alison, 106
burial rites and tombstones, 26, 130n80, 133n8
Burian, Peter, 46
Burkert, W., 144n41
Burns, Alfred, 117
Buxton, R., 144n35

Cahill, N., 175n199, 175n208
Carawan, E., 149n107, 151n138
census: agricultural vs. military basis for, 103–6, 170nn105–6; changing status in, 107; citizen and soil linked in, 12, 87, 102–3, 106, 121; income and, 103; numbers of (317/307), 152n160; political and class functions of, 106–9
Children of Heracles (Euripides), 135n37
Christ, M., 153n180
citizen autochthony. *See* autochthony
citizens: as artisans, 111; benefits and wages for, 51–53; census categories of, 12, 87, 102–7; definitions of, 6, 50, 54–55, 58, 101, 124–25; examination (*dokimasiai*) of male would-be, 27–28, 29, 138nn99–100; *misthos* paid to (state payments), 18; number of (adult males), 19; in oratory, demonstrative pronouns used, 135–36n46; polis-wide military muster of, 140n117; voting by, 123. *See also* agrarian citizen farmer; Argives; Athenians; autochthony; census; collective identity; free local person, redefined; natives/newcomers/land relationship
citizenship: direct descent insufficient for, 29; geographical and genealogical components of, 58; insider/outsider construction in, 141n145; manpower concerns and, 150n136; metoikia's relation to, 8; "refracted nature" of, 4, 127n5; restrictions in, as response to metic speech, 50; speech norms, Pericles's law, and, 49–57. *See also* Pericles's citizenship law (451/50)
citizen speech: in assembly, 47–49; norms formulated in, 153n179; Pelasgus as exemplifying, 34, 45–47; successful type of, 49. See also *isegoria*; speech norms
citizen sponsors (*prostatai*): failure to have (*graphai aprostasiou*), 9, 129n60; requirement for, 8, 115
civic incorporation: anxieties about and limits to, 5, 18; dramaturgy

and, 20, 23; as theme of play, 57–58, 60, 140n133. *See also* assimilation
Cleisthenes: democracy instituted by, 102; foreigners and slaves incorporated by, 18, 133n13, 133n15; free residents enfranchised by, 20, 46; intermarriages under, 86; land ownership under, 106; reforms of, 3; tribal reorganization of, 17–18
Clerc, Michel, 7
Cohen, Edward, 8–9, 129n57, 129n59, 139n109, 165n2
coinage, 18, 71–72, 159n89. *See also* Cypriote stamp
Cole, S. G., 138nn879, 139n112, 140n115
collective identity: exclusionary component of, 3, 34–35; insider/outsider construction in, 141n145; Pelasgus and city identical in, 45–46; self-definition of, 5–7. *See also* citizens; Pericles's citizenship law (451/50)
colonization myths, 163n170
Conacher, D. J., 134n29
Connor, W. R., 150n119, 150n127
Copenhagen Polis Centre, 6
corporate ownership of land, 106, 114–15
council (*boule*): daily meetings of, 132n4; metics barred from, 35; *prytaneis* and, 36–37, 143n22; structure of, 37
Cylon conspiracy, 149n115
Cypriotes: Danaids perceived as, 67–68; non-Greeks among, 71
Cypriote stamp: Danaids as coins struck with, 67, 71–73, 143n25; historical details of, 158–59n86. *See also* coinage

Danaids: appearance and clothing of, 21–22, 25, 65–66, 70, 89; approach to, 10–11; border crossing of, 26–29; claims to Argive descent, 26–28, 67–68, 145n59 (*see also* Io); concept of, 5; Danaus characterized by, 42–45; departure from Egypt, 23–26, 59, 102; elocutionary advice for, 40–42, 147n83; entry into Argos city center, 32–33; fears of, 59–60, 65; fertility brought by, 155n21; foreignness and exoticism of, 11–12, 20–23, 60–61, 67–73, 135n40; historical context of, 17–19; housing for, 87–88, 113–19; husbands killed by, 12, 43, 73, 75, 76–77, 88, 113; independence of, 11–12, 60–67; invention of metoikia status for, 19–20; limits of incorporation in Argos, 57–58; metoikia granted by Argive assembly, 4, 30–32, 34, 101–2; myth of, summarized, 3–4, 17, 73; other tragic female characters compared with, 81–85; patrilineal descent traced, 60, 155n13; Pelasgus's cross-examination of, 27–29, 38, 88–89; serpents juxtaposed to, 94–95, 168n52; sexual desirability highlighted, 72–73; speech as intelligible to land but not current inhabitants, 35–36; suppliant boughs ("daggers") of, 22, 40–41, 62–63, 65; Themistocles compared with, 97–98, 168n65; threats (suicide and pollution) of, 35–40, 58, 65, 98–100, 144n32; Zeus invoked by, 37, 79–81, 134n30, 141n145. *See also* marriage; *metics*; metic speech; *metoikia* charter myth; natives/newcomers/land relationship
Danaids (Aeschylus): fragments of, 60, 73–76, 113; outline of, 15–16; title of, 132n98. *See also* Danaid trilogy
Danaid trilogy: Argives summoned to fight Egyptians, 140n117; assumptions about, 11; Danaids' housing as relevant to, 113; Danaus's description key to, 44; dating of, 10, 130n63; Hypermestra's role in, 16, 73–77, 136n47, 157n56;

Danaid trilogy (*continued*)
incongruity of alleged trial in, 74–76; lack of control by Danaus in, 157n56; order and reconstruction of plays, 60, 73, 146n73, 159n96; outline of, 15–16, 132n99, 132n100, 132n103; proposed outcomes of, 12; purification and remarriage of Danaids in, 76–79; women's ethnicity as theme in, 67–73. See also *Danaids*; *Sons of Aegyptus*; *Suppliant Women* (Aeschylus)
Danaus: advice on daughters' speech and behavior, 40–42, 147n83; ancestors of, 26–28, 145n59; appeal for daughters to remain chaste, 66–67; on Argive assembly proceedings, 48–49, 149n114; as Argos ruler, 15–16, 44–45; on assembly's decision, 30; athletic contest references and, 76–77; bodyguards requested by, 34, 42, 44, 77–78, 116, 146n72; characteristics of, 42–45, 74–75; daughters' relationship to, 59–60; death foretold by oracle, 23, 38, 74, 154n7; *dolos* ("cunning") in speech of, 39, 40, 42–45, 144n46; Egyptians spotted by, 32–33; housing advice of, 116, 118; lack of control by, 157n56; marriage views of, 61–62; seafaring and ship of, 24–25; stage absences of, 66, 165n6; stage entrance/exit of, 20–21, 135n32, 156n41, 176n219
Davidson, James, 69
Davies, J. K., 18, 177n13
decrees: formula for, 30–31, 48, 140nn123–24; on protections for Acheloion, 140n125
Delian League, 18, 19, 53, 167n42
demes ("local villages"): of *asty*, listed, 32; function of, 6; male would-be citizens examined by (*dokimasiai*), 27–28, 29, 138nn99–100; recorded laws of (Scambonidae), 20
Demetrius of Phaleron, 152n160
democracy: Cleisthenes's institution of, 102; Danaids' antipathy to and subversion of, 35–40, 143n28; ideological shifts in, 7; *peitho* in, 123–24; tragedy's role in citizens' thinking about, 5–6; xenophobia and autochthony in relation to, 167n32
Demosthenes, 91, 173n155, 174n185
de Ste. Croix, G. E. M., 103, 104, 105
Diamantopoulos, A., 131n88
dikasteria. *See* law courts
dolos ("cunning"): gendered female, 39; in metic speech, 40, 42–45, 144n46. *See also* persuasion
Draco's homicide law, 133n8
Dunbabin, T. J., 172n154
Duncan-Jones, R. P., 54, 152n157

earth. *See* land; natives/newcomers/land relationship
earthborn. *See* Pelasgus
Easterling, Patricia, 36, 37, 131n95
economic realm: aristocratic vs. democratic systems of exchange, 136n57; boards' spending authority in, 37–38; citizenship benefits and, 51–53; fear of metics' effects in, 13–14, 34–35; immigrant opportunities in, 18–19; Medea's marriage in context of, 84–85; metics' roles in, 87, 110–12, 131n83, 172n151; writing in, 25–26. *See also* agriculture; land; political realm; religious realm; sexual realm; socioeconomic groups
Effenterre, Henri van and Micheline van, 21–22
Egypt: Danaids' departure from, 23–26, 59, 102; Danaids' failure to mention laws of, 38; Danaus's quarrel about ruling, 43; gender roles in, 69; Greek emporium in, 24; Io's flight to, 27; writing in, 25
Egyptian herald: as barbarian, 46, 65, 75; departure and threat of, 66–67,

80, 89, 96–97; Pelasgus's interaction with, 22–23, 25–26, 44, 45, 92, 95, 147n80, 147n88; task of, 147n95
Egyptians (Aegyptids): approaching walls of Argos, 32–33, 89; Danaids' murder of, 12, 43, 73, 75, 76–77, 88, 113; Danaids perceived as, 67–68, 69; proper marriage sought by, 157n43
ekklesia. *See* assembly
enktesis (ownership of real property): metics banned from, 12, 87, 109–10, 112–13; reflected in housing offered to Danaids, 113–17 *See also* housing; land
Epaphus, 3–4, 27, 91, 94, 136n47
ephebes: board games for, 147n78; examined before joining citizen body (*dokimasiai*), 27–28, 29, 138nn99–100
Ephialtes, 17, 47, 52, 92, 133n6
Epicurus, 112–13
epitaphios (genre), 165n4
equal speech. See *isegoria*
Erechtheum, building accounts of, 111, 173nn157–58
Erechtheus (Euripides), 90–91, 146n75
Erichthonius, 91
Eumenides (Aeschylus): Apollo's exit unremarked, 176n219; Athena in, 169n83; beginning of, 167n30; chorus's farewell in, 123, 177n7; Danaid trilogy in relation to, 159–60n105; Furies in, 76, 160n112, 168–69n67; newcomers in, 20, 162n148; prosecution of Orestes in, 160n106; *Suppliant Women* compared with, 122–23, 124; territorial definitions in, 93, 167n42. See also *Oresteia*
Euripides, works: *Children of Heracles*, 135n37; *Erechtheus*, 90–91, 146n75; *Hecuba*, 149–50n119; *Phoenician Women*, 159n94; *Suppliant Women*, 13, 135n37, 144n45. See also *Medea*
Eustathius, 147n85
family values, as *kyrios*-centered, 12, 60–61. *See also* gender norms; marriage
Farenga, Vincent: on citizenship, 4, 127n5; on ephebes, 139n108; on Pelasgus and Argive assembly, 49, 149n114; on Pelasgus's cross-examination and *dokimasiai*, 27–28, 29, 138n99
FJW. See *Aeschylus: The Suppliants*
Foley, Helene, 84, 155n22, 156n30, 164n179
Föllinger, S., 160n106
foreigners: dramaturgy as emphasizing difference of, 20–23, 135n40; metics distinguished from, 134n25; putative sexual practices of various, 67–73; as suppliants, 41. *See also* immigrants; *metics*; natives/newcomers/land relationship
Forrest, W., 131n38
Forsdyke, S., 171n115
Foxhall, L., 170n101
Fraenkel, E., 138n88, 166n15
free local person, redefined, 9. *See also* citizens
free speech, 45–46. *See also* speech norms
French, Alfred, 103–4, 153n172
Friis Johansen, Holger. See *Aeschylus: The Suppliants*
Fritz, Kurt von, 76, 81

game playing, 44–45, 147n78, 147n81
Gantz, T., 159n87
Garvie, A. F.: on *Amymone*, 159n95; on Danaids' housing, 113; on Danaids' refusal to marry, 154n2, 156n30; on Danaids' trial, 75; on Danaid trilogy, 73, 76, 131–32n97, 132nn98–100, 132n103; on dating of plays, 10; on end of plays, 160n122; on Pelasgus's death, 132n102

gender norms: aristocratic vs. democratic systems of exchange and, 136n57; Danaids' departure from Egypt and, 23; Danaids' independence as threat to, 60–67; divorce and, 159n93; foreign women and practices as challenge to, 67–73; land as female and, 166n27; reversals in, 39–40, 80–81; tragic women's disruption of, 81–85. *See also* marriage; sexual realm
Geometric Attica, burial rites in, 133n8
Glazebrook, Allison, 135–36n46, 139n106, 157–58n63, 176n213
Gödde, Susanne, 41, 136n50
Goldhill, Simon, 5–6, 141n145
Graham, A. J., 172n142
gravestones and burial rites, 26, 130n80, 133n8
Greece: commonalities throughout, 19; Egyptian trade with, 24–25; Persian conflict with, 96; *Urvolk* of, 90; wool-tipped olive boughs as symbol of, 22
Grethlein, J., 59, 127n12, 137n79, 147n88, 167n39
Griffith, Mark, 10, 16, 82, 130n73, 163n159
Grossmann, G., 132n1
Gruppe (scholar), 160n114
guest-friendship (*xenia*), 7, 11, 31–32, 122, 141n135. *See also* suppliant tradition

Hall, Edith, 6, 90, 144n40
Hall, J., 142n7, 166n24
Halliwell, S., 133–34n22
hands and handiwork: emphasis on, 22–23; suppliant boughs ("daggers") and, 22, 40–41, 62–63, 65; voting via, 30, 140n120, 140n123
Hansen, Mogens H., 6, 19, 52, 133n6, 143n22, 169n74
Hanson, Victor, 105
Harrison, J., 167n36
Heath, John, 49–50, 99
Hecataeus, 93
Hecuba (Euripides), 149–50n119
Helen of Troy, 96, 159n93
Hellanicus of Lesbos, 167n29
Henderson, John, 159n94
Hera, 78, 91, 167n29
Heraclitus, 44
Hermarchus, 112–13
Hermes, 76–77
Herodotus: contemporaries' belief in veracity of, 157n61; on *gemoroi*, 101; on Greek-Persian conflict, 96; on non-Greek groups, 68–70; on Peisistratus, 146n71; on Pelasgians, 90; on poleis involved in Hellenion, 136n60; Thesmophoria and, 60
Hesychius, 35
hippeis, 102–3, 104–5, 170n105. *See also* census
Hippias, 18
Hippodamus of Miletus, 117–18
Hoepfner, Wolfram, 118, 175n207
"holy line," 44–45, 147nn84–85
Homer: absence of coinage in epics, 24
—WORKS: *Hymn to Demeter*, 155n22; *Iliad*, 96, 148n100; *Odyssey*, 29–30, 44
honor, concept and bestowal of, 47
hoplites, 54, 105, 107, 152n157
horoi (stone markers), 107–8, 171n129, 171–72n133, 172n137
Hose, M., 159n96
housing: corporate ownership of, 106, 114–15; of Danaids in Argos, 87–88, 113–19; Hippodameian style of, 117–18; of metics, 12, 130n80; of military leaders, 174n185
Hurwit, J., 132n3
Hymn to Demeter (Homer), 155n22
Hypermestra, 16, 73–77, 136n47, 157n56

Iliad (Homer), 96, 148n100
immigrants: citizens' suspicions of motives of, 56–57; diversity of, 8;

livelihoods of, 87, 110–12, 128n33, 131n83, 172n151; military role of, 53–54; number of, 19; self-interests of, 57–58; substantial role in Athens, 7; as *xenoi*, 20. *See also* civic incorporation; foreigners; *metics*; natives/newcomers/land relationship
immigration: beliefs underlying, 172n149; early U. S. law on, 134n23; increased in fifth century BCE, 3, 7, 17, 18–19; modern dangers of, 134n24; Pericles's law linked to, 53–54; Solon's restrictions on, 110. *See also* border crossings; Pericles's citizenship law (451/50)
Inarus, 26, 137n79
Indians, Danaids likened to, 67–68, 69, 72
Io: Danaids as descendants of, 27–28, 67–68, 91; Danaids' references to, 80, 120, 142n3; Pelasgus's version of story, 35; sexual practices of, 69–70; symbolism in story of, 162n149; wanderings of, 167n40, 168n58
Iphigenia, 156n29, 157n57
isegoria ("equal right to speech"): cherished by Athenians, 148n97; emergence of, 46; "frank speech" linked to, 57; implications of, 148n99; limits of, 57; metics excluded from, 153–54n186; Pelasgus as embodiment of, 11, 34. *See also* citizen speech; persuasion

Jenkins, Ian, 65, 157n47
Johnstone, Christopher, 49
Jones, Nicholas, 110

Keesling, C., 107, 171n127
Kennedy, R., 167n42
King, Helen, 66, 157n51
Kraay, C., 153n178
Kretschmer (scholar), 142n6
Kurke, Leslie, 44, 72, 147n81, 147n84

land: census categories and, 103–6; citizenship linked to, 12, 87, 102–3, 106, 121; city-state distinguished from, 50; corporate ownership of, 106, 114–15; Danaids' threat to pollute, 36, 38–40, 58, 65, 98–100, 144n32; defense of, 92–93; equality myth of, 108–9; as female, 166n27; *horoi* marking boundaries of, 107–8, 171n129, 171–72n133, 172n137; inheritance issues and, 51; loss of, 102, 107n86; metics banned from owning, 12, 87, 109–10, 112–13; Pelasgus as son of, 12, 45, 87, 89–92, 108–9, 120; Solon's rejection of redistributing, 105–6. *See also* autochthony; *enktesis*; natives/newcomers/land relationship
language: dialect scenes and, 133–34n22; ethnicity linked to, 142n7. *See also* speech norms; *and specific terms and plays*
Laureion mines, 18, 105
law courts (*dikasteria*): asset appropriation powers of, 106, 173n167; citizens' role as jurymen, 55, 57; metics barred from, 35; pay for jurors, 52, 133n6; Philon's trial in, 110; women's identities in, 139n106
laws: on betrothal, 62; Ephialtes's reforms (462/61), 17, 47, 133n6; on homicide, 133n8; on mixed-status marriages, 163n173; obedience to, 55–57, 153n130; of Scambonidae (deme), 20. *See also* Pericles's citizenship law (451/50)
Lebeck, A., 134n29
Lee, Mireille, 65, 135n40
Leiwo, Martti, 112–13
Lewis, David, 20, 134n25, 172n143
Libation Bearers (Aeschylus), 100, 135n43, 173n173. See also *Oresteia*
Libyans, women perceived as, 67–69, 72
literacy, 107, 137n72
Loomis, William, 52, 152n153

Loraux, Nicole, 91, 92, 166n23, 166n25
Lucian, 137n78, 145n54, 151n146, 153n177
Lysias, 55–56, 136n54, 163n156, 172n148, 176n211

MacKinnon, J. K., 154n2, 154n6
Maitland, J., 164–65n190
Manville, Philip, 106, 128n32, 133n8, 133n15, 165n5, 172n137
marriage: approach to issue, 11–12; citizenship issues and, 54, 153n173; ending a bad, 156n39; *epithalamion* and, 79–80; *eros* vs. practical considerations in, 163n169; foreign practices as threat to, 67–73; mixed-status type of, 85–86, 163n173; as political bond of polis, 130n77, 155n19; virilocal type of, 70, 83, 155n2; women's disruptive effects on norms, 81–85; women's lack of power in, 157n47. *See also* sexual realm
—OF DANAIDS: departure from Egypt and, 23; to Egyptians, 73–76; independence concerning, 11–12, 60–61; opposition later moderated, 61–67, 79–81, 154n2, 156n30; purification and remarriage, 76–79; reluctance and fears, 59–60, 65; reversal of norms, 80–81
Mastronarde, D., 163–64n174, 164n177, 164n188
McClure, Laura, 41
McMahon, John, 69
Medea (Euripides): Danaids compared with, 61, 83–85, 161n130; foreigners and citizens in, 163–64n174; Medea's appeal to Aegeus in, 164n188
Meier, Christian, 5
Meiggs, R., 134n25, 172n143
men: bride-grabbing by, 65; as ephebes examined before joining citizen body (*dokimasiai*), 27–28, 29, 138nn99–100, 139n108; tragic women used to think about themselves, 15; as women's guardians, 61–62
Mesatus, 10
metatheater, 15, 131n93. *See also* tragedy
metics ("livers with"): as anti-citizens, 139n108; appearance of, 176–77n6; banned from *enktesis*, 12, 87, 109–10, 112–13; citizen sponsors of, 8, 9, 115, 129n60; Cleisthenes's incorporation of, 18, 133n13, 133n15; communities and deities of, 26, 118, 137n83, 176nn211–12; definitions and use of term, 3, 5, 8, 50, 163n159, 163n164; Egyptians as, 26; foreigners distinguished from, 134n25; independence of Danaids as, 11–12, 60–67; legal status of, 7, 30–32, 101, 124–25; livelihoods of, 87, 110–12, 128n33, 131n83, 172n151; motivations of, 23–24; number, *demes*, and dwellings of, 19, 32, 54, 86, 118; other tragic women as, 81–85; *pessoi* compared with, 146n75; political activities restricted for, 34–35; roles envisioned for, 13–14, 153–54n186; studies of, 7–10; suspected in taking of walled cities, 169n76. *See also* citizen sponsors; civic incorporation; Danaids; foreigners; housing; immigrants; natives/newcomers/land relationship
metic speech: *bia* ("force") in, 35–40; citizens' fears concerning, 34–35, 50; *dolos* ("cunning") in, 39, 40, 42–45, 144n46; elocutionary advice for, 40–42, 147n83. *See also* speech norms
metoikia (metic status): Argive assembly's grant of, 4, 30–32, 34, 101–2; Athenian model of, 14–15; definition and use of term, 3, 5; festival participation and, 141–42n146; ideological founda-

tions of, 128–29n37; legal description of, 7, 30–32, 101, 124–25; persuasion and mutual benefit as basis for, 123–24; studies of, 7–10; *Suppliant Women* and legitimization of, 122–25; tenor and tenure of, 12–14
metoikia charter myth: approach to, 10–11; Argive assembly's role in, 4, 30–32, 34, 101–2; border crossing in, 26–29; departure from Egypt in, 23–26, 59, 102; dramaturgy and, 20–23; entry into Argos city center, 32–33; historical context of, 17–19; invention of status in, 19–20; story of, 3–4, 17, 73
metoikion (annual payment), 8, 18
Meyer, Elizabeth, 9, 174n187
Michelini, Ann, 69
military: approach to walled cities, 169n76; Athenian successes in, 18–19, 133n14; autochthony and, 92–93; benefits and wages for, 51–52; board games for ephebes of, 147n78; census categories and, 104–6, 170nn105–6; food scarcity and activities of, 151n143; generals' independence and vulnerability, 143n26, 169n74; hoplites of, 54, 105, 107, 152n157; housing of leaders of, 174n185; number of citizens available, 53–54; polis-wide muster of, 140n117; political strife and, 100, 169nn73–74
Miltiades, 47, 174n185
Mitchell, L., 127n13, 131n84, 135n33, 158n72
Möller, A., 136nn60–61, 136n63
Monoson, Sara, 57, 148n99
Müller, C. W., 10
Munn, M., 147n78
Murnaghan, S., 160n129, 163n156
Murray, R. D., 4
myths: autochthony, 91–93, 167n32; colonization, 163n170; equality, 108–9. See also *metoikia* charter myth; religious realm

Naiden, F. S., 143–44n30, 144n37
nation (*ethnos*), 8–9
native inhabitants, defined, 101. *See also* citizens
natives/newcomers/land relationship: approach to, 12; categories and characterization of, 100–109; complexity of, 87–88; Danaids and danger in relation to, 98–100; Pelasgus's relation to land and polis in, 88–98; territorial definition and, 87, 92–94, 167n42. *See also* border crossings
Naucratis (Egypt): courtesans of, 136n63; Greek emporium at, 24; papyrus exported from, 25; tombstone of metic from, 26
Neaera (courtesan), 163n173, 164n189, 165n193
Neils, Jennifer, 141n144, 177n7
Nicomenes, 125
non-citizens: ban on striking at Athens, 13; Cleisthenes's incorporation of, 13, 133n13, 133n15; as *xenoi*, 20. *See also* foreigners; immigrants; *metics*; slaves

Ober, J., 130n76, 148n97, 153n179, 171n129
Odyssey (Homer), 29–30, 44
Oedipus at Colonus (Sophocles), 135n37, 138n91, 161n130
Oedipus the King (Sophocles), 159n94
Ogden, Daniel, 54, 151n138, 151n146, 153n175
oligarchy, game playing in, 44–45
Olynthus housing, 175n199, 175n208
Oresteia (Aeschylus): chorus and political strife linked in, 43; coup d'état in, 100; scene building of, 135n38; *Suppliant Women* in relation to, 132n100, 155n17. See also *Agamemnon*; *Eumenides*; *Libation Bearers*
Ormand, K., 163n169
Osborne, Robin, 114, 125, 129n57
Ostwald, Martin, 109

Oxyrhynchus Papyrus 2256, 10, 131–32n97

Palaichthon, Pelasgus linked to, 45, 89–92, 120
Papadopoulos, J., 172n151
papyrus, uses of, 25–26
Parker, Robert, 26, 137n83
Parthenon, 141n144
Patterson, Cynthia: on citizenship, 152n167; on citizens in relation to metics, 50; on courtesans and collective identity, 165n193; on food scarcity and military activities, 151n143; on marriage and audience, 155n19; on marriage as political bond, 130n77; on Pericles's law, 53–54, 150n135; on population pressures, 152n164
Pausanias (Greek geographer): on Aphrodite and Persuasion, 140n117, 153n178; Danaid trilogy and, 15; on Hypermestra, 74, 159n104; sources of, 75–76
Pausanias (Spartan king), 97
Pearson, M., 165n3
Pecirka, Jan, 112
Peisistratids, 3, 46, 110, 125, 146n71
Peisistratus, 42, 146n71
peitho. *See* persuasion
Peitho (deity), 55, 140n117, 153n178
Pelasgus: accommodation for Danaids offered by, 113–17; accusations feared by, 47–48, 100, 148n100, 149n107; ancestry and land of, 12, 45, 87, 89–92, 108–9, 120; Apis compared with, 94–96, 108, 120; armed men accompanying, 88–89, 171n113; as Athenian ideal, 132n1; attitude toward sea, 24; choice to place decision before assembly, 13–14, 29–30, 38, 46–48; citizen speech exemplified by, 34, 45–47; citizen speech for assembly, 48–49; Danaids' characterization of role, 36–38; Danaids cross-examined by, 27–29, 38, 88–89; Danaids' foreignness perceived by, 21–22, 67–69, 70–73; democratic rhetorical ethos and *isegoria* of, 11; Egyptian herald's interaction with, 22–23, 25–26, 44, 45, 92, 95, 147n80, 147n88; on Io's story, 35; on marriage issue, 62–64; Palaichthon linked to, 45, 89–92, 120; staff carried by, 89; ultimate failure of, 15, 96, 100, 132n102
Peloponnesian War: beginning of, 167n29; extent of, 99; losses in, 109, 125, 173n158; military strength before, 52; tragedy in context of, 5–6
Pentecontaetea, 51–52
pentecosiomedimnoi, 102–3, 104, 170n105. *See also* census
Pericles: accusations feared by, 149n108; census and, 169n76; as *choregus* in *Persians*, 152n152; death of, 150n119; mentioned, 17; pay for military and for jurors, 52; son's enrollment and, 151n138
Pericles's citizenship law (451/50): Athenian self-definition linked to, 6; caliber of citizenry and, 54–57; citizen body regulated by, 34–35; citizen-to-newcomer ratio and, 51–54; implementation date of, 151n148; lack of recorded debate on, 150n135; metics as target of, 11, 153n172; as morale booster, 153n176; motivation for, 50–51, 124–25, 151n142; *Suppliant Women* in relation to, 50, 58; text of, 150n134. *See also* collective identity
Periegesis (Hecataeus), 93
Persephone, 155n22
Persians (Aeschylus), 93, 134n26, 143n18, 152n152
Persian Wars: Athens after, 175n197, 175n203; immigration after, 3, 17, 19; population growth of Attica after, 52–53
persuasion ("*peitho*"): concept of, 35, 144n35; Danaids' disregard for

norms of, 36, 38–40, 58, 144n32; implemented in assembly, 47–49; Pelasgus as embodiment of, 34; polis activities and reliance on, 55; primacy in democracy, 123–24. See also *dolos*; Peitho (deity)
Petre, Z., 140n125
Philon, 56, 110
Phoenician Women (Euripides), 159n94
Pindar, 73, 77, 117, 144n39
Piraeus, 18, 19, 26, 117–18
Plato, 25, 55, 56–57, 109, 173n167
Plutarch, 10, 50, 128n35, 133n8, 150n127, 151n138
Podlecki, Anthony, 97, 98, 152n152
polemarch, 8
polis (*poleis*): archonship in, 52, 104, 106–7, 152n156; *astoi* vs. *politai* in, 9, 139n109; Athens as nation and, 8–9; boundaries of, 88–89; center and perimeter defined for, 7; fringe areas of, 29, 139n112; game playing in, 44–45, 147n81; individual interests subordinated to, 55–57, 153n180; *kyrios*-centered values of, 12, 60–61; male and female members compared, 139nn105–6; marriage as political bond of, 83, 130n77, 155n19; metics' participation in festivals of, 141–42n146; reshaping studies of, 6–7; tragedy's implications for, 5–6; women's disruptive effects on, 81–85. *See also* assembly; autochthony; citizenship; council; *demes*; law courts; *and specific poleis*
polites, 9, 128–29n37, 139n109
political realm: archonship in, 52, 104, 106–7, 152n156; Athenian structure in, 37; census distinctions in, 106–9; citizen's roles in, 55; expanded opportunities in, 46; fear of metics' effects in, 13–14, 34–35, 50; foreign ideas about, 35–36; game playing in, 44–45, 147n81; land ownership and status in, 103–5; marriage as bond in, 83, 130n77, 155n19; military defeats' impact on, 100, 169nn73–74; as subject in tragedy, 5–6. *See also* assembly; council; economic realm; law courts; religious realm; sexual realm; suppliant tradition
potters, metics as, 110, 172n151. *See also* vase paintings
Pritchett, W. K., 52, 152n153, 173n162
prostitutes, 69–70, 72, 165n193
Psammetichus, 51
Pseudo-Apollodorus, 76–77
Pseudo-Xenophon, 13, 153–54n186
public shrines: attitudes toward precincts of, 114; Danaids' stop at, 26–27; description of, 138n87; location of, 138n88; private hearth vs., 29–30; rituals for entering, 27, 138n89. *See also* religious realm; rituals

Raaflaub, Kurt, 45, 46, 105
Randall, Richard, 111, 173nn157–58
Reden, S. von, 176n212
Rehm, R., 135n34, 164n174
religious realm: act of supplication in, 29–30; Danaids' attitude toward, 119–20; Danaids' shifting allegiance in, 33. *See also* economic realm; myths; political realm; public shrines; rituals; sexual realm; *and specific deities*
Remes, Pauliina, 112–13
Rhodes, P. J.: on Aristotelian *Athenaion Politeia*, 6; on citizen categories, 170n93, 170n105, 171n126; on metic population, 86; on military wage, 52, 152n153; on Pericles's law, 54, 151n145, 153n173
rituals: demesmen and metics' roles in, 20; for entering shrine, 27, 138n89; gods and altar placement in, 138n86; of marriage, 73–74; of supplication, 21, 136n50. *See also* public shrines; religious realm; sanctuary; suppliant tradition
Robertson, D. S., 75

Rosivach, Vincent, 91–92, 104
Rösler, Wolfgang, 10, 115, 116–18, 148n104
"ruler" (*prytanis*), 36–37

Saïd, Suzanne, 15
Salamis, battle of (480), 19, 20, 53
sanctuary: previously private requests for, 29–30, 31–32; ratification of, 33. *See also* public shrines; suppliant tradition
Sandin, Pär: on "cures," 95; on Cyprus reference, 71; on Danaus's entrance, 135n32; on gods and altar placement in play, 138n86; mentioned, 10; on Pelasgus, 93, 94; on women's speech, 35
Sappho, 161n137, 162n146
satyr drama (tragicomedy), 73, 159n95
Saxonhouse, A., 167n32
Schlesinger, E., 134n31
Schuck, P., 134nn23–24
Schwandner, E.-L., 118, 175n207
Scullion, Scott, 10, 130n68
Seaford, Richard, 24, 59, 79, 155n14, 162n146
Sealey, R., 128n31, 133n14
serpents: Danaids compared with, 94–95, 168n52; deities as, 144n41; plague of, in "Apian" Argos, 39–40, 87, 94–95, 108
Seven against Thebes (Aeschylus), 10, 96, 135n43, 141n143, 148–49n105
sexual realm: Athenians' fear of metics' effects in, 13–14; Danaids' realistic view of, 120; foreign women and practices in, 67–73, 165n193; skin color and, 69, 70; strangulation vs. unwanted sex, 157n51; titillating images in play, 65–66, 157n57; women's disruptive effects on norms, 81–85. *See also* economic realm; gender norms; marriage; political realm; religious realm
Shanks, M., 165n3
Sicherl, Martin, 10, 154n7, 157n56
slaves: Cleisthenes's incorporation of, 18, 133n13, 133n15; confiscated from individuals, 173n167; free people distinguished from, 128n32; male would-be citizens rejected, then sold as, 29; metics without sponsors sold as, 115
snakes. *See* serpents
social life: citizens vs. metics in, 129n59; degree of mobility in, 9; women's role in, 61–62. *See also* gender norms; marriage
socioeconomic groups: agricultural yield and acreage in, 103–4; census categories in relation to, 102–3, 106–9; citizen definition and, 101; citizen-metic marriages and, 85–86, 163n173; of foreign residents (artists and laborers), 128n33; tragedies' depiction of, 164–65n190. *See also* economic realm
Solon: defense of actions by, 108; enslaved Athenians freed and exiles returned under by, 107, 128n35, 142n4, 172n135; *horoi* removed by, 107–8, 171n129, 171–72n133; immigration under, 110; reforms of, 128n32. *See also* census
Sommerstein, Alan: on Cyprus reference, 71; on Danaids, 77, 143n28; on Danaus, 43–44, 145n65; dowries and, 156n35; on ending a bad marriage, 156n39; on *Eumenides*, 123, 176–77n6, 177n7; interpretative study of, 10, 141n143; on metic terminology, 169n83; on Pelasgus, 149n112, 156n31; on Pelasgus and Argive assembly, 48; on two choruses' exchanges, 161n132
Sons of Aegyptus (Aeschylus), 15–16, 60, 73, 131–32n97. *See also* Danaid trilogy

Sophocles: contests of plays and, 10
—WORKS: *Aegeus*, 164n188; *Antigone*, 61, 81–83, 143n24, 163n156; *Oedipus at Colonus*, 135n37, 138n91, 161n130; *Oedipus the King*, 159n94; *Trachiniae*, 162n153
Sourvinou-Inwood, C., 157n46
Sown Men (Spartoi) of Thebes, 91
Sparta: equality myth of, 108–9; as foil, 131n91; foreigners driven out of, 131n89. *See also* Pausanias (Spartan king)
speech norms: approach to, 11; citizenship concepts underlying, 54–57; free speech in, 45–46; function of, 130n76; gender issues in, 41–42; persuasion vs. bold speech and guile in, 35, 39–40; political hierarchies linked to, 49–50; summary of, 57–58. *See also* citizen speech; *isegoria*; metic speech
Stewart, Andrew, 70, 86, 158n67
subjectivity, female: Danaids' insistence on, 119–20; metic women's independence and, 61–67; metic women's mixed-status marriage and, 86; as problem for male citizens, 83; scholarly interest in, 59–60
suppliant tradition: commitment to, 97; criteria of, 143–44n30; displacement of, 140n115; elocutionary advice for, 40–42, 147n83; etymology of, 134n31; foreign mediation linked to, 141n136; metoikia linked to, 122–25; other plays including, 29–30, 135n37; threats rare in, 144nn37–38; types of suppliants in, 41. *See also* rituals
Suppliant Women (Aeschylus): approach and methodologies for, 10–12, 14–16; Athenian events compared with, 97–98; border-crossing theme of, 26–29, 88–89; in context of other Aeschylean works, 9–10; corrupted lines in, 141n138; date, text, and commentary on, 9–10; discordant notes in, 26; dominant theme of, 4–5; dramaturgy emphasizing foreignness in, 20–23, 136n48; ending of, 67; historical context of, 3, 17–19; metic terminology of, 5; patrilineal nature of, 60, 155n13; public expectations of, 135n36; purification and remarriage referenced in, 76–79; role of choruses in, 77–78, 161n132; significance summarized, 122–25; story summarized, 3–4, 17, 73; visual structure of, 66. *See also* Argos; Danaids; Danaid trilogy; Danaus; marriage; *metoikia* charter myth; natives/newcomers/land relationship; Pelasgus; speech norms
Suppliant Women (Euripides), 13, 135n37, 144n45

Taplin, Oliver: on chorus, 146n70; on Danaus, 134n30, 156n41, 165n6; on *exeunt*, 33; on metatheater, 131n93; on Pelasgus and armed men, 88; on Pelasgus and Egyptian herald, 22, 168n55; on stagecraft, 66, 135n38, 161n134
Telesicrates (runner), 77
Thebes, as foil, 15
Themistocles: Danaids compared with, 97–98, 168n65; mentioned, 143n17; navy and, 17–18, 105; ostracized by Athens and flight of, 4, 20, 97–98
Theseus, 70, 140n117, 153n178
Thesmophoria, 60, 154–55n12, 155n14, 155n16
thetes, 102–3, 105, 106, 167n32, 170n105. *See also* census
Tholos, construction of, 132n4
Thomas, R., 137n72, 170n86
Thompson, H., 175n197
Thomson, G. D., 59

Thrasyboulus, 110, 111, 125
Thucydides: on Alcibiades, 109, 170n87; autochthony idea rejected by, 165n2; on census categories, 169n76; commitment to suppliant tradition, 97; dating of, 167n29; on early migrations, 172n149; on extent of conflict, 99; methodology of, 131n94; on Pericles's fears, 149n108; population numbers of, 52, 152n157
Thür, Gerhard, 115
Timocrates, 112
Todd, S., 153n183, 170n86
tombstones and burial rites, 26, 130n80, 133n8
Trachiniae (Sophocles), 162n153
tragedy: act of supplication in, 29–30, 135n37; approach to past in, 15, 131n95; Athenocentric nature of, 15, 97; barbarian stereotype in, 6; characteristics of figures in, 22; class differences in, 164–65n190; contests of, 10; democratic interests vs. mythical content in, 148n104; displacement strategy in, 6; disruptive women in, 81–85; female experience and subjectivity in, 59–60; financial concerns and, 23–24; language differences disregarded in, 35; messenger's role in, 149n114; metic terminology in, 127n11; political and ideological nature of, 5–6, 15; roles of chorus and music in, 43–44; scene building in, 135n38; sexual metaphors in, 159n94; stichomythia in, 28, 144n36; suppliant ritual in, 21, 41; *Suppliant Women* in context of, 9–10
tragicomedy (satyr drama), 73, 159n95
Turner, C., 143–44n30, 157n43
Tyrrell, W., 162n141
Tzakirgis, B., 175n203
Tzanetou, A., 155n16

Ulpian, 52
urban metic artisan stereotype, 87, 111–12. See also *metics*

vase paintings: Amazons on, 70, 158n67; "freedom" vases (*phialai exeleutherikai*), 9, 174n187; oriental cult scenes on, 137n83; symbol of fleeing girl on, 65, 157n46. *See also* potters, metics as
Vasunia, Phiroze, 25, 147n80, 157n62
Veness, Ruth, 158n72
Vernant, J.-P., 162n150
Vidal-Naquet, P., 127n11, 139n108

Wasps (Aristophanes), 138n100
West, M. L., 28, 148n101, 148n103, 148–49n105
Whitehead, David: on Aristotle, 133n13; on Athenian attitudes, 13, 131n83, 131n87; on census, 104; on the deme ("local village"), 6; metic studies of, 7–8, 9, 14, 16, 32, 118; on metic terminology, 5, 127n12, 128n16, 139n108, 139n110, 163n164; on metoikia, 128–29n37; on *zeugites*, 170n106
Whittle, Edward. See *Aeschylus: The Suppliants*
Wilamowitz-Möllendorf, Ulrich von, 7, 59, 113, 127n12, 129n39
Wilson, P., 43, 146n68, 146n70
Winnington-Ingram, R. P., 76, 155n15
Winton, R., 152n157
Wohl, Victoria, 15, 136n57, 162n153
women: abductions of, as source of conflict, 96–97; citizenship of Athenian, 28; Danaids' appeal for power for, 80–81; disruptive effects in tragedy, 81–85; dowries of, 156n35; foremost virtue of, 176n213; as "furrows," 159n94; in public and non-family spaces, 69–70, 139n106, 158n65, 165n193; textile production of, 65–66. *See*

also gender norms; marriage; subjectivity, female
writing and writing materials, 25–26

xenoi. *See* immigrants
xenophobia, 167n32
Xenophon, 13, 112, 125
Xerxes, 19, 39, 93, 98, 143n18

Zeitlin, Froma: on *astoxenoi* to *metoikoi* transformation, 128n17; on Athenocentric nature of tragedy, 15; on Danaids, 12, 39, 57, 140n133; on displacement strategy, 6; interpretative study of, 10; on suppliant tradition as foreign relations, 141n136; on themes of *Suppliant Women*, 4, 60, 127n8; on Thesmophoria, 60, 154–55n12
zeugitae, 46, 102–5, 152n156, 170nn105–6. *See also* census
Zeus: Danaids' attitude toward, 119–20; Danaids' invocation of, 37, 79–81, 134n30, 141n145; Danaids' purification and, 76–77; Danaus's invocation of, 48; daughter given to Hades by, 155n22

WISCONSIN STUDIES IN CLASSICS

William Aylward and Patricia A. Rosenmeyer, General Editors

E. A. THOMPSON
Romans and Barbarians: The Decline of the Western Empire

H. I. MARROU
A History of Education in Antiquity
Histoire de l'Education dans l'Antiquité, translated by George Lamb

JENNIFER TOLBERT ROBERTS
Accountability in Athenian Government

ERIKA SIMON
Festivals of Attica: An Archaeological Commentary

WARREN G. MOON, editor
Ancient Greek Art and Iconography

G. MICHAEL WOLOCH
Roman Cities: Les villes romaines by Pierre Grimal, translated and edited by G. Michael Woloch, together with A Descriptive Catalogue of Roman Cities by G. Michael Woloch

KATHERINE DOHAN MORROW
Greek Footwear and the Dating of Sculpture

JOHN KEVIN NEWMAN
The Classical Epic Tradition

JEANNY VORYS CANBY, EDITH PORADA, BRUNILDE SISMONDO RIDGWAY, and TAMARA STECH, editors
Ancient Anatolia: Aspects of Change and Cultural Development

ANN NORRIS MICHELINI
Euripides and the Tragic Tradition

WENDY J. RASCHKE, editor
The Archaeology of the Olympics: The Olympics and Other Festivals in Antiquity

PAUL PLASS
Wit and the Writing of History: The Rhetoric of Historiography in Imperial Rome

BARBARA HUGHES FOWLER
The Hellenistic Aesthetic

F. M. CLOVER and R. S. HUMPHREYS, editors
Tradition and Innovation in Late Antiquity

BRUNILDE SISMONDO RIDGWAY
Hellenistic Sculpture I: The Styles of ca. 331–200 B.C.

BARBARA HUGHES FOWLER, editor and translator
Hellenistic Poetry: An Anthology

KATHRYN J. GUTZWILLER
Theocritus' Pastoral Analogies: The Formation of a Genre

VIMALA BEGLEY and RICHARD DANIEL DE PUMA, editors
Rome and India: The Ancient Sea Trade

RUDOLF BLUM
HANS H. WELLISCH, translator
Kallimachos: The Alexandrian Library and the Origins of Bibliography

DAVID CASTRIOTA
Myth, Ethos, and Actuality: Official Art in Fifth Century B.C. Athens

BARBARA HUGHES FOWLER, editor and translator
Archaic Greek Poetry: An Anthology

JOHN H. OAKLEY and REBECCA H. SINOS
The Wedding in Ancient Athens

RICHARD DANIEL DE PUMA and JOCELYN PENNY SMALL, editors
Murlo and the Etruscans: Art and Society in Ancient Etruria

JUDITH LYNN SEBESTA and LARISSA BONFANTE, editors
The World of Roman Costume

JENNIFER LARSON
Greek Heroine Cults

WARREN G. MOON, editor
Polykleitos, the Doryphoros, and Tradition

PAUL PLASS
The Game of Death in Ancient Rome: Arena Sport and Political Suicide

MARGARET S. DROWER
Flinders Petrie: A Life in Archaeology

SUSAN B. MATHESON
Polygnotos and Vase Painting in Classical Athens

JENIFER NEILS, editor
Worshipping Athena: Panathenaia and Parthenon

PAMELA A. WEBB
Hellenistic Architectural Sculpture: Figural Motifs in Western Anatolia and the Aegean Islands

BRUNILDE SISMONDO RIDGWAY
Fourth-Century Styles in Greek Sculpture

LUCY GOODISON and CHRISTINE MORRIS, editors
Ancient Goddesses: The Myths and the Evidence

JO-MARIE CLAASSEN
Displaced Persons: The Literature of Exile from Cicero to Boethius

BRUNILDE SISMONDO RIDGWAY
Hellenistic Sculpture II: The Styles of ca. 200–100 B.C.

PAT GETZ-GENTLE
Personal Styles in Early Cycladic Sculpture

CATULLUS
DAVID MULROY, translator and commentator
The Complete Poetry of Catullus

BRUNILDE SISMONDO RIDGWAY
Hellenistic Sculpture III: The Styles of ca. 100–31 B.C.

ANGELIKI KOSMOPOULOU
The Iconography of Sculptured Statue Bases in the Archaic and Classical Periods

SARA H. LINDHEIM
Mail and Female: Epistolary Narrative and Desire in Ovid's "Heroides"

GRAHAM ZANKER
Modes of Viewing in Hellenistic Poetry and Art

ALEXANDRA ANN CARPINO
Discs of Splendor: The Relief Mirrors of the Etruscans

TIMOTHY S. JOHNSON
A Symposion of Praise: Horace Returns to Lyric in "Odes" IV

JEAN-RENÉ JANNOT
Religion in Ancient Etruria
Devins, Dieux et Démons: Regards sur la religion de l'Etrurie antique, translated by Jane K. Whitehead

CATHERINE SCHLEGEL
Satire and the Threat of Speech: Horace's "Satires," Book 1

CHRISTOPHER A. FARAONE and LAURA K. MCCLURE, editors
Prostitutes and Courtesans in the Ancient World

PLAUTUS
JOHN HENDERSON, translator and commentator
Asinaria: The One about the Asses

PATRICE D. RANKINE
Ulysses in Black: Ralph Ellison, Classicism, and African American Literature

PAUL REHAK
JOHN G. YOUNGER, editor
Imperium and Cosmos: Augustus and the Northern Campus Martius

PATRICIA J. JOHNSON
Ovid before Exile: Art and Punishment in the "Metamorphoses"

VERED LEV KENAAN
Pandora's Senses: The Feminine Character of the Ancient Text

ERIK GUNDERSON
Nox Philologiae: Aulus Gellius and the Fantasy of the Roman Library

SINCLAIR BELL and HELEN NAGY, editors
New Perspectives on Etruria and Early Rome

BARBARA PAVLOCK
The Image of the Poet in Ovid's "Metamorphoses"

PAUL CARTLEDGE and FIONA ROSE GREENLAND, editors
Responses to Oliver Stone's "Alexander": Film, History, and Cultural Studies

AMALIA AVRAMIDOU
The Codrus Painter: Iconography and Reception of Athenian Vases in the Age of Pericles

SHANE BUTLER
The Matter of the Page: Essays in Search of Ancient and Medieval Authors

ALLISON GLAZEBROOK and MADELEINE HENRY, editors
Greek Prostitutes in the Ancient Mediterranean, 800 BCE–200 CE

NORMAN AUSTIN
Sophocles' "Philoctetes" and the Great Soul Robbery

SOPHOCLES
A verse translation by DAVID MULROY, with introduction and notes
Oedipus Rex

JOHN ANDREAU and RAYMOND DESCAT
The Slave in Greece and Rome
Esclave en Grèce et à Rome, translated by Marion Leopold

AMANDA WILCOX
The Gift of Correspondence in Classical Rome: Friendship in Cicero's "Ad Familiares" and Seneca's "Moral Epistles"

MARK BUCHAN
Perfidy and Passion: Reintroducing the "Iliad"

SOPHOCLES
A verse translation by DAVID MULROY, with introduction and notes
Antigone

GEOFFREY W. BAKEWELL
Aeschylus's "Suppliant Women": The Tragedy of Immigration

ELIZABETH P. BAUGHAN
Couched in Death: "Klinai" and Identity in Anatolia and Beyond